## Early Praise for *Programming Machine Learning*

As a developer with more than 20 years of experience but with no background in machine learning, I found this book to be pure gold. It explains the math behind machine learning in a very intuitive way that is easy to understand.

➤ **Giancarlo Valente**
  Agile Coach and auLAB Co-Founder

Let me say that I think this is a brilliant book. It takes the reader step by step through the thinking behind machine learning. Combine that with Paolo's fun approach and this is the book I'd suggest every machine learning neophyte start with.

➤ **Russ Olsen**
  Author, *Getting Clojure* and *Eloquent Ruby*

This book is totally engaging. I love the humor, and the way Paolo talks as a buddy who understands your fears and guides you through as someone who has gone through the same learning process.

➤ **Alberto Lumbreras**
  Research Scientist, Criteo AI Lab

*Programming Machine Learning* is a well-organized and accessible introduction to machine learning for programmers. The book eschews traditional mathematically centric explanations for programming centric ones, and as a result, it makes foundational concepts readily accessible.

➤ **Dan Sheikh**
  Lead Engineer, BCG Digital Ventures

# Programming Machine Learning

From Coding to Deep Learning

Paolo Perrotta

The Pragmatic Bookshelf

Raleigh, North Carolina

Many of the designations used by manufacturers and sellers to distinguish their products are claimed as trademarks. Where those designations appear in this book, and The Pragmatic Programmers, LLC was aware of a trademark claim, the designations have been printed in initial capital letters or in all capitals. The Pragmatic Starter Kit, The Pragmatic Programmer, Pragmatic Programming, Pragmatic Bookshelf, PragProg and the linking *g* device are trademarks of The Pragmatic Programmers, LLC.

Every precaution was taken in the preparation of this book. However, the publisher assumes no responsibility for errors or omissions, or for damages that may result from the use of information (including program listings) contained herein.

For our complete catalog of hands-on, practical, and Pragmatic content for software developers, please visit *https://pragprog.com*.

The team that produced this book includes:

Publisher: Andy Hunt
VP of Operations: Janet Furlow
Executive Editor: Dave Rankin
Development Editor: Katharine Dvorak
Copy Editor: Jasmine Kwityn
Indexing: Potomac Indexing, LLC
Layout: Gilson Graphics

For sales, volume licensing, and support, please contact *support@pragprog.com*.

For international rights, please contact *rights@pragprog.com*.

ISBN-13: 978-1-68050-660-0
Book version: P2.0—March 2021

*To my wife Irene,*

*making my every day.*

# Contents

## Part I — From Zero to Image Recognition

## Part II — Neural Networks

## Part III — Deep Learning

# Acknowledgments

A shout out to my tech reviewers: Alessandro Bahgat, Arno Bastenhof, Roberto Bettazzoni, Guido "Zen" Bolognesi, Juan de Bravo, Simone Busoli, Pieter Buteneers, Andrea Cisternino, Sebastian Hennebrüder, Alberto Lumbreras, Russ Olsen, Luca Ongaro, Pierpaolo Pantone, Karol Przystalski, Dan Sheikh, Leonie Sieger, Gal Tsubery, l'ùmarèin pugnàtta di Casalecchio, and Giancarlo Valente. All of them should be thanked for making this book better with their insightful comments, with the exception of Roberto Bettazzoni. Like a good friend, he should instead take the blame for any mistake in these pages.

Thank you to the generous readers who sent errata and beta comments: Marco Arena, Mahib Arnob, Glen Aultman-Bettridge, Juanjo Bazan, Zbynek Bazanowski, Jamis Buck, Charles de Bueger, Leonardo Carotti, Amir Ebrahimi, Helge Eichhorn, George Ellis, Bruno Girin, Elton Goci, Dave Halliday, Paul Hanchett, Darren Hunt, Randle Kashuba, Peter Lin, Karen Mauney, Daniel Meneses, Bradley Mirly, Richard Murnane, Vasileios Ntarlagiannis, Volkmar Petschnig, David Pinto, Conlan Rios, Roman Romanchuk, Benjamin Rosemann, Alexander Shevelev, Ionut Simion, Drew Thomas, Michal Trzcinka, Jeroen Wenting, and Xiang Zhang. If you ever cross me at a conference, or anywhere else, tap my shoulder. Beer (or your favorite beverage) will follow.

Thanks to my friend Annamaria Di Sebastiano, who shared with me the story that opens the first chapter. Long time no see!

Thank you to Marc Schnierle for his excellent LaTeX4technics[1] web app that I used to generate formulae; to Kimberly Geswein, who designed the Indie Flower font that I used in the diagrams; to the team that designed DejaVu Sans and DejaVu Sans Mono, which I used extensively throughout the book; and to the Brisbane City Council, which published the beautiful echidna picture[2] that appears, in a slightly modified version, in one of the last chapters.

---

1. https://www.latex4technics.com
2. https://www.flickr.com/photos/brisbanecitycouncil/6971519658

This book went through three editors. Lucky me, all three were great. Thank you, Meghan Blanchette and Susan Conant, for getting me from scratch to half a book. You'll forgive me if I play favorites here, and give special thanks to Katharine Dvorak—for the sheer amount of work she poured into the book, and for her sure-handed, but always very patient direction. You're an amazing editor, Katie.

Thank you to my very spread-out village—Dad, Mom, Anna, Susanna, and my extended family of friends and relatives, living all around the globe. It's a perpetual joy to have you around.

Finally, to my wife Irene: you were there when I started writing, supporting me in the throes of a harsh summer. Now that the book is going to the printers, you're still there, unswerving and unflinching as ever. I owe you everything, and this book is dedicated to you.

# How the Heck Is That Possible?

Machine learning can seem like magic. How can a computer recognize the objects in an image? How can a car drive itself?

Those feats are baffling—not just to the layman, but to many software developers like you and me. Even after writing code for many years, I had no idea how machine learning could possibly work. While I tinkered with the latest web framework, someone out there was writing amazing software that looked like science fiction—and I couldn't even comprehend it.

I wanted in on the action. I wanted to be able to build those things myself.

I knew how to write software, so I assumed that I would grok machine learning quickly. I mean, how hard could it be? I put on a confident smile and started studying. Then I kept smiling confidently as I slammed my muzzle into a long sequence of brick walls.

To us developers, machine learning feels… *foreign*. The field is teeming with math jargon, researchy conventions, and frankly, bad code. Instead of tutorials, people point you at lectures and research papers. For many of us, machine learning is as intimidating as it's intriguing.

This is the book I missed when I got started with machine learning: an introduction for developers, written in our own language. After reading it, you'll be comfortable with the fundamentals, and able to write machine learning programs. No, you probably won't be able to build your own self-driving car just yet—but at least you will know how the heck that's possible.

Come in.

## About This Book

This is a book for developers who want to learn machine learning from scratch.

Machine learning is a broad field, and no book can cover it all. We'll focus on the three facets of machine learning that are most important today: *supervised learning, neural networks*, and *deep learning*. We'll look into those terms as we go through the book, but here's a picture and a few quick definitions to get you started:

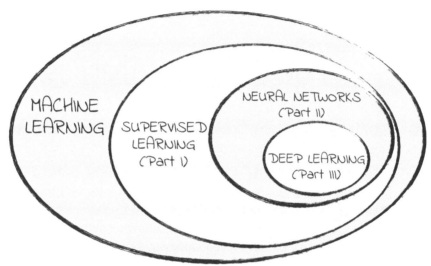

*Supervised learning* is a specific type of machine learning. Machine learning comes in a few different flavors, but supervised learning is the most popular one these days. Part I of this book, *From Zero to Image Recognition*, is a hands-on supervised learning tutorial. Within a couple of chapters, we'll write a minimal learning program. Then we'll evolve this program step by step, progressively turning it into a machine learning system called a *perceptron*. Our perceptron will be a bona fide computer vision program, powerful enough to recognize handwritten characters. We'll craft it all by ourselves, without using machine learning libraries. You'll understand each single line of its code.

There are many ways to implement a supervised learning system. The most popular of those is the *neural network*—a brilliant algorithm that was loosely inspired by the connections of neurons in our own brains. Part II of this book is dedicated to neural networks. We'll grow the program from Part I into a full-fledged neural network. We'll have to overcome a few challenges along the way, but the payoff will be worth it: the final neural network will be way more powerful than the fledgling program we'll start off with. Once again, we'll write the code ourselves, line by line. Its inner workings will be open for you to play with.

Neural networks got a big boost in recent years, when researchers came up with breakthrough techniques to design and use them. This souped-up technology is vastly more powerful than the simple neural networks of old—so much so that it got its own name: *deep learning*. That's also the title of Part III of this book. In it, we'll rewrite our neural network using a modern machine learning library. The resulting code will be our starting point to understand what deep learning is about. Finally, as we wrap up the book, we'll take a look at a few advanced deep learning techniques, paving the way for your future explorations.

In truth, things aren't quite as clean-cut as our picture implies. For example, neural networks can be used in other fields of machine learning, not just in supervised learning. However, the diagram just shown is a good starting point to get a sense of the topics in this book, and how they fit together.

## Before We Begin

This book cannot turn you into a machine learning pro overnight, but it can give you an intuitive, practical understanding of how machine learning works. I want to open the hood of this discipline, show you the gears, and demystify the magic. Once you grasp the fundamental principles of machine learning, you'll find it much easier to dig deeper, incorporate these techniques in your daily job, and maybe even embark on a career as a machine learning engineer.

You don't need to be a senior developer to read this book. However, you should be comfortable writing short programs. If you know Python, then you just lucked out: that's the language that I will use throughout, so you'll feel right at home. Even if you don't know Python yet, no worries. It's a friendly language, and the code in this book will never get too complicated. Read Appendix 1, Just Enough Python, on page 275 to get up to speed, and be ready to Google for more information if you get stuck.

Machine learning involves a lot of mathematics. I won't dumb down the math, but I'll make it as intuitive as I can. To go through this book, you need some high school level concepts: I'm going to assume that you can read a Cartesian chart, that you know what the "axes" and their "origin" are, and that you can make sense of a function plot. Other than that, you don't need much math knowledge. In fact, you might be able to read through even if you consider yourself terrible at math... But be ready to be proven wrong about that!

On the other hand, if you have a solid background in linear algebra and calculus, then you might find some of the math obvious. In that case, feel free to breeze over the explanations you don't need.

**Math Deep Dives**

We all love intuitive mathematics, but sometimes you might strive for a more formal explanation. If you ever feel lost while parsing a formula, or if you like math and want to dig deeper, then look for "Math Deep Dive" boxes like this one. They'll point you at relevant math screencasts on the excellent Khan Academy.[1] No matter what your current level of math is, this site has got you covered.

Just to be clear, these additional lessons are optional. You don't need them to read this book—only if you wish to really wrap your mind around the mathematics of machine learning.

Machine learning has a rich and specific vocabulary. You're likely to stumble upon new words, or new meanings for old words. Take it easy and don't feel like you have to remember everything. I will remind you of many of those words' meaning the next time we encounter them. Whenever a term gives you that obnoxious "I cannot quite remember what this means" feeling, you can look it up in Appendix 2, The Words of Machine Learning, on page 293.

One word about the datasets that I'll use in the examples: many of them are collections of images. Rest assured that machine learning can do much more besides image recognition: it can analyze text, generate music, or even hold conversations. However, image recognition makes for very intuitive examples, so it will be our go-to application throughout the book.

Finally, there are a couple of online resources that you should know about. One is this book's official page[2] on the Pragmatic Bookshelf. From there, you can download the examples' source code and report errata—typos, bugs, and factual mistakes.

This book also has a companion website called ProgML[3] that contains a few additional explanations that I couldn't fit in these pages. Every now and then, you'll find references to ProgML in the page margins, pointing you at those optional explanations. Go read them if you're eager for more details.

References to ProgML look like this.

That's enough public service announcements. Let's dive into Part I.

1.  www.khanacademy.org
2.  https://pragprog.com/book/pplearn/programming-machine-learning
3.  www.progml.com

# Part I

# From Zero to Image Recognition

*We're about to get an introduction to supervised learning. Within a couple of chapters, we'll code our first machine learning system. Then we'll evolve this system, one small step at a time, until it becomes powerful enough to read handwritten digits.*

*You read that right: in the next 100 pages, we'll build an image recognition program. Even better, we're not going to use any machine learning library. Other than a few general-purpose functions for arithmetic and plotting, we'll write all of that code by ourselves.*

*In your future career, you're unlikely to ever write machine learning algorithms from scratch. But doing it once, to grok the fundamentals... that's priceless. You will understand every line in the final program. Machine learning will never look like magic again.*

# CHAPTER 1

# How Machine Learning Works

Software developers like to share war stories. As soon as a few of us sit down in a pub, somebody asks: "What project are you working on?" Then we nod our heads off as we listen to each other's amusing, and sometimes horrible, tales.

In the mid-90s, during one of those evenings of bantering, a friend told me about the impossible mission she was on. Her managers wanted a program that would analyze X-ray scans and identify diseases, such as pneumonia.

My friend had warned management that the task was hopeless, but they refused to believe her. If a radiologist could do it, they reasoned, then why not a Visual Basic program? They even paired my friend with a professional radiologist, so that she could learn the job and turn it into code. That experience only reinforced her opinion that radiology required human judgment and intelligence.

We laughed at the futility of the task. A few months later, the project was canceled.

Fast-forward to more recent times: in late 2017, a research team at Stanford University published an algorithm to diagnose pneumonia from X-ray scans.[1] The algorithm wasn't just okay—it was more accurate than professional radiologists. That was supposed to be impossible! How the heck could they write that code?

The answer is that they didn't. Instead of writing code, they cracked the problem with machine learning. Let's see what that means.

---

1.  news.stanford.edu/2017/11/15/algorithm-outperforms-radiologists-diagnosing-pneumonia

## Programming vs. Machine Learning

Here's an example of the difference between machine learning (or simply "ML") and regular programming. Imagine building a program that plays video games. With traditional programming, that program might look something like this:

```
enemy = get_nearest_enemy()
if enemy.distance() < 100:
  decelerate()
  if enemy.is_shooting():
    raise_shield()
  else:
    if health() > 0.25:
      shoot()
    else:
      rotate_away_from(enemy)
else:
  # ...a lot more code
```

...and so on. Most of the code would be a big collection of if..else statements, mixed with imperative commands such as shoot().

Granted, modern languages give us the means to replace those ugly nested ifs with more pleasant constructs—polymorphism, pattern matching, or event-driven calls. The core idea of programming, however, stays the same: you tell the computer what to look for, and you tell it what to do. You must list every condition and define every action.

This approach has served us well, but it has a few flaws. First, you must be exhaustive. You can probably imagine dozens or hundreds of specific situations that you'd have to cover in that video game–playing program. What happens if the enemy is approaching, but there is a power-up between you and the enemy, and the power-up is shielding you from enemy fire? A human player would quickly notice the situation and take advantage of it. Your program... well, it depends. If you coded for that special case, then your program will deal with it—but we know how hard it is to cover all special cases, even in structured domains like accounting. Good luck listing each and every possible special case in complex domains like playing video games, driving a truck, or recognizing an image!

Even if you could list all those decisions, you'd have to know how to take them in the first place. That's a second limitation of programming, and a showstopper in some domains. For example, take a *computer vision* task like our original problem: identifying pneumonia in chest scans.

We don't *really* know how a human radiologist recognizes pneumonia. Yes, we have a high-level idea of it, like: "the radiologist looks for opaque areas." However, we don't know how the radiologist's brain recognizes and evaluates an opaque area. In some cases, the expert herself cannot tell you how she came to a diagnosis, except for a rather vague: "I know by experience that pneumonia doesn't look like this." Since we don't know how those decisions happen, we cannot instruct a computer to take them. That is a problem shared by all typically human tasks, such as tasting beer, or understanding a sentence.

Machine learning, on the other hand, turns traditional programming on its head: instead of giving *instructions* to the computer, ML is about giving *data* to the computer, and asking it to figure out what to do:

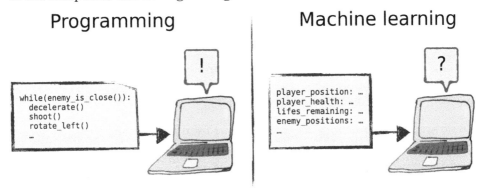

The idea of a computer "figuring out" anything sounds like wishful thinking, but there are actually a few different ways to make it happen. In case you're wondering, all of them still require running code. That code, however, isn't a step-by-step procedure to solve the problem, like in traditional programming. Instead, the code in machine learning tells the computer how to crunch the data, so that the computer can solve the problem by itself.

As an example, here is one way that a computer can figure out how to play a video game. Imagine an algorithm that learns how to play by trial and error. It starts by giving random commands: "shoot," "decelerate," "rotate," and so on. If those commands eventually lead to success, such as a higher score, the algorithm remembers this experience. If they lead to failure, such as death, the algorithm also takes note. At the same time, it also takes note of the state of the game: where are the enemies, the obstacles, and the power-ups? How much health do we have? And so on.

From then on, whenever it encounters a similar game state, the algorithm is a bit more likely to attempt the successful actions than the unsuccessful ones. After many cycles of trial and error, such a program would become a competent player. In 2013, a system using this approach reached superhuman skills in a bunch of old Atari games.[2]

This style of ML is called *reinforcement learning*. Reinforcement learning works pretty much like dog training: "good" behavior is rewarded so that the dog does more of it.

(I also tried the same approach with my cat. So far, I failed.)

Reinforcement learning is just one way to let a computer figure out a problem. In this book, we'll focus on another style of machine learning—arguably the most popular one. Let's talk about it.

## Supervised Learning

Among the various approaches to ML, *supervised learning* is the one that reaped the most impressive results so far. Here is how supervised learning solves a problem like diagnosing pneumonia.

To do supervised learning, we need to start from a set of *examples*, each carrying a *label* that the computer can learn from. For instance:

| What are we building? | Each example could be... | Each label could be... |
| --- | --- | --- |
| A system that identifies a dog's breed from its barking. | ...a .wav recording of a dog. | ...the dog's breed, like "greyhound" or "beagle." |
| A system that detects pneumonia. | ...an X-ray scan. | ...a boolean flag: 1 if the scan shows pneumonia, 0 if it doesn't. |
| A system that predicts the earnings of a lemonade stand from the weather. | ...the recorded temperatures on a day in the past. | ...the recorded earnings on the same day. |
| A system that recognizes the sentiment in a politician's tweet. | ...the tweet. | ...emotional states such as "indignant," "angry," or "absolutely furious." |

As you can see, examples can be a lot of different things: data, text, sound, video, and so on. Also, labels can be either *numerical* or *categorical*. Numerical labels are just a number, as in the case of the temperature-to-lemonade converter. Categorical labels represent a category in a pre-defined set, as in the case of the dog breed detector. With some imagination, you can come up with many other examples of predicting something, be it numerical or categorical, from something else.

So, let's assume that we already put together a collection of labeled examples. Now we can dive into the two phases of supervised learning:

*Phase 1: Training*

During this phase, we feed the labeled examples to an algorithm that's designed to spot patterns. For example, the algorithm might notice that all pneumonia scans have certain common characteristics—maybe certain opaque areas—that are missing from non-pneumonia scans. This is called the *training phase*, because the algorithm is looking at the examples over and over, and learning to recognize those patterns.

*Phase 2: Prediction*

Now that the algorithm knows what pneumonia look like, we switch to the *prediction phase*, where we reap the benefits of our work. We show an *unlabeled* X-ray scan to the trained algorithm, and the algorithm tells us whether it contains signs of pneumonia or not.

Here comes another example of supervised learning—a system that recognizes animals. Each input is the picture of an animal, and each label is the species. During the training phase, we show labeled images to the algorithm. During the prediction phase, we show it an unlabeled image, and the algorithm guesses the label:

## Training phase            Prediction phase

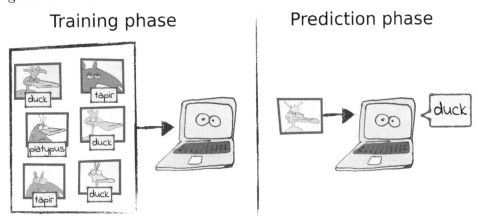

I told you that in machine learning, a computer "figures out" data. Supervised learning is an example of that process: in traditional programming, you code a computer to go from the input to the output; in supervised learning, you give examples of the input and the output to the computer, and it gets the hang of how to go from one to the other on its own.

Now that you've read this high-level explanation of supervised learning, you might have more questions than you started out with. We said that a supervised learning program "notices common characteristics" in the data and "spots patterns"—but how? Let's step down one level of abstraction, and see how that magic happens.

## The Math Behind the Magic

To understand the relation between a piece of data and its label, a supervised learning system exploits a mathematical concept—the idea of *approximating a function*. Let's see how that idea works, with a concrete example.

Imagine that you have a solar panel on your roof. You'd like a supervised learning system that learns how the solar panel generates energy, and predicts the amount of energy generated at some time in the future.

There are a few variables that impact the solar panel's output: the time of day, the weather, and so on. The time of day looks like an important variable, so you decide to focus on that one. In true supervised learning fashion, you start by collecting examples of power generated at different times of the day. After a few weeks of random sampling, you get a spreadsheet table that looks like this:

| Time of day | Power (in Watts/hour) |
| --- | --- |
| 09:01 | 153 |
| 11:48 | 280 |
| 05:20 | 0 |

...and so on.

Each line in the table is an example. It includes an *input variable* (the time of day) and a label (the generated power)—just like in the system that recognizes animals, the picture is the input, and the name of the animal is the label.

If you plot the examples on a chart, such as the one shown here, you can visualize how the time of day relates to the energy produced:

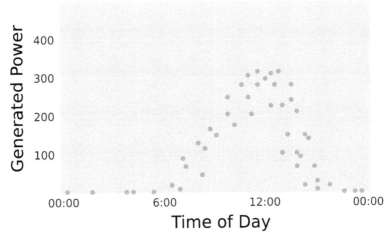

At a glance, our human brains can see that the solar panel doesn't generate power during the night, and that its power peaks around noon. Lacking the luxury of a brain, a supervised learning system can understand the data by approximating them with a function, as shown in the next chart:

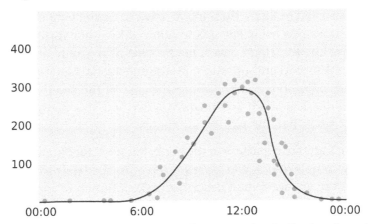

Finding the function that approximates the examples is the hard part of the job—what I called the "training phase" earlier. The prediction phase that follows is easier: the system forgets all about the examples, and uses the function to predict the power generated by the solar panel—for example, on any day at noon, as illustrated in the following chart on page 10.

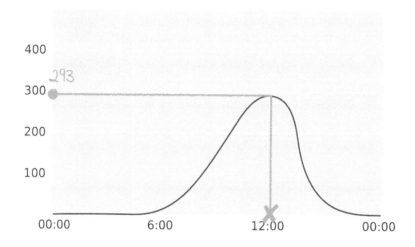

That's what I meant when I said that supervised learning works by approximating functions. The system receives real-world data that's generally messy and incomplete. During the training phase, it approximates that complicated data with a relatively simple function. During the prediction phase, it uses that function to predict unknown data.

As a programmer, you're always thinking of the many ways something could go wrong—so you're likely thinking of ways to complicate our example. For one, the output of a solar panel is influenced by other variables besides the time of day, like the cloud cover, or the time of the year. If we collected all those variables, we'd end up with a multidimensional cloud of points that we couldn't visualize on a chart. Also, in the case of the solar panel, we're predicting a numerical label. You might wonder how this method translated to categorical labels like the names of animals.

We'll discuss all those matters in the book. For now, just know this: no matter how many complications you layer on top of it, the basic idea of supervised learning is the one we've just described: take a bunch of examples, and find a function that approximates them.

Modern supervised learning systems are very good at this approximation job. They can approximate complicated relations, like the one between an X-ray scan and a diagnosis. A function that approximates that relation would look maddeningly complicated to us humans, but it's par for the course for those systems.

And that's supervised learning in a nutshell. As for the details… well, the rest of this book is all about them. Let's set up our computers and start coding.

## What About Unsupervised Learning?

There are a few different types of ML. Most tutorials list three of them in particular: reinforcement learning, supervised learning, and a third flavor called *unsupervised learning*. We used reinforcement learning to introduce the basics of ML, and we'll talk about supervised learning for the rest of this book. So, what about unsupervised learning?

The technical difference between supervised and unsupervised learning is that the second is about learning from *unlabeled* data. In practice, unsupervised learnings has little to do with our intuitive idea of "learning," and looks more like a sophisticated form of data processing.

Here is an example of unsupervised learning: imagine that you're doing market research for an online shop. You have all the data for the shop's customers: how much they spent, how many times they visited, and so on. An unsupervised learning algorithm could help you make sense of those data, by grouping similar customers together—a process known as *clustering*.

Unsupervised learning can be very useful, but it doesn't grab as many headlines as the other flavors of ML these days. Having to choose one, this book focuses on supervised learning.

## Setting Up Your System

We're about to embark on an ML tutorial that spans the entire first part of this book. We'll start from scratch and end with a working computer vision program. Later on, that same program will be our starting point toward higher peaks: neural networks in Part II of this book, and deep learning in Part III.

You might want to approach this tutorial hands-on, running the source code for this book, and solving the exercises at the end of most chapters. Alternatively, you might prefer to read through and get the big picture before you grab the keyboard. Both approaches are feasible, although programmers often go for the first.

If you prefer the hands-on approach, it won't take long to set up your system and run this book's code. Even though ML tends to require a lot of computing power, the code in this book runs fine on a regular laptop. You just need to install some software.

Just a note before we set up your system: I hope that most information in this book will stay valid for years—but when it comes to machine learning libraries, all bets are off. Some of these libraries seem to introduce breaking changes every time you look away. If you get errors while installing the libraries or running the examples, look for updated set-up instructions on this book's companion site.[3]

First and foremost, you need Python. It's the most popular language in the ML community, and the language that all of this book's examples are written in. Don't worry if you never coded in Python before—you'll be surprised by how readable this language is. If Python code perplexes you, then read Appendix 1, Just Enough Python, on page 275. That will be enough knowledge to get you through this book.

## A Note for Experienced Pythonistas

If you're steeped in Python, you might notice that the code in this book deviates from common conventions. For example, I actively avoid language-specific idioms (such as list comprehension) that complicate the code for newcomers to the language. With the same intent of making the code more accessible, I might use slightly imprecise language, such as the word "function" in place of "method."

I apologize in advance for those transgressions to the Pythonic canon.

Let's get down to business and check that you have Python installed. Run:

```
python3 --version
```

If you don't have Python 3.7 or later, then stop reading for a minute and go get it. The introduction to Appendix 1, Just Enough Python, on page 275 gives you a few pointers to install the language.

One thing to note: on some systems, you can also execute Python 3 by typing `python`, without the 3 at the end. On other systems, however, the `python` command executes Python 2. To avoid confusing errors related to older Pythons, I'll always use the more explicit `python3` command in this book.

Now that you have the language, let's talk libraries. You'll need three of them to begin with. The big one is NumPy, a library for scientific computing. We'll also use two libraries to plot charts. Matplotlib is the de facto standard for chart-plotting in Python. Seaborn sits on top of Matplotlib, and focuses on making the charts look pretty.

There are two ways to install those libraries: you can use *pip*, Python's official package manager, or you can use Conda, a more sophisticated environment manager that is popular in the ML community. If you're curious, Installing

---

3.   www.progml.com

Packages with Conda, on page 289 delves deeper into the differences between pip and Conda. If you're in doubt, then just use pip.

On Python 3.7, you can install the libraries with pip by running these commands:

```
pip3 install numpy==1.19.5
pip3 install matplotlib==3.2.2
pip3 install seaborn==0.11.1
```

...and you're done. If you'd rather use Conda, then look in the source code's root folder for a readme.txt with the necessary instructions.

Finally, you need some kind of coding environment. Many ML tutorials use a system called Jupyter Notebooks to edit and run code in the browser. You don't have to use Jupyter to run the examples in this book. Being a developer, you know how to write and run a program, so go ahead and use your favorite text editor or IDE. On the other hand, if you already know and like Jupyter, that's fine: look into the notebooks directory for a Jupyter version of the book's code.

Let's double-check: you have Python, a few essential libraries, and your favorite editor. That's all you need to get started.

And now, let's build a program that learns.

### Becoming Familiar with ML

As a developer, you're accustomed to learning at a rapid pace. With ML, however, you're entering a new field. I'm not going to lie: the next three or four chapters are going to be tough. As you read them, you might feel like an absolute beginner—an exciting, but sometimes frustrating, place to be.

I know that feeling, and I can tell you that it's worth getting through. I remember my excitement when, for the first time, I ran a machine learning program that came up with accurate predictions. Hold on, and soon enough you'll know that geeky joy.

# CHAPTER 2

# Your First Learning Program

Welcome to our first stepping stone in machine learning. In this chapter, we're going to build a tiny supervised learning program. It will be a long haul from this program to our goal of image recognition—in fact, at first it won't have anything to do with computer vision at all. However, we'll improve its code over the next chapters, until it gets sophisticated enough to tackle images.

We'll base the first version of our program on a technique called *linear regression*. Remember what I said in the previous chapter? Supervised learning is about approximating data with a function. In linear regression, that function is as simple as it could be: a straight line.

However simple linear regression is, don't underestimate the challenge ahead. To introduce linear regression, this chapter will touch on many different concepts—so many that you might feel slightly overwhelmed. Take it slow and easy. Even if it looks like we're just writing a short program, we're actually laying the foundation of our ML knowledge. What you learn here will stay useful throughout this book, and beyond. Let's start with a practical problem.

## Getting to Know the Problem

Our friend Roberto owns a cozy little pizzeria in Berlin. Every day at noon, he checks the number of reserved seats and decides how much pizza dough to prepare for dinner. Too much dough, and it goes wasted; too little, and he runs out of pizzas. In either case, he loses money.

It's not always easy to gauge the number of pizzas from the reservations. Many customers don't reserve a table, or they eat something other than pizza. Roberto knows that there is some kind of link between those numbers, in that more reservations generally mean more pizzas—but other than that, he's not sure what the exact relation is.

Roberto dreams of a program that looks at historical data, grasps the relation between reserved seats and pizzas, and uses it to forecast tonight's pizza sales from today's reservations. Can we code such a program for him?

## Supervised Pizza

Remember what I said back in Supervised Learning, on page 6? We can solve Roberto's pizza forecasting problem by training a supervised learning algorithm with a bunch of labeled examples. To get the examples, we asked Roberto to jot down a few days' worth of reservations and pizzas, and collected those data in a file. Here's what the first four lines of that file look like:

```
02_first/pizza.txt
Reservations  Pizzas
13            33
2             16
14            32
23            51
```

The file contains 30 lines of data. Each is an example, composed of an input variable (the reservations) and a numerical label (the pizzas). Once we have an algorithm, we can use these examples to train it. Later on, during the prediction phase, we can pass a specific number of reservations to the algorithm, and ask it to come up with a matching number of pizzas.

Let's start with the numbers, like a data scientist would.

## Making Sense of the Data

If we glance at Roberto's examples, it seems that the reservations and pizzas are correlated. Let's fire up a Python shell (with the python3 command) and take a deeper look.

The NumPy library has a convenient function to import whitespace-separated data from text:

```
import numpy as np
X, Y = np.loadtxt("pizza.txt", skiprows=1, unpack=True)
```

The first line imports the NumPy library, and the second uses NumPy's loadtxt() function to load the data from the pizza.txt file. I skipped the headers row, and I "unpacked" the two columns into separate arrays called X and Y. X contains the values of the input variable, and Y contains the labels. I used uppercase names for X and Y, because that's a common Python convention to indicate that a variable should be treated as a constant.

Let's peek at the data, to make sure they loaded okay. If you wish to follow along, start a Python interpreter, send the two lines given before, and then check out the first few elements of X and Y:

```
⇒ X[0:5]
❮ [ 13.   2.  14.  23.  13.]
⇒ Y[0:5]
❮ [ 33.  16.  32.  51.  27.]
```

The numbers are consistent with Roberto's file, but it's still hard to make sense of them. Plot them on a chart, though, and they become clear:

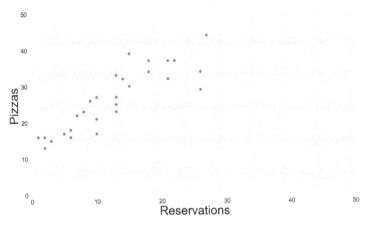

Now the correlation jumps out at us: the more reservations, the more pizzas. To be fair, a statistician might scold us for drawing conclusions from a handful of hastily collected examples. However, this is no research project—so let's ignore the little statistician on our shoulder, and build a pizza forecaster.

## Coding Linear Regression

To recap our goal: we want to write a program that calculates the number of pizzas from the number of reservations. That program should follow the approach we discussed in The Math Behind the Magic, on page 8: during the training phase, the program approximates the data with a function; then, during the prediction phase, it uses the function to infer the number of pizzas.

In the general case, finding a function that approximates the data can be a lot of work. In our specific case, however, we lucked out. Our data points are roughly aligned, so we can approximate them with an especially simple function: a line.

## The Plotting Code

In case you're curious, here's the code that generates the plot in Making Sense of the Data, on page 16:

`02_first/plot.py`

```python
import numpy as np
import matplotlib.pyplot as plt
import seaborn as sns

sns.set()                                                  # activate Seaborn
plt.axis([0, 50, 0, 50])                                   # scale axes (0 to 50)
plt.xticks(fontsize=15)                                    # set x axis ticks
plt.yticks(fontsize=15)                                    # set y axis ticks
plt.xlabel("Reservations", fontsize=30)                    # set x axis label
plt.ylabel("Pizzas", fontsize=30)                          # set y axis label
X, Y = np.loadtxt("pizza.txt", skiprows=1, unpack=True)    # load data
plt.plot(X, Y, "bo")                                       # plot data
plt.show()                                                 # display chart
```

Besides NumPy, this code uses two libraries: Matplotlib draws charts, and Seaborn makes them look pretty. The plot() function plots the examples as blue circles (that's what 'bo' stands for), while the rest of the code sets up the axes, loads the data points, and displays them. If you wish, you can run this program yourself with python3 plot.py.

You don't need to understand the plotting code here, but sooner or later you'll probably write similar code yourself. Maybe set aside a rainy Sunday to learn the basics of Matplotlib and Seaborn—or just do it bit by bit, as you need them.

In the rest of this book, I'll skip the code that generates the plots. You can always find it in the book's accompanying source code.

Let's see what that line would look like. For now, let's pick a line that passes by the origin of the axes, as shown in the following chart, because that will make things easier to begin with.

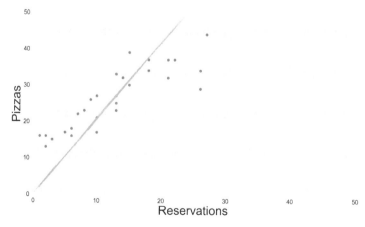

Once we've found the line, the training phase is over. You can say that the line is our *model* of the relation between reservations and pizzas.

Now we can move on to the prediction phase, where we use the line to predict the label from the input variable. Here is an example: we have 20 reservations; how much pizza do we expect to sell? To answer that question, I picked the point x = 20 on the "Reservations" axis. From there I traced up until I crossed the line, and then I traced left until I crossed the "Pizzas" axis. I ended up at y = 42, as shown in this chart:

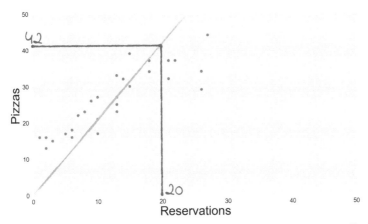

So, there you have it: with 20 reservations, we can expect to sell about 42 pizzas.

This method has been used by statisticians since way before supervised learning existed. It's called *linear regression*. "Linear" means that we're tracing a straight line rather than a curve, and "regression" is a statistician's way of saying: "find the relation between two variables."

To recap, here is how you do supervised learning with linear regression:

*Training phase*
   Trace a line that approximates the examples.

*Prediction phase*
   Use the line to predict the label from the input variable.

Admittedly, not every relation can be approximated well with a straight line. If your examples fall along a curve, or lack a discernible shape, then you can't get away with this simple method. However, Roberto's examples roughly fall on a line, so linear regression should be good enough for this particular problem.

Now let's find a way to implement linear regression with code.

## Defining the Model

To turn linear regression into running code, we need some way to represent the line numerically. That's where mathematics comes into the picture.

Here is the mathematical equation of a line that passes by the origin of the axes:

$$y = x * w$$

You might remember this equation from your studies—or a similar one with a different notation. However, don't fret if it looks unfamiliar. Here is what it means: each line passing by the origin is uniquely identified by a single value. I called this value w, short for *weight*. You can also think of w as the *slope* of the line: the larger w is, the steeper the line. Check out the following graph:

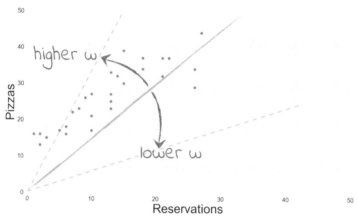

Before we move on, let me rewrite the equation of the line with a slightly different notation:

$$\hat{y} = x * w$$

I changed the symbol y to $\hat{y}$ (read "y-hat"), because I don't want to confuse this value with the y values that we loaded from Roberto's file. Both symbols represent the number of pizzas, but there is a crucial difference between the two. $\hat{y}$ is a forecast—our prediction of how many pizzas we hope to sell. By contrast, the labels y are real-life observations—what machine learning practictioners call the *ground truth*.

After this short digression about notation, let me go back to the important concept here: w is a constant that identifies the line. In other words, w is all we need to represent a line in code.

So, let's write that code. We'll start from the prediction phase, because it's easier than the training phase. We will tackle the training phase soon after.

**Math Deep Dive: Linear Equations**

If the equation y = x * w confuses you, then you might want to watch Khan Academy's screencasts on linear equations.[1] These optional videos offer much more content than you need to read this book —so don't feel like you have to watch them all.

## Implementing Prediction

Imagine that somebody came to you with a line (that is, a value of w), and asked you to use that line to predict the value of $\hat{y}$ from x—like, pizzas from reservations. That's a one-liner:

02_first/linear_regression.py
```
def predict(X, w):
    return X * w
```

The predict() function predicts the pizzas from the reservations. To be more precise, it takes the input variable and the weight, and it uses them to calculate $\hat{y}$.

This tiny function is more powerful than you may think. In particular, X can be either a single number, or an entire array of reservations. NumPy comes with its own array type, that supports *broadcast* operations: if we multiply an array of reservations by w, then NumPy multiplies each element of the array by w, and returns an array of predicted pizzas. That's a handy way of making multiple predictions at once.

In the beginning of Coding Linear Regression, on page 17, we used a hand-drawn line to match reservations to pizzas. The predict() function does the same thing that we did by hand, but it's more precise. How many pizzas do we expect to sell if we have 20 reservations? Let's say that our line is w = 2.1. Call predict(20, 2.1), and you get back the predicted number of pizzas: 42.

That's all we need for the second phase of linear regression. Now let's take care of the more complicated first phase. It will take us four intense pages to do that, so hold on tight.

## Implementing Training

Now we want to write code that implements the first part of linear regression: given a bunch of examples (X and Y), it finds a line w that approximates them. Can you think of a way to do that? Feel free to stop reading for a minute and think about it. It's a fun problem to solve.

---

1.   www.khanacademy.org/math/algebra/two-var-linear-equations

You might think that there is one simple way to find w: just use math. After all, there must be some formula that takes a list of points and comes up with a line that approximates them. We could Google for that formula, and maybe even find a library that implements it.

As it turns out, such a formula does indeed exist... but we won't use it, because that would be a dead end. If we use a formula to approximate these points with a straight line, then we'll get stuck later, when we tackle datasets that require twisty model functions. We'd better look for a more generic solution—one that works for any model.

So much for the mathematician's approach, then. Let's look at a programmer's approach instead.

### How Wrong Are We?

Here is one strategy to find the best line that approximates the examples. Imagine if we had a function that takes the examples (X and Y) and a line (w), and measures the line's error. The better the line approximates the examples, the lower the error. If we had such a function, we could use it to evaluate multiple lines, until we find a line with a low enough error.

Except that instead of "error," the cool ML kids have another name for this function: they call it the *loss*.

Here is how we can write a loss function. Assume that we've come up with a random value of w—say, 1.5. Let' use this w to predict how many pizzas we'd sell if we had, say, 14 reservations. Call predict(14, 1.5), and you get $\hat{y} = 21$ pizzas.

But here is a crucial point: this prediction doesn't match the ground truth— that is, the real-world examples from Roberto's file. Look back at the first few examples:

02_first/pizza.txt

| Reservations | Pizzas |
|---|---|
| 13 | 33 |
| 2 | 16 |
| 14 | 32 |
| 23 | 51 |

On that night with 14 reservations, Roberto sold 32 pizzas, not 21. So we can calculate an error that is the difference between the predicted value $\hat{y}$ and the ground truth—that thick orange segment shown in the graph on page 23.

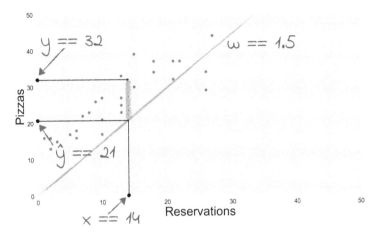

Here is what that calculation would look like in code:

```
error = predict(X, w) - Y
```

There's a wrinkle in this calculation: error could be zero, positive, or negative. However, an error should always be positive. If you add multiple errors together, which we're going to do soon, you don't want two opposite-sign wrongs to make one right. To guarantee that the error is always positive, let's square it:

```
squared_error = error ** 2
```

We could also use the absolute value of the error instead of squaring it. However, squaring the error has additional benefits that will become obvious in the next chapter.

Now let's average the squared errors of all the examples, and *voilà!* We finally have our loss. This way to calculate the loss is called the *mean squared error*, and it's pretty popular among statisticians. Here's what it looks like in code:

02_first/linear_regression.py
```
def loss(X, Y, w):
    return np.average((predict(X, w) - Y) ** 2)
```

Remember that we used NumPy to load X and Y? Both variables are NumPy arrays, which makes for pretty terse code. In the span of the first line of loss(), we multiply each element of X by w, resulting in an array of predictions; for each prediction, we compute the error—the difference between the prediction and the ground truth; we square each error with the ** power operator; and finally, we ask NumPy to average the squared errors. And there you have it: our mean squared error.

Now that we're done with the loss() function, we can write the last function of our learning program.

## Lingo Overload

"Mean squared error," "model," "loss"... in these first few pages of the book, new names are coming up fast and hard. Here's a friendly reminder: if you forget what a term means, look it up in Appendix 2, The Words of Machine Learning, on page 293. If you don't find the term in there, check out the book's index.

### Closer and Closer

Remember what the training phase of linear regression is about: we want to find a line that approximates the examples. In other words, we want to calculate w from the values in X and Y. We can use an iterative algorithm to do that:

02_first/linear_regression.py
```
def train(X, Y, iterations, lr):
    w = 0
    for i in range(iterations):
        current_loss = loss(X, Y, w)
        print("Iteration %4d => Loss: %.6f" % (i, current_loss))

        if loss(X, Y, w + lr) < current_loss:
            w += lr
        elif loss(X, Y, w - lr) < current_loss:
            w -= lr
        else:
            return w

    raise Exception("Couldn't converge within %d iterations" % iterations)
```

The train() function goes over the examples over and over, until it learns how to approximate them. Its arguments are X, Y, a number of iterations, and a value called lr (that I will explain in a moment). The algorithm begins by initializing w to an arbitrary value of 0. This w represents a line on the chart. It's unlikely to be a good approximation of the examples, but it's a start.

Afterwards, train() gets into a loop. Each iteration starts by calculating the current loss. Then it considers an alternative line—the one that you get when you increase w by a small amount. We could call that amount the "step size," but in this code I borrowed a term from machine learning, and called it the *learning rate*—lr for short.

We just added the learning rate to w, that results in a new line. Does this new line result in a lower loss than our current line? If so, then w + lr becomes the new current w, and the loop continues. Otherwise, the algorithm tries another line: w - lr. Once again, if that line results in a lower loss than the current w, the code updates w and continues the loop.

If neither w + lr nor w - lr yield a better loss than the current w, then we're done. We've approximated the examples as well as we can, and we return w to the caller.

To put it in more concrete terms, this algorithm rotates the line, making it either a tad steeper or a tad less steep at each iteration, while keeping an eye on the loss. The higher the learning rate, the faster the system rotates the line. Picture a radio operator of old, slowly turning a knob to make the voice in his headset that tiny little bit clearer—until, eventually, it's as clear as it gets.

Iterative algorithms can sometimes get stuck in an infinite loop. (They don't *converge*). A computer scientist could prove that this particular algorithm doesn't have that problem: given enough time and iterations, it will always converge. However, the algorithm might run out of iterations before that happens. In that case, train() gives up and exits with an exception.

I know that you're itching to run this code. Let's do it.

## Let's Do This!

The following code loads Roberto's examples and feeds them to train(). It uses Python's named arguments, explained in Named Arguments, on page 284, to be more explicit. After calling train(), it prints out the resulting weight, plus the predicted pizzas for 20 reservations:

```
02_first/linear_regression.py
# Import the dataset
X, Y = np.loadtxt("pizza.txt", skiprows=1, unpack=True)

# Train the system
w = train(X, Y, iterations=10000, lr=0.01)
print("\nw=%.3f" % w)

# Predict the number of pizzas
print("Prediction: x=%d => y=%.2f" % (20, predict(20, w)))
```

When we call train(), we need to pick values for iterations and lr. For now, we can do that by trial and error. I asked for 10000 iterations, that feels like a good value to begin with. As for lr, remember what it does: it decides how much w changes at each step of training. I set it to 0.01, that seems precise enough for counting pizzas.

Indeed, running the program shows that train() converges on a result in less than 200 iterations:

```
Iteration     0 => Loss: 812.866667
Iteration     1 => Loss: 804.820547
Iteration     2 => Loss: 796.818187
...
Iteration   184 => Loss: 69.123947

w=1.840
Prediction: x=20 => y=36.80
```

Success! The loss decreased at each iteration, until the algorithm gave up at squeezing it further. The weight at that point is 1.84, so that's the number of pizzas that Roberto can expect to sell for each reservation. In the case of 20 reservations, he can expect to sell around 36.80 pizzas. (Pizzas are not really sold in fractions, but Roberto is the precise type who likes the extra decimals).

By computing w, our code did the equivalent of "drawing a line on the chart." Check out the following graph (as usual, you'll find the plotting code in the book's source code):

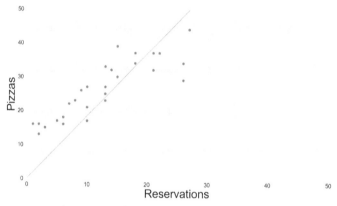

Nice. But we can make it even better.

## Adding a Bias

Look at the chart we just plotted. Our line is not quite the best approximation of the examples, is it? The perfect line would have less slope, and it wouldn't pass by the origin. Give or take, it would cross the "Pizzas" axis around the value of 10.

So far, we forced the line to pass by the origin to keep our model as simple as we could. It's time to remove that constraint. To draw a line that is *not* constrained to pass by the origin, we need one more parameter in our model:

```
ŷ = x * w + b
```

You might experience *déjà vu* here. This equation is the classic linear function which you may have studied in 8th grade. Most people would remember it as

$y = m * x + b$, where m is called the "slope" and b is called the "y-intercept." Here, we'll use the vocabulary of ML instead. We already called w the "weight," and we will call b the *bias*.

Intuitively, the bias measures the "shift" of the line up or down the chart, as shown in the following graph. The line crosses the y axis at a value equal to b. If the bias happens to be 0, then we're back at our previous case, with a line passing by the origin.

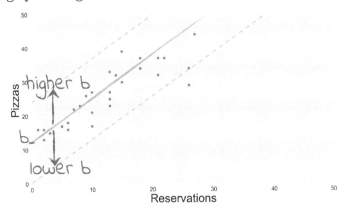

Here is the entire linear regression program, updated to use the new model with two parameters. The small arrows in the left margin mark changes:

02_first/linear_regression_with_bias.py

```
import numpy as np

def predict(X, w, b):
    return X * w + b

def loss(X, Y, w, b):
    return np.average((predict(X, w, b) - Y) ** 2)

def train(X, Y, iterations, lr):
    w = b = 0
    for i in range(iterations):
        current_loss = loss(X, Y, w, b)
        print("Iteration %4d => Loss: %.6f" % (i, current_loss))

        if loss(X, Y, w + lr, b) < current_loss:
            w += lr
        elif loss(X, Y, w - lr, b) < current_loss:
            w -= lr
        elif loss(X, Y, w, b + lr) < current_loss:
            b += lr
        elif loss(X, Y, w, b - lr) < current_loss:
            b -= lr
```

```
        else:
➤           return w, b

    raise Exception("Couldn't converge within %d iterations" % iterations)

# Import the dataset
X, Y = np.loadtxt("pizza.txt", skiprows=1, unpack=True)

# Train the system
➤ w, b = train(X, Y, iterations=10000, lr=0.01)
➤ print("\nw=%.3f, b=%.3f" % (w, b))

# Predict the number of pizzas
➤ print("Prediction: x=%d => y=%.2f" % (20, predict(20, w, b)))
```

Most lines have changed, but all of those changes are about introducing b. The most notable changes are in predict(), that uses the new model, and train(), that tweaks b the same way that it tweaks w, increasing or decreasing it while keeping an eye on the loss. I wasn't sure how to tweak w and b at the same time, so I went for one of those temporary hacks that we all love: I just added a couple of new branches to the if. Let's give this program a shot. The train() function takes longer to converge this time, but eventually it does:

```
Iteration    0 => Loss: 812.867
Iteration    1 => Loss: 804.821
Iteration    2 => Loss: 796.818
...
Iteration 1551 -> Loss: 22.864

w=1.100, b=12.930
Prediction: x=20 => y=34.93
```

And here is what we get if we plot the data and the line:

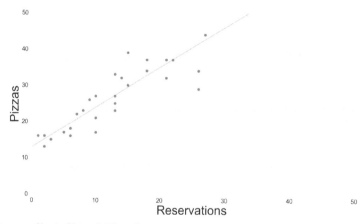

Now we're really talking! This line approximates the examples much better, and it crosses the y axis at a value equal to b. Even better, our final loss is lower than it used to be, which means that we're more accurate than ever at forecasting pizza sales. Roberto will be delighted!

That was a lot of work for a first version of our program. Let's catch our breath, take a step back, and take a look at the bigger picture.

### "Hyperparameters"?

In supervised learning, the training phase returns a set of values that we can use in the model—in our case, a weight and a bias that we can use in the equation of a line. Those values are called "parameters." That's unfortunate for us programmers, because we already use the name "parameter" for something different. It's easy to get confused between parameters such as w and b, and the parameters of a function such as train().

To avoid the confusion, ML practitioners use another name for the parameters of the train() function: they call them *hyperparameters*, meaning "higher level parameters." To recap: we set *hyperparameters* such as iterations and lr, so that the train() function can find *parameters* such as w and b.

## What You Just Learned

We went through a lot of information in these first two chapters, and I introduced many new terms. Let's recap.

In this chapter we wrote our first *supervised learning* program. A supervised learning system learns from *examples* composed of *input variables* and *labels*. In our case, the input variables were the number of reservations, and the labels were the number of pizzas.

Supervised learning works by approximating the examples with a function, also called the *model*. In our first program, the model is a line identified by two *parameters*—the *weight* and the *bias*. This idea of approximating the examples with a line is called *linear regression*.

The first phase of supervised learning is the *training phase*, when the system tweaks the parameters of the model to approximate the examples. During this search, the system is guided by a *loss function* that measures the distance between the current model and the *ground truth*: the lower the loss, the better the model. Our program calculates the loss with a formula called the *mean squared error*. The result of training are a weight and a bias—the ones that result in the lowest loss that the system could find.

The parameters found during the training phase are then used during the second phase of supervised learning: the *prediction phase*. This phase passes an unlabeled input through the parametrized model. The result is a forecast, such as: "Tonight, you can expect to sell 42 pizzas."

You can find an analogy between the training and prediction phases of supervised learning, and the *compilation* and *runtime* phases of programming. Training tends to be hungry for data and require a lot of computation, while prediction tends to be cheap. Even in our little program, the train() function takes a discernible time to find a line that fits the examples, while predict() is a blazing fast multiplication.

The differences between training and prediction become even more obvious for large systems: training a speech recognition system might involve weeks of number crunching through millions of audio files on multiple GPUs. Then you could conceivably deploy the system to a smartphone, and use it to cheaply predict the meanings of individual samples.

Phew! That was a lot of knowledge. I promise that no other chapter will introduce so many new terms at once.

On the plus side, in this chapter we've coded a supervised learning program from scratch, and that's quite an achievement. Most ML software today, including most of those amazing deep learning systems, uses supervised learning. Granted, those systems are way more complicated than our pizza forecaster. Rather than a list of reservations, they might eat high-resolution images for breakfast; and rather than a simple model with two parameters, they might have a complex model with tens of thousands of parameters. Still, they work on the same basic premises of our tiny Python program.

In the next chapter, we'll build on those premises, getting familiar with one of the most important algorithms in machine learning.

## Hands On: Tweaking the Learning Rate

Before you move on, you might want to play with the code for a little while. That's optional, but it's a good way to make these concepts stick.

To begin with, you can start getting familiar with the system's hyperparameters. (If you don't know what a "hyperparameter" is, read "Hyperparameters"?, on page 29.) Try changing the value of the lr argument to train(). What happens if you set lr to a very small value? What if you set it to a large value? What are we gaining and losing in the two cases? After you're done experimenting, check out the content of the 02_first/solution directory for straight answers to those questions.

# CHAPTER 3

# Walking the Gradient

In the previous chapter, we achieved something to be proud of: we wrote a piece of code that learns. If we got that code reviewed by computer scientists, however, they would find it lacking. In particular, they'd raise an eyebrow at the sight of the train() function. "This code might work okay for this simple example," the stern computer scientist would say, "but it won't scale to real-world problems."

Fair enough. In this chapter, we're going to address those concerns in two ways. First, we're *not* going to get our code reviewed by a computer scientist. Second, we're going to analyze the shortcomings of the current train() implementation and solve them with one of machine learning's key ideas: an algorithm called *gradient descent*. Like our current train() code, gradient descent is a way to find the minimum of the loss function—but it's faster, more precise, and more general than the code from the previous chapter.

Gradient descent isn't just useful for our tiny program. In fact, you cannot go very far in ML without gradient descent. In different forms, this algorithm will accompany us all the way to the end of this book.

Let's start with the problem that gradient descent is meant to solve.

## Our Algorithm Doesn't Cut It

Our program can successfully forecast pizza sales, but why stop there? Maybe we could use the same code to forecast other things, such as the stock market. We could get rich overnight! (Spoiler: that wouldn't really work.)

If we tried to apply our linear regression program to a different problem, however, we'd bump into an impediment. Our code is based on a simple line-shaped model with two parameters: the weight w and the bias b. Most real-life problems require complex models with more parameters. As an example, remember our goal for Part I of this book: we want to build a system that recognizes images. An image is way more complicated than a single number, so it needs a model with many more parameters than the pizza forecaster.

Unfortunately, if we added more parameters to our model, we'd kill its performance. To see why, let's review the train() function from the previous chapter:

```
def train(X, Y, iterations, lr):
    w = b = 0
    for i in range(iterations):
        current_loss = loss(X, Y, w, b)
        print("Iteration %4d => Loss: %.6f" % (i, current_loss))

        if loss(X, Y, w + lr, b) < current_loss:
            w += lr
        elif loss(X, Y, w - lr, b) < current_loss:
            w -= lr
        elif loss(X, Y, w, b + lr) < current_loss:
            b += lr
        elif loss(X, Y, w, b - lr) < current_loss:
            b -= lr
        else:
            return w, b

    raise Exception("Couldn't converge within %d iterations" % iterations)
```

At each iteration, this algorithm tweaks either w or b, looking for the values that minimize the loss. Here is one way in which that approach could go wrong: as we tweak w, we might be increasing the loss caused by b, and the other way around. To avoid that problem and get as close as possible to the minimum loss, we should tweak both parameters *at once*. The more parameters we have, the more important it is to tweak them all at the same time.

To tweak w and b together, we'd have to try all the possible combinations of tweaks: increase w and b; increase w and decrease b; increase w and leave b unchanged; decrease w and... well, you get the point. Do the math, and you'll find that the total number of tweaking combinations, including the one where all the parameters stay unchanged, would be 3 to the power of the number of parameters. With two parameters, that would be $3^2$—that is, nine combinations.

Calling loss() nine times per iteration doesn't sound like a big deal—but increase the number of parameters to 10, and you get $3^{10}$ combinations, which is almost 60,000 calls per iteration. You might think that 10 parameters are far-fetched, but they aren't. Later in this book we'll use models with *hundreds of thousands* of parameters. With such large models, an algorithm that tries every combination of parameters is never going to fly. We should nip this slow code in the bud.

There is also a more urgent problem in the current implementation of train(): it tweaks parameters in increments that are equal to the learning rate. If lr is large, then the parameters change quickly, which speeds up training—but the final result is less precise, because each parameter has to be a multiple of that large lr. To increase precision, we need a small lr, which results in even slower training. We're trading off speed for precision, when we actually need both.

That's why our current code is basically a hack. We should replace it with a better algorithm—one that makes train() both fast *and* precise.

## Gradient Descent

Let's look for a better train() algorithm. The job of train() is to find the parameters that minimize the loss, so let's start by focusing on loss() itself:

```
def loss(X, Y, w, b):
    return np.average((predict(X, w, b) - Y) ** 2)
```

Look at this function's arguments. X and Y contain the input variables and the labels, so they never change from one call of loss() to the next. To make the upcoming discussion easier, let's also temporarily fix b at 0. So now the only variable is w.

How does the loss change as w changes? I put together a program that plots loss() for w ranging from -1 to 4, and draws a green cross on its minimum value. Check out the following graph (as usual, that code is among the book's source code):

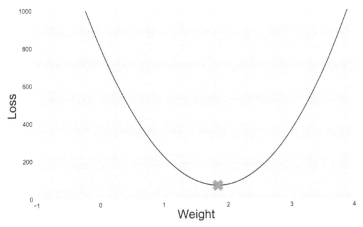

Nice curve! Let's call it the *loss curve*. The entire idea of train() is to find that marked spot at the bottom of the curve—the value of w that gives the minimum loss. At that w, the model approximates the data points as well as it can.

Now imagine that the loss curve is a valley, and there is a hiker standing somewhere in this valley. The hiker wants to reach her basecamp, right where the marked spot is—but it's dark, and she can only see the terrain right around her feet. To find the basecamp, she can follow a simple approach: walk in the direction of the steepest downward slope. If the terrain doesn't contain holes or cliffs—and our loss function doesn't—then each steps will take the hiker closer to the basecamp.

To turn that idea into running code, we need to measure the slope of the loss curve. In mathspeak, that slope is called the *gradient* of the curve. By convention, the gradient at a certain point is an arrow that points directly uphill from that point, like this:

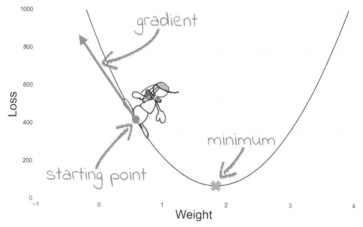

To measure the gradient, we can use a mathematical tool called "the *derivative* of the loss with respect to the weight," written $\partial L/\partial w$. More formally, the derivative at a certain point measures how the loss $L$ changes at that point for small variations of $w$. Imagine increasing the weight just a tiny little bit. What happens to the loss? In the case of the diagram here, the derivative would be a negative number, meaning that the loss is decreasing. If the derivative were positive, that would mean that the loss is increasing. At the minimum point of the curve—the point marked with the cross—the curve is level, and the derivative is zero.

In the case of the diagram here, the derivative would be a negative number, meaning that the loss decreases when $w$ increases. If the hiker were standing on the right side of the diagram, the derivative would be positive, meaning that the loss *increases* when $w$ increases. At the minimum point of the curve—the point marked with the cross—the curve is level, and the derivative is zero.

Note that the hiker would have to walk in the direction opposite to the gradient to approach the minimum—so, in the case of a negative derivative like the one in the picture, she'd take a step in the positive direction. The size of the hiker's steps should also be proportional to the derivative. If the derivative is a big number (either positive or negative), that means the curve is steep, and the basecamp is far away. So the hiker can take big steps with confidence. As she approaches the basecamp, the derivative becomes smaller, and so do her steps.

The algorithm I just described is called *gradient descent*, or GD for short. Implementing it requires a tiny bit of math.

## A Sprinkle of Math

Here is how to crack gradient descent with math. First, let's rewrite the mean squared error loss in good old-fashioned mathematical notation:

$$L = \frac{1}{m} \sum_{i=1}^{m} ((wx_i + b) - y_i)^2$$

If you're not familiar with this notation, know that the $\sum$ symbol stands for "sum." Also, the m in the preceding formula stands for "the number of examples." In English, the formula reads: add the squared errors of all the examples, from the example number one to the example number m, and divide the result by the number of examples.

Remember that the xs and ys are constants—they are the values of the input variable and the labels, respectively. m is also a constant, because the number of examples never changes. So is b, because we temporarily fixed it at zero. We'll reintroduce b in a short while, but for the moment, the only value that varies in this formula is w.

Now we have to calculate the direction and size of the gradient—that is, the derivative of L with respect to w. If you remember calculus from school, you might be able to calculate this derivative on your own. Otherwise, don't worry about it. Somebody already did it for us:

$$\frac{\partial L}{\partial w} = \frac{2}{m} \sum_{i=1}^{m} x_i ((wx_i + b) - y_i)$$

The derivative of the loss is somewhat similar to the loss itself, except that the power of 2 is gone, each element of the sum has been multiplied by x, and the final result is multiplied by 2. We can plug any value of w into this formula, and get back the gradient at that point.

Here's the same formula converted to code. I fixed b at 0 as planned:

03_gradient/gradient_descent_without_bias.py
```
def gradient(X, Y, w):
    return 2 * np.average(X * (predict(X, w, 0) - Y))
```

Now that we have a function to calculate the gradient, let's rewrite train() to do gradient descent.

## Downhill Riding

Here is train(), updated for gradient descent:

03_gradient/gradient_descent_without_bias.py
```
def train(X, Y, iterations, lr):
    w = 0
    for i in range(iterations):
        print("Iteration %4d => Loss: %.10f" % (i, loss(X, Y, w, 0)))
        w -= gradient(X, Y, w) * lr
    return w
```

This version of train() is much terser than the previous one. With GD, we don't need any if. We just initialize w, and then step repeatedly in the opposite direction of the gradient. (Remember, the gradient is pointing uphill, and we want to go downhill). The lr hyperparameter is still there, but now it tells how large each step should be in proportion to the gradient.

When you do gradient descent, you have to decide when to stop it. The old version of train() returned after a maximum number of iterations, or when it failed to decrease the loss further—whichever came first. With GD, the loss could in theory decrease forever, inching toward the minimum in smaller and smaller steps, without ever quite reaching it. So, when should we stop making those ever-tinier steps?

We could decide to stop when the gradient becomes small enough, because that means that we're very close to the minimum. This code, however, follows a less refined approach: when you call train(), you tell it for how many iterations to run. More iterations lead to a lower loss, but since the loss decreases progressively more slowly, at a certain point we can just decide that the additional precision isn't worth the wait.

Later in this book (in Chapter 15, Let's Do Development, on page 177), you will learn how to choose good values for hyperparameters such as iterations and lr. For now, I just tried a bunch of different values and ended up with these ones, which seem to result in a low enough, precise enough loss:

```
X, Y = np.loadtxt("pizza.txt", skiprows=1, unpack=True)
w = train(X, Y, iterations=100, lr=0.001)
print("\nw=%.10f" % w)
```

Here is what we get by running this code:

```
Iteration     0 => Loss: 812.8666666667
Iteration     1 => Loss: 304.3630879787
Iteration     2 => Loss: 143.5265791020
...
Iteration    98 => Loss: 69.1209628275
Iteration    99 => Loss: 69.1209628275

w=1.8436928702
```

The loss drops at each iteration, as it should. After 100 iterations, GD got so close to the minimum that you can't see the difference between the last two losses. It seems like our gradient descent algorithm is doing its job.

But wait—remember that we're only using the w parameter. Let's see what happens when we put b back in the game.

## Escape from Flatland

Take a look at the loss function in math notation again:

$$L = \frac{1}{m} \sum_{i=1}^{m} ((wx_i + b) - y_i)^2$$

So far, we treated all the values in this function as constants, except for w. In particular, we fixed b at a value of 0. If we change b from a constant to a variable, the loss is not a two-dimensional curve anymore. Now it's a surface as shown in the graph on page 38.

Our hiker doesn't live in flatland anymore—she's free to walk around in three dimensions. The two horizontal axes are the values of w and b, and the vertical axis is the value of the loss. In other words, each point on this surface represents the error of a line in our linear regression model, and we want to find the line with the lowest error: the point marked with a cross.

Even if the loss is now a surface, we can still reach its minimum point with gradient descent—only, now we need to calculate the gradient of a function of multiple variables. Fortunately for us, there is a way to do that with a technique called *partial derivatives*.

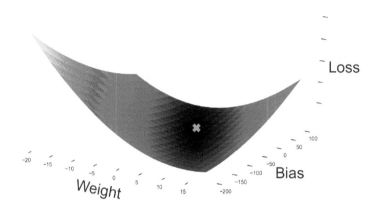

## Partial Derivatives

Let's see what partial derivatives are, and how they can help us. Taking a partial derivative is like slicing a function with a katana, and then calculating the derivative of the slice. (It doesn't have to be a katana, but using a katana makes the process look cooler.) For example, when we fixed b at 0, we sliced the loss like this:

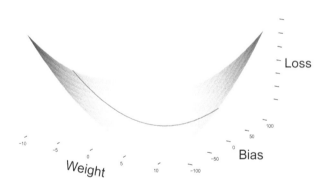

The slice shown here is the same loss curve that we plotted in Gradient Descent, on page 33. It looks squashed because I used different ranges and scales for the axes, but it's exactly the same function. For each value of b, you have one such curve, which has w as its only variable. Likewise, for each value of w you have a curve with variable b. Here is the one with w = 0 as shown in the graph on page 39.

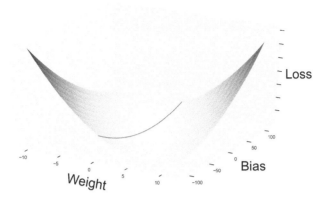

Once we have those one-dimensional slices, we can calculate the gradients on them, just like we did for the original curve. And here's the good news: if we combine the gradient of the slices, then we get the gradient of the surface. The following graph visualizes that concept:

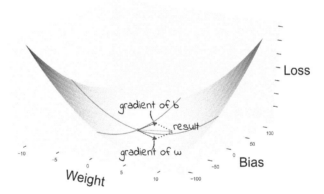

Thanks to partial derivatives, we just split a two-variables problem into two one-variable problems. That means that we don't need a new algorithm to do GD on a surface. Instead, we just slice the surface using partial derivatives, and then do GD on each slice.

---

**Math Deep Dive: Derivatives and Calculus**

 The branch of mathematics that deals with gradients, derivatives, and partial derivatives is called *calculus*. If you want to dig deeper into calculus, check out Khan Academy.[1] As usual, it contains way more information on the subject than you need to read this book.

---

1.   www.khanacademy.org/math/differential-calculus

In concrete, you can calculate partial derivatives by taking each variable (in our case, w and b) and pretending that it's the *only* variable in the function. Just imagine that everything else is constant, and calculate the derivative with respect to that sole variable. We already did half of that work when we fixed b and calculated the derivative of L with respect to w:

$$\frac{\partial L}{\partial w} = \frac{2}{m} \sum_{i=1}^{m} x_i((wx_i + b) - y_i)$$

Now we need to do the same, only the other way around: pretend that w is a constant, and take the derivative of L with respect to b. Feel free to calculate that partial derivative by yourself if you studied calculus. For the rest of us, here it is:

$$\frac{\partial L}{\partial b} = \frac{2}{m} \sum_{i=1}^{m}((wx_i + b) - y_i)$$

Let's recap how GD works on a two-dimensional loss surface. Our hiker is standing at a specific spot—that is, a specific value of w and b. She's armed with the formulas to compute the partial derivatives of L with respect to w and b. She plugs the current values of w and b into those formulas, and she gets one gradient for each variable. She applies GD to both gradients, and there you have it! She's descending the gradient of the surface.

Enough math for this chapter. Let's put this algorithm in code.

## Putting Gradient Descent to the Test

Here is the two-variables version of our gradient descent code, with the changes marked by little arrows in the left margin:

03_gradient/gradient_descent_final.py

```
import numpy as np

def predict(X, w, b):
    return X * w + b

def loss(X, Y, w, b):
    return np.average((predict(X, w, b) - Y) ** 2)

def gradient(X, Y, w, b):
    w_gradient = 2 * np.average(X * (predict(X, w, b) - Y))
    b_gradient = 2 * np.average(predict(X, w, b) - Y)
    return (w_gradient, b_gradient)

def train(X, Y, iterations, lr):
    w = b = 0
```

```
      for i in range(iterations):
➤         print("Iteration %4d => Loss: %.10f" % (i, loss(X, Y, w, b)))
➤         w_gradient, b_gradient = gradient(X, Y, w, b)
➤         w -= w_gradient * lr
➤         b -= b_gradient * lr
➤     return w, b

   X, Y = np.loadtxt("pizza.txt", skiprows=1, unpack=True)
➤  w, b = train(X, Y, iterations=20000, lr=0.001)
   print("\nw=%.10f, b=%.10f" % (w, b))
   print("Prediction: x=%d => y=%.2f" % (20, predict(20, w, b)))
```

The gradient() function now returns the partial derivatives of the loss with respect to both w and b. Those values are used by train() to update both w and b, at the same time. I also bumped up the number of iterations, because the program takes longer to get close to the minimum now that it has two variables to tweak.

Let's make an apples-to-apples comparison between this new version of the program and the one from the previous chapter. First, let's run the earlier version with plenty of iterations and a pretty low lr of 0.0001, to get four decimal digits of precision:

```
…
Iteration 157777 -> Loss: 22.842737

w=1.081, b=13.171
Prediction: x=20 => y=34.80
```

Our new GD-based implementation runs circles around that result. With just 20,000 iterations, we get:

```
…
Iteration 19999 => Loss: 22.8427367616

w=1.0811301700, b=13.1722676564
Prediction: x=20 => y=34.79
```

Higher precision in almost one tenth of the iterations. Good stuff! This faster, more precise learner might be wasted for our pizza forecasting problem—after all, nobody buys one hundredth of a pizza. However, that additional speed will prove essential to tackle more advanced problems.

Finally, I wrote a quick visualization program to plot the algorithm's path, from an arbitrary starting point to the minimum loss. I tried to give you an intuitive understanding of gradient descent in the previous few pages, but nothing beats watching it in motion as shown in the graph on page 42.

The hiker didn't take the optimal route to the basecamp, because she couldn't know that route in advance. Instead, she let the slope of the loss function

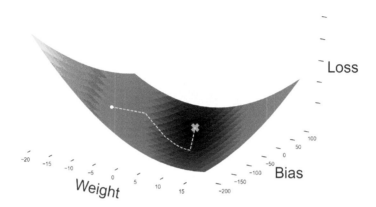

guide her every step. After two abrupt changes of direction, she finally reached the bottom of the valley, and proceeded along a gently sloping trail down to the basecamp.

## When Gradient Descent Fails

GD doesn't give you many guarantees. By using it, we could follow a longer route than the shortest possible one. We could step *past* the basecamp, and then have to backtrack. We could even step further away from the basecamp, as the crow flies.

There are also a few unlucky cases where gradient descent might miss its target entirely. One such case has to do with the learning rate, and we'll explore it in the Hands On exercise at the end of this chapter. Most GD failures, however, have to do with the shape of the loss surface.

With some imagination, you can probably think of a surface that trips up the hiker on her way to the basecamp. What if the loss surface includes a sudden cliff like the one in following graph, and the hiker ends up making her best Wile E. Coyote impression?

this gap is bad for GD

Here is another example: what if the hiker reaches a *local minimum*, like the one in this graph, instead of the *global minimum* that it's supposed to reach?

The gradient at the bottom of the local minimum is zero. If gradient descent gets in there, it gets stuck.

Long story short, GD works well as long as the loss surface has a few characteristics. In mathspeak, a good loss function should be *convex* (meaning that it doesn't have bumps that result in local minima); *continuous* (meaning that it doesn't have vertical cliffs or gaps); and *differentiable* (meaning that it's smooth, without cusps and other weird spots where you cannot even calculate a derivative). Our current loss function ticks all those boxes, so it's ideal for GD. Later on, we will apply GD to other functions, and we will vet those functions for such prerequisites.

GD is also the main reason why we implemented our loss with the mean squared error formula. We could have used the mean *absolute value* of the error—but the mean absolute value doesn't work well with GD, because it has a non-differentiable cusp around the value 0. As a bonus, squaring the error makes large errors even larger, creating a really steep surface as you get further away from the minimum. In turn, that steepness means that GD blazes toward the minimum at high speed. Because of both its smoothness and its steepness, the mean squared error is a great fit for GD.

## What You Just Learned

In this chapter we investigated *gradient descent*, the most widely used algorithm to miminize loss. No matter how complicated our model and dataset are, gradient descent always works the same way: it takes a step in the opposite direction as the *gradient* of the loss, and keeps doing that until the gradient becomes small. To find the gradient, we took the *partial derivatives* of the loss with respect to w and b.

GD has a few limitations. In particular, being based on derivatives, it expects that the loss function is smooth and without gaps, so that you can calculate its derivative anywhere. Also, GD can get stuck in a *local minimum*, failing to reach the *global minimum*. To avoid those problems, we'll try to use smooth loss functions that have only one minimum.

GD is not the be all and end all of the algorithms that minimize loss. Researchers are exploring alternative algorithms that do better in some circumstances. There are also variations of plain vanilla GD, some of which we'll meet later in this book. Nonetheless, GD is still a crucial algorithm in modern ML, and it's likely to keep that spot for a while.

And now, prepare for a challenge. At the beginning of this chapter, I told you that GD allows our code to scale to more interesting models that approximate complicated datasets. In the next chapter, we'll see one such model.

## Hands On: Basecamp Overshooting

Let's talk about the learning rate again. In the final example of this chapter, I used a learning rate of 0.001. Try increasing the learning rate, and you might notice that at some point the loss starts to *increase* instead of decreasing. Can you imagine why?

If you can't picture the answer in your mind, try drawing the loss function on paper. What happens with a very large learning rate? As usual, check the content of the 03_gradient/solution directory if you're stuck.

# CHAPTER 4

# Hyperspace!

In the previous two chapters, we predicted an output from an input: a restaurant's pizza sales from its reservations. Most interesting real-world problems, however, have more than one input. Even something as simple as pizza sales isn't likely to depend on reservations alone. For example, if there are many tourists in town, then the restaurant will probably sell more pizzas, even if it got as many reservations as yesterday.

If pizza sales have many variables, imagine how many variables we'll have to consider once we get into complex domains, like recognizing pictures. A learning program that only supports one variable is never going to solve those hairy problems. If we ever want to tackle them, we'd better upgrade our program to support multiple input variables.

We can learn from multiple input variables with a souped-up version of linear regression: *multiple linear regression*. In this chapter, we will extend our program to support multiple linear regression. We'll also add a few tricks to our bag, including a couple of useful matrix operations and several NumPy functions. Let's dive right in!

### A Tough Chapter

Public service announcement: for most readers, this may be the hardest chapter in the entire book. There are two reasons for that difficulty. First, the next few pages are relatively heavy on math. Second, the code in this chapter is minimal, but deep: at one point, we'll go through almost two pages to explain a single line of code.

Don't let those challenges put you off. The concepts and techniques in this chapter are pivotal to ML, and very much worth learning. Also, consider that after this chapter, the rest of the book will look easy!

## Adding More Dimensions

In the previous chapter, we coded a gradient descent-based version of our learning program. This souped-up program can potentially scale to complex models with more than one variable.

In a moment of weakness, we mentioned that opportunity to our friend Roberto. That was a mistake. Now Roberto is all pumped up about forecasting pizza sales from a bunch of different input variables besides reservations, such as the weather, or the number of tourists in town.

This is going to be more work for us—and yet, we can't blame Roberto for wanting to add variables to the model. After all, the more variables we consider, the more likely it is that we'll get accurate predictions of pizza sales.

Let's start with a souped-up version of the old pizza.txt file. Here are the first few lines of this new dataset:

```
04_hyperspace/pizza_2_vars.txt
Reservations  Temperature  Pizzas
13            26           44
2             14           23
14            20           28
```

Roberto suspects that more people drop into his pizzeria on warmer days, so he kept track of the temperature in degrees Celsius. (For reference, 2 °C is almost freezing; 26 °C is about 78 Fahrenheit). Now the third column contains labels (the pizzas), and the first two contain input variables.

First, let's see what happens to linear regression when we move from one to two input variables. You know that linear regression is about approximating the examples with a line, like this:

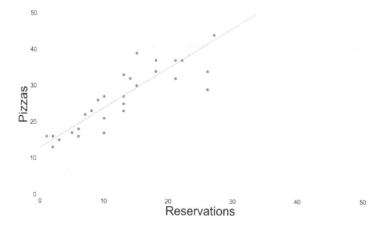

As a reminder, here is the formula of that line:

$\hat{y} = x * w + b$

If we add a second input variable (in our case, the temperature), then the examples aren't laying on a plane anymore—they're points in three-dimensional space. To approximate them, we can use the equivalent of a line, with one more dimension—a plane, as shown in the next graph:

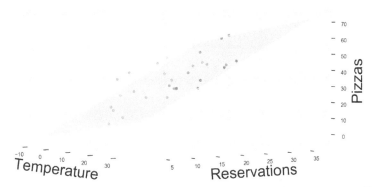

Like we did for the line, we can calculate $\hat{y}$ by using the equation of a plane. That's similar to the equation of a line—but it has two input variables, x1 and x2, and two weights, w1 and w2:

$\hat{y} = x1 * w1 + x2 * w2 + b$

If you're not convinced that we need a separate weight for each input variable, consider this fact: in Roberto's dataset, x1 is the number of reservations and x2 is the temperature. It makes sense that the reservations and the temperature have different impacts on the number of pizzas, so they must have different weights.

In the equation of a line, the bias b shifts the line away from the origin. The same goes for a plane: if we didn't have b, then the plane would be constrained to pass by the origin of the axes. If you want to prove that, just set all the input variables to 0. Without a bias, $\hat{y}$ would also be 0. Thanks to the bias, the plane is free to shift vertically and find the position where it approximates the points as well as it can.

Now see what happens when Roberto adds yet another column to his dataset:

04_hyperspace/pizza_3_vars.txt

| Reservations | Temperature | Tourists | Pizzas |
|---|---|---|---|
| 13 | 26 | 9 | 44 |
| 2 | 14 | 6 | 23 |
| 14 | 20 | 3 | 28 |

This new input variable shows the density of tourists in town, downloaded from the local tourist office's website. It ranges from 1 ("not a soul in town") to 10 ("tourist invasion").

We started by approximating bi-dimensional examples with a one-dimensional model. Then we moved on to approximate three-dimensional examples with a bi-dimensional model. Now that we have four-dimensional examples, we have to approximate them with a three-dimensional model… and this process continues as we add more input variables. In general, to approximate examples with n dimensions, we need an (n - 1)-dimensional shape.

With the exception of H. P. Lovecraft's characters, humans cannot perceive more than three spatial dimensions. However, math has no problem dealing with those sanity-bending multidimensional spaces—it just calls them *hyperspaces*, and describes them with the same equations as bi-dimensional and three-dimensional spaces. However many dimensions we have, we can just add input variables and weights to the formula of the line and the plane:

ŷ = x1 * w1 + x2 * w2 + x3 * w3 + … + b

This formula is called the *weighted sum* of the inputs. The equation of a line is just a special case of this equation—the weighted sum of a single input. So, here's a simple plan to upgrade our learning program from one to many input variables: we'll replace the equation of a line with the more generic formula of the weighted sum.

To implement that plan, however, we'll need a couple more mathematical operations. Let's take a short detour to learn them.

## Matrix Math

To upgrade our system to multiple variables, you'll need to know about two operations on matrices. I don't want to introduce those operations at the last moment, while we're busy coding. Instead, we'll take a few pages to get them out of the way now.

A *matrix* is a bi-dimensional array. For example, here is a (4, 3) matrix, meaning that it has four rows and three columns:

| 2 | 3 | 5 |
|----|----|----|
| 11 | 13 | 19 |
| 31 | 27 | 1 |
| -3 | 14 | 9 |

The two operations that we'll cover are *matrix multiplication* and *matrix transpose*. Both are ubiquitous in ML, and each deserves its own section.

## Multiplying Matrices

Did you ever wonder why ML is usually done on those big racks of GPUs? That's because ML systems spend most of their time doing one operation that happens to be particularly fast on a GPU: they multiply big matrices.

To introduce matrix multiplication, let me tell you its "golden rule" first: we can multiply two matrices if (and only if) the second matrix has as many rows as the first matrix has columns, like this:

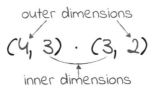

M1 is (4, 3) and M2 is (3, 2). Can we multiply them? To answer this question, write down the operation like this:

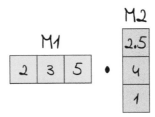

Look at the *inner* dimensions in the multiplication. If they're equal, as in this case, then the multiplication is valid, and the result will be a matrix that has the *outer* dimensions—in this case, (4, 2):

$$(4, 3) \cdot (3, 2) = (4, 2)$$

Let's look at concrete cases, starting with a simple one: a matrix with a single row, multiplied by a matrix with a single column, like this:

First, let's check whether this multiplication is a valid one. The first matrix is (1, 3), and the second is (3, 1). By the golden rule, the multiplication (1, 3) · (3, 1) is legit, and it will return a (1, 1) matrix—a matrix that contains only one element.

To calculate that one element, you multiply each element of M1 with the corresponding element of M2—the first with the first, the second with the second, and so on. Then you add them all together:

```
2 * 2.5 + 3 * 4 + 5 * 1 = 22
```

So, that's the result of the multiplication:

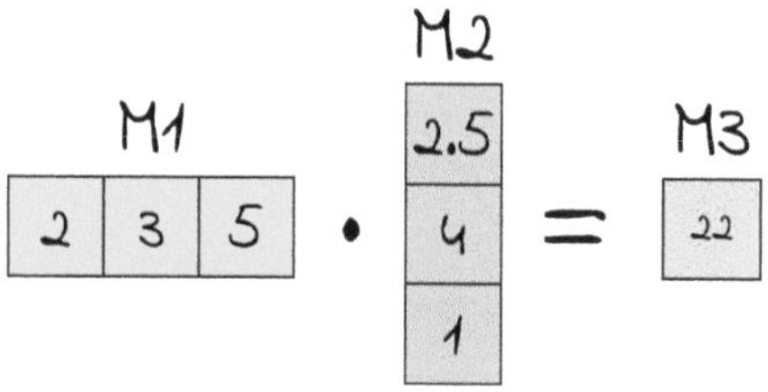

Spoiler alert: astute readers (that's all of you) might notice a similarity between the multiplication here and the formula at the end of Adding More Dimensions, on page 46. As you've probably guessed, that similarity isn't a coincidence: after we're done talking about matrix multiplication, we'll use it to implement our multiple linear regression model.

What happens if the matrices involved have multiple rows and columns? In that case, we perform the same row-by-column calculation that we've just seen, but we do it for each row of the first matrix and each column of the second. Each element (i, j) in the result is the multiplication of row i from M1 and column j from M2:

```
M3[i][j] = i-th_row_of_M1 · j-th_column_of_M2
```

Here's a concrete example:

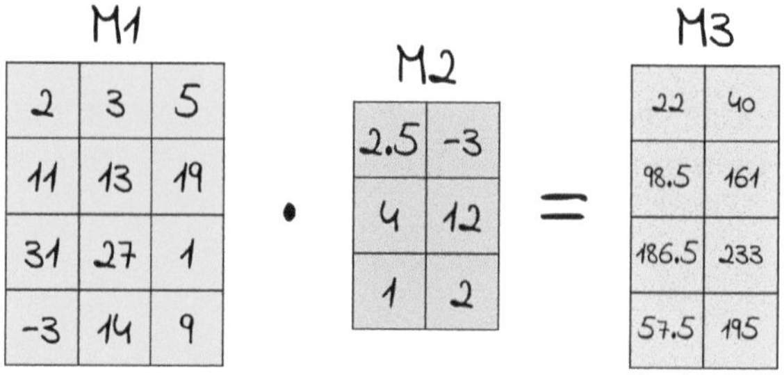

Let's double-check one of M3's elements—say, M3[0][1], which is 40. The rule says that M3[0][1] should be equal to row 0 of M1 by column 1 of M2 as shown in the figure on page 51.

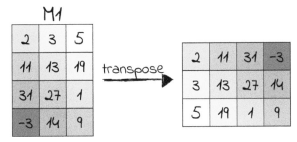

The product of that row and column is 2 * -3 + 3 * 12 + 5 * 2 = 40, as we expected. Repeat the process for each element of M3, and there you have it—matrix multiplication.

Note that in matrix multiplication, different than regular multiplication, order matters. If we swap M1 and M2, then we generally get a different result, and in most cases we cannot complete the multiplication at all. For example, we couldn't multiply M2 by M1, because the inner dimensions in (3, 2) · (4, 3) differ.

We'll have plenty of matrix multiplications in this book, but we'll use NumPy to calculate the results rather than do it by hand. However, you'll have it easier if you remember the golden rule: in matrix multiplication, the inner dimensions must be equal, and the outer dimensions are the dimensions of the result. In our example, we multiplied (4, 3) · (3, 2), so the result is a (4, 2) matrix.

And that's how matrix multiplication works. Let's move on to matrix transpose.

## Transposing Matrices

Compared to matrix multiplication, matrix transpose is easy. When you transpose a matrix, you flip it around the diagonal that goes from top left to bottom right. This diagram uses graduated cell colors to show what a transposed matrix looks like:

Transposing a matrix means that row data become column data, and the other way round. As a result, the matrix's dimensions are swapped. This matrix is (4, 3). When we transpose, it becomes (3, 4).

Now you know about matrix multiplication and transpose. Both operations will come useful in the next few pages. Let's go back to the code.

---

### Math Deep Dive: Linear Algebra

 Matrix operations such as multiplication and transpose belong to a branch of math called *linear algebra*. If you want to really wrap your head about linear algebra, check out the lessons on Khan Academy.[1]

---

## Upgrading the Learner

After this mathematical detour, we can come back to the work at hand. We want to upgrade our learning program to deal with multiple input variables. Let's make a plan of action so that we don't get lost in the process:

1. First, we'll load and prepare the multidimensional data, so that we can feed them to the learning algorithm.

2. After preparing the data, we'll upgrade all the functions in our code to use the new model: we'll switch from a line to a more generic weighted sum, as I described in Adding More Dimensions, on page 46.

Let's step through this plan. Feel free to type the commands in a Python interpreter and make your own experiments. If you don't have an interpreter handy, fear not: I will show you the output of all important commands (sometimes slightly edited, to spare space).

### Preparing Data

I wish I could tell you that ML is all about building amazing AIs and looking cool. The reality is that a large part of the job is preparing data for the learning algorithm. To do that, let's start from the file that contains our dataset:

## pizza_3_vars.txt

| Reservations | Temperature | Tourists | Pizzas |
|---|---|---|---|
| 13 | 26 | 9 | 44 |
| 2 | 14 | 6 | 23 |
| 14 | 20 | 3 | 28 |
| ... | ... | ... | ... |
| 13 | 20 | 3 | 28 |

---

1. www.khanacademy.org/math/linear-algebra

In the previous chapters, this file had two columns, which we loaded into two arrays with NumPy's loadtxt()—and that was it. Now that we have multiple input variables, X needs to become a matrix, like this:

pizza_3_vars.txt

| | Reservations | Temperature | Tourists | Pizzas |
|---|---|---|---|---|
| | 13 | 26 | 9 | 44 |
| | 2 | 14 | 6 | 23 |
| | 14 | 20 | 3 | 28 |
| | ... | ... | ... | ... |
| | 13 | 20 | 3 | 28 |

Each row in X is an example, and each column is an input variable.

If we load the file with loadtxt(), like we did before, we'll get a NumPy array for each column:

```
import numpy as np
x1, x2, x3, y = np.loadtxt("pizza_3_vars.txt", skiprows=1, unpack=True)
```

Arrays are NumPy's killer feature. They're very flexible objects that can represent anything from a *scalar* (a single number) to a multidimensional structure. That same flexibility, however, makes arrays somewhat hard to grasp at first. I'll show you how to mold those four arrays into the X and Y variables that we want—but when you get around to do this on your own, you'll probably want to keep NumPy's documentation handy.

To see which dimensions an array has, we can use its shape() operation:

```
x1.shape   # => (30, )
```

All four columns have 30 elements, one for each example in pizza_3_vars.txt. That dangling comma is NumPy's way of saying that these arrays have just one dimension. In other words, they're what you probably think about when you hear the word "array," as opposed to "matrix."

Let's build the X matrix by joining the first three arrays together:

```
X = np.column_stack((x1, x2, x3))
X.shape   # => (30, 3)
```

Here are the first two rows of X:

```
X[:2]   # => array([[13., 26., 9.], [2., 14., 6.]])
```

NumPy's indexes are powerful, and sometimes confusing. The notation [:2] in this code is a shortcut for [0:2], that means "the rows with index from zero to 2, excluded"—that is, the first two rows.

Now that we took care of X, let's look at y, that still has that one-dimensional (30, ) shape. Here is one trick that saved my bottom multiple times: avoid mixing NumPy matrices and one-dimensional arrays. Code that involves both can have surprising behavior. For this reason, as soon as you have a one-dimensional array, it's a good idea to reshape it into a matrix with the reshape() function:

```
Y = y.reshape(-1, 1)
```

reshape() takes the dimensions of the new array. If one dimension is -1, then NumPy will set it to whatever makes the other dimensions fit. So the preceding line means: "reshape Y so that it's a matrix with 1 column, and as many rows as you need to fit the current elements." The result is a (30, 1) matrix:

| pizza_3_vars.txt | | | |
|---|---|---|---|
| Reservations | Temperature | Tourists | Pizzas |
| 13 | 26 | 9 | 44 |
| 2 | 14 | 6 | 23 |
| 14 | 20 | 3 | 28 |
| ... | ... | ... | ... |
| 13 | 20 | 3 | 28 |

```
Y.shape   # => (30, 1)
```

So now we have our data neatly arranged into an X matrix for input variables, and a Y matrix for labels. Preparing data... check! Let's move to update the functions of our learning system, starting with the predict() function.

## Upgrading Prediction

Now that we have multiple input variables, we need to change the prediction formula—from the simple equation of a line, to a weighted sum:

```
ŷ = x1 * w1 + x2 * w2 + x3 * w3 + …
```

You might have noticed that something is missing in this formula. To simplify it, I temporarily removed the bias b. It will be back soon.

Now we can translate the weighted sum to a multidimensional version of predict(). As a reminder, here is the old mono-dimensional predict() (without the bias):

```
def predict(X, w):
    return X * w
```

The new predict() should still take X and w—but those variables have more dimensions now. X used to be a vector of m elements, where m is the number of examples. Now X is a matrix of (m, n), where n is the number of input variables. In the specific case that we're tracking now, we have 30 examples and 3 input variables, so X is a (30, 3) matrix.

What about w? Just as we need one x per input variable, we also need one w per input variable. Different from the xs, though, the ws will be the same for each example. So we could make the weights a matrix of (n, 1), or a matrix of (1, n). For reasons that will become clear in a moment, it's better to make it (n, 1): one row per input variable, and a single column.

Let's initialize this matrix of (n, 1). Do you remember that we used to initialize w at zero? Now w is a matrix, so we must initialize all its elements to zeros. NumPy has a zeros() function for that:

```
w = np.zeros((X.shape[1], 1))
w.shape   # => (3, 1)
```

Remember that X.shape[0] is the number of rows in X, and X.shape[1] is the number of columns. The code here says that w has as many rows as the columns in X—in our case, 3.

And this is where matrix multiplication finally becomes useful. Look back at the weighted sum:

```
ŷ = x1 * w1 + x2 * w2 + x3 * w3
```

If X had just one row, this formula would be the multiplication of X by w:

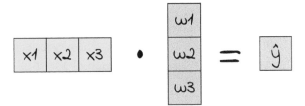

In our case, X doesn't have one row. It has one row for each example—a (30, 3) matrix. When we multiply X by w, which is (3, 1), we get a (30, 1) matrix: one row per example, and a single column that contains the prediction for that example. In other words, a single matrix multiplication gets us the predictions for all the examples in one fell swoop!

So it turned out that rewriting prediction for multiple input variables is as simple as multiplying X and w, with a little help from NumPy's matmul() function:

```
def predict(X, w):
    return np.matmul(X, w)
```

It took us a while to get through this tiny function. Also, we cut a corner by temporarily ignoring the bias, which I'll reintroduce later. So far, however, the result was worth it: predict() implements the model of multiple linear regression in a single teeny line of code.

## Upgrading the Loss

Moving on to the loss() function—remember that we used the mean squared error to calculate the loss, like this:

```
def loss(X, Y, w):
    return np.average((predict(X, w) - Y) ** 2)
```

Once again, I removed the bias b from loss(), so that we have one less thing to worry about. We'll reintroduce the bias in a short while. First, let's see how we should change this stripped-down version of loss() to accomodate multiple dimensions.

I remember how frustrated I got with matrix operations when I wrote my first ML programs. Matrix dimensions, in particular, never seemed to add up. With time, I learned that matrix dimensions could actually be my friends: if I tracked them carefully, they could help me piece my code together. Let's do the same here: we can use matrix dimensions to guide us through the code.

Let's start from the labels. We have two matrices of labels in the previous code: Y, that contains the ground truth from the dataset, and the y_hat matrix calculated by predict(). Both Y and y_hat are (m, 1) matrices, meaning that they have one row for example, and one column. In our case, we have 30 examples, so they're (30, 1). If we subtract Y from y_hat, NumPy checks that the two matrices have the same size, and subtracts each element of Y from each element of y_hat. The result is still (30, 1).

Then we want to square all the elements in this (30, 1) matrix. Because the matrix is implemented as a NumPy array, we can make use of a feature of NumPy called *broadcasting*, which we already used in the previous chapters: when we apply an arithmetic operation to a NumPy array, the operation is "broadcast" over each element of the array. In other words, we can square the entire matrix, and NumPy dutifully applies the "square" operation to each of its elements. The result of this operation is a matrix of squared errors, and is still (30, 1).

Finally, we call average(), which averages all the elements in the matrix, returning a single scalar number:

```
a_number = loss(X, Y, w)
a_number.shape  # => ()
```

The empty parentheses are NumPy's way of saying: "this is a scalar, so it has no dimensions."

Here's the bottom line: we don't need to change the way we calculate the loss at all. Our mean squared error code works with multiple input variables just as well as it did with one variable.

## Upgrading the Gradient

We just have one last thing to do: we need to upgrade the gradient of the loss to multiple variables. I'll cut straight to the chase and give you a matrix-based version of the gradient() function:

```
def gradient(X, Y, w):
    return 2 * np.matmul(X.T, (predict(X, w) - Y)) / X.shape[0]
```

X.T means "X transposed"—the operation that we talked about in Transposing Matrices, on page 51.

See "Of Gradients and Matrices" on ProgML.

It took me a while to go from the old version of gradient() to this new matrix-based one. For once, I won't give you all the details about this function, simply because they'd take up too much space—but if you're curious, you can read them on the book's companion site, ProgML.[2] If you're so inclined, you can even check by yourself that this new version of gradient() is just the same as the older gradient(), except that it works with multiple input variables.

## Putting It All Together

Let's check that we have everything in order:

- We wrote the code that prepares the data.
- We upgraded predict().
- We came to the conclusion that there is no need to upgrade loss().
- We upgraded gradient().

Check... check... check... and check. We can finally apply all those changes to our learning program:

---

2.  www.progml.com

04_hyperspace/multiple_regression_without_bias.py

```python
import numpy as np


def predict(X, w):
    return np.matmul(X, w)


def loss(X, Y, w):
    return np.average((predict(X, w) - Y) ** 2)


def gradient(X, Y, w):
    return 2 * np.matmul(X.T, (predict(X, w) - Y)) / X.shape[0]


def train(X, Y, iterations, lr):
    w = np.zeros((X.shape[1], 1))
    for i in range(iterations):
        print("Iteration %4d => Loss: %.20f" % (i, loss(X, Y, w)))
        w -= gradient(X, Y, w) * lr
    return w


x1, x2, x3, y = np.loadtxt("pizza_3_vars.txt", skiprows=1, unpack=True)
X = np.column_stack((x1, x2, x3))
Y = y.reshape(-1, 1)
w = train(X, Y, iterations=100000, lr=0.001)
```

We took quite a few pages to get it done, but this code is very similar to the code from the previous chapter. Aside from the part that loads and prepares the data, we changed just three lines. Also note that the functions are generic: not only they can process Roberto's three-variables dataset—they'd work just as well with an arbitrary number of input variables.

If we run the program, here's what we get:

```
Iteration      0 => Loss: 1333.56666666666660603369
Iteration      1 => Loss: 151.14311361881479456315
Iteration      2 => Loss: 64.99460808656147037254
…
Iteration 99999 => Loss: 6.89576133146784187034
```

The loss decreases at each iteration, and that's a hint that the program is indeed learning. However, our job isn't quite done yet: you might remember that we removed the bias parameter in the beginning of this discussion, to make things easier—and we know that we shouldn't expect good predictions without the bias. Fortunately, putting the bias back in is easier than you might think.

## Bye Bye, Bias

So far, we implemented this prediction formula:

ŷ = x1 * w1 + x2 * w2 + x3 * w3

Now we want to add the bias back to the system, like this:

ŷ = x1 * w1 + x2 * w2 + x3 * w3 + b

We could rush to the code and add the bias everywhere, like we had in the previous chapter—but hold on a minute. I can teach you a trick to roll the bias into the code more smoothly.

Give another look at the previous formula. What's the difference between the bias and the weights? The only difference is this: the weights are multiplied by some input variable x, and the bias is not. Now imagine that there is one more input variable in the system (let's call it x0) that always has a value of 1. We can rewrite the formula like this:

ŷ = x1 * w1 + x2 * w2 + x3 * w3 + x0 * b

Now there's no difference at all between bias and weights. The bias is just the weight of an input variable that happens to have the constant value 1. So, here's the trick I was talking about: we can add a dummy input variable with the constant value 1, and we won't need an explicit bias anymore.

We could add this constant input variable by slipping a column of 1s into the pizza_3_vars.txt file, like this:

### pizza_3_vars.txt

| Bias | Reservations | Temperature | Tourists | Pizzas |
|------|--------------|-------------|----------|--------|
| 1 | 13 | 26 | 9 | 44 |
| 1 | 2 | 14 | 6 | 23 |
| 1 | 14 | 20 | 3 | 28 |
| ... | ... | ... | ... | ... |
| 1 | 13 | 20 | 3 | 28 |

However, it's generally a good idea to avoid messing with the original data. Instead, let's insert a column of ones into X *after* we load the data. The position of this *bias column* doesn't really matter, but it's a common convention to insert it as the first column, like this:

```
04_hyperspace/multiple_regression_final.py
x1, x2, x3, y = np.loadtxt("pizza_3_vars.txt", skiprows=1, unpack=True)
➤ X = np.column_stack((np.ones(x1.size), x1, x2, x3))
Y = y.reshape(-1, 1)
w = train(X, Y, iterations=100000, lr=0.001)

➤ print("\nWeights: %s" % w.T)
➤ print("\nA few predictions:")
➤ for i in range(5):
➤     print("X[%d] -> %.4f (label: %d)" % (i, predict(X[i], w), Y[i]))
```

I took this chance to add a few printouts to the program. First, they print the weights matrix (transposed, to fit it on a single line). Then they print the predicted values and labels for the first five examples, so we can compare them.

With that, our multiple linear regression program is complete. And now...

## A Final Test Drive

If we run the program, we get this output:

```
Iteration     0 => Loss: 1333.56666666666660603369
Iteration     1 => Loss: 152.37148173674077611395
...
Iteration 99999 => Loss: 6.69817817063803833122

Weights: [[ 2.41178207  1.23368396 -0.02689984  3.12460558]]

A few predictions:
X[0] -> 45.8717 (label: 44)
X[1] -> 23.2502 (label: 23)
X[2] -> 28.5192 (label: 28)
X[3] -> 58.2355 (label: 60)
X[4] -> 42.8009 (label: 42)
```

First, look at the loss. As we expected, it's lower than the one that we got without a bias.

The weights are interesting in their own right. The first weight is actually the bias, which we turned into a regular weight with the "column of ones" trick. The remaining weights match the three input variables—reservations, temperature, and tourist density, respectively. Tourist density has a large weight, and temperature has a tiny one. That's a hint that pizza sales are strongly impacted by tourist density, while they don't seem to change much with the temperature.

Finally, the last few lines of output show predictions and labels for the first five examples. No prediction is more than a pizza or two off the mark. It seems that Roberto was right: upgrading to multiple variables boosted our ability to forecast pizzas.

Congratulations! You worked through the hardest chapter in this book. Let's wrap up what you learned.

## What You Just Learned

This chapter was all about *multiple linear regression*. We extended our program to datasets with more than one input variable—using multiple weights to match the input variables. We also got rid of the explicit bias, turning it into just another weight. Our learning program is now powerful enough to tackle real-world problems, although it doesn't look any more complicated than it did before.

Along the way, you also learned about *matrix multiplication* and *matrix transpose*. These pieces of math sit right at the core of ML. Now that they're in your toolbox, they'll serve you well for years to come.

Finally, in this chapter we started delving deeper into NumPy. I personally have a love–hate relationship with NumPy: I love its power, but I keep getting confused by its interface. Say what you want, NumPy is a must-have ML tool, so it's important to get familiar with it. We'll keep using it throughout this book.

It's time for a plot twist: everything that we talked about in these first few chapters was just groundwork for something different and cooler. In the next chapter, we'll abandon the beaten track of linear regression, and set on the road less traveled... the one that leads to computer vision.

## Hands On: Field Statistician

Now that we have a program that deals with multiple variables, you might want to try it on real-life data. In the data/life-expectancy directory of the book's source code, you'll find a dataset that lists life expectancy in many countries.

In the same directory you'll also find a readme.txt that contains additional information, including an experiment that you can run on this dataset. You'll be asked to train the multiple linear regression program on these data, and to compare the program's predictions to the ground truth.

Have fun playing with real data!

# CHAPTER 5

# A Discerning Machine

We started our journey in machine learning by way of linear regression. Now we're going to use that knowledge (and that code) to branch off toward our goal: a program that recognizes images.

This chapter covers the first step toward image recognition. We'll build a *classifier*—a program that assigns data to one of a limited number of *classes*. Instead of *numerical* labels, classifiers work with *categorical* labels. As an example, consider the difference betwen our pizza predictor and a system that recognizes plants. The pizza predictor outputs a number. By contrast, the plant classifier would output the name of a plant, taken from a predefined list of possible species.

In this chapter, we'll start off small: our classifier will be a *binary classifier* that only recognizes two classes. Many useful real-life systems are based on binary classification. For example, the pneumonia detector that we described in the first chapter assigns X-ray scans to either the class "pneumonia" or the class "no pneumonia."

In the next few pages, we'll replace the linear regression in our program with binary classification. We'll start with a classification problem that has nothing to do with computer vision—however, in the next chapter we'll turn around and apply that binary classifier to an image recognition problem.

Before we dive in, be aware of a slight change in vocabulary. So far, I said that a learning system works in two phases: training and prediction. From now on, I'll call those two phases "training" and "classification" instead, to emphasize that the result of our prediction is a categorical label. "Classification" is just a specific type of prediction, so I'll use the more specific term.

## Where Linear Regression Fails

Our friend Roberto asked us to help him one last time. (He *swears* it's the last time.) Roberto's pizzeria is located in a hip Berlin neighborhood. On busy nights, it's common for noisy customers to hang out in front of the pizzeria, until the neighbors eventually call the police. (If you ever lived in Berlin, then you're likely to appreciate both the customers' reasons, and those of the neighbors.)

Roberto suspects that the same input variables that impact the number of pizzas sold, such as temperature and tourists, also affect the number of loud customers by the entrance, and hence the likelihood of a police call. He wants to know in advance whether a police call is likely to happen, so that he can set up counter-measures—such as walk outside and beg people to lower their voices.

As usual, Roberto sent us a file of labeled data. Here are the first few lines:

05_discerning/police.txt

| Reservations | Temperature | Tourists | Police |
|---|---|---|---|
| 13 | 26 | 9 | 1 |
| 2 | 14 | 6 | 0 |
| 14 | 20 | 3 | 1 |
| 23 | 25 | 9 | 1 |
| 13 | 24 | 8 | 1 |
| 1 | 13 | 2 | 0 |

These are the same data that we used to train our linear regression program, except for one difference: the labels are either 0 (meaning a quiet uneventful night) or 1 (meaning that the police arrived on the scene). Roberto would like a system that forecasts those binary values in the last column.

This is a classification problem, because we want to classify data as either 0 or 1. We might be tempted to solve this problem with the same code that we used so far. Unfortunately, that approach would fail, and here is why.

Linear regression is all about approximating data with a line, like this:

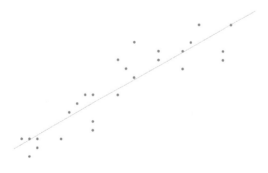

There's a hidden assumption in linear regression: we assume that the data points are roughly aligned to begin with. If the points are arranged on a curve, or scattered around randomly, then we cannot approximate them with a line—and without the line, we cannot make a prediction. The same reasoning applies with multiple input variables: whether we draw a line, a plane, or a higher-dimensional space, we need points that can be reasonably approximated by that shape. Otherwise, we cannot use linear regression.

Now let's take a look at Roberto's file. To make our life easier, let's ignore the "Temperature" and "Tourists" columns for now, and just plot the "Reservations" column against the label, as shown in the graph that follows:

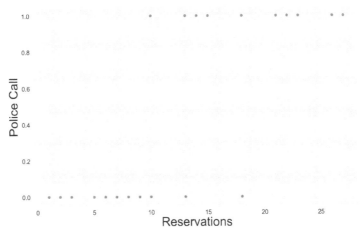

Even by looking at this one input variable, we can guess that linear regression wouldn't work well on categorical data such as these. How are we supposed to draw that line, if the points aren't aligned at all?

Not only is linear regression a bad approximation for categorical data—it's also an *unstable* approximation. To understand what that means, imagine that Roberto's data contain an *outlier*—that is, a data point that's very far away from the others. Maybe there was one day when the pizzeria had a very high number of reservations, but the police was busy with a major operation in Alexanderplatz, and never arrived on the scene. If you add this outlier example to the dataset, the line generated by linear regression moves around a lot, as shown in the graph on page 66.

See? The presence of the outlier leads linear regression to generate a very different line, that results in very different predictions. So not only is this model a bad approximation of the points—it's also extremely sensitive to anomalous data.

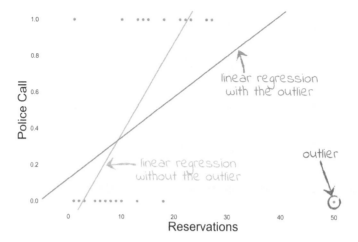

Long story short, linear regression isn't a good fit for categorical data such as these. Let's look for a model that is.

## Invasion of the Sigmoids

Even though linear regression isn't a natural fit for binary classification, that doesn't mean that we have to scrap our linear regression code and start from scratch. Instead, we can adapt our existing algorithm to this new problem, using a technique that statisticians call *logistic regression*.

Let's start by looking back at $\hat{y}$, the *weighted sum* of the inputs that we introduced in Adding More Dimensions, on page 46:

```
ŷ = x1 * w1 + x2 * w2 + x3 * w3 + …
```

In linear regression, $\hat{y}$ could take any value. Binary classification, however, imposes a tight constraint: $\hat{y}$ must not drop below 0, nor raise above 1. Here's an idea: maybe we can find a function that wraps around the weighted sum, and constrains it to the range from 0 to 1—like this:

```
ŷ = wrapper_function(x1 * w1 + x2 * w2 + x3 * w3 + …)
```

Let me repeat what the wrapper_function() does. It takes whatever comes out of the weighted sum—that is, any number—and squashes it into the range from 0 to 1.

We have one more requirement: the function that we're looking for should work well with gradient descent. Think about it: we use this function to calculate $\hat{y}$, then we use $\hat{y}$ to calculate the loss, and finally we descend the loss with gradient descent. For the sake of gradient descent, the wrapper function should be smooth, without flat areas (where the gradient drops to zero) or gaps (where the gradient isn't even defined).

To wrap it up, we want a function that smoothly changes across the range from 0 to 1, without ever jumping or flatlining. Something like this:

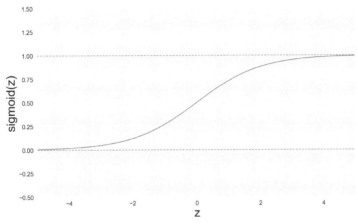

As it happens, this is a well-known function that we can use. It's called the *logistic function*, and it belongs to a family of S-shaped functions called *sigmoids*. Actually, since "logistic function" is a mouthful, people usually just call it the "sigmoid," for short. Here is the sigmoid's formula:

$$\sigma(z) = \frac{1}{1 + e^{-z}}$$

The greek letter sigma ($\sigma$) stands for "sigmoid." I also used the letter z for the sigmoid's input, to avoid confusion with the system's inputs x.

The formula of the sigmoid is hard to grok intuitively, but its picture tells us everything that we need to know. When its input is 0, the sigmoid returns 0.5. Then it quickly and smoothly falls toward 0 for negative numbers, and raises toward 1 for positive numbers—but it never quite reaches those two extremes. In other words, the sigmoid squeezes any value to a narrow band ranging from 0 to 1, it doesn't have any steep cliffs, and it never goes completely flat. That's the function we need!

Let's return to the code and apply this newfound knowledge.

## Confidence and Doubt

I took the formula of the sigmoid and converted it to Python, using NumPy's exp() function to implement the exponential. The result is one-line function:

```
def sigmoid(z):
    return 1 / (1 + np.exp(-z))
```

As usual with NumPy-based functions, sigmoid() takes advantage of broadcasting: the z argument can be a number, or a multidimensional array. In the second case, the function will return an array that contains the sigmoids of all the elements of z.

Then I went back to the prediction code—the point where we used to calculate the weighted sum. The original function looked like this:

```
def predict(X, w):
    return np.matmul(X, w)
```

I modified that function to pass the result through the sigmoid() function:

```
def forward(X, w):
    weighted_sum = np.matmul(X, w)
    return sigmoid(weighted_sum)
```

Later in this book, we'll see that this process of moving data through the system is also called *forward propagation*, so I renamed the predict() function to forward().

The result of forward() is our prediction $\hat{y}$, that is a matrix with the same dimensions as the weighted sum: one row per example, and one column. Only, each element in the matrix is now constrained between 0 and 1.

Intuitively, you can see the values of y_hat as forecasts that can be more or less certain. If a value is close to the extremes, like 0.01 or 0.98, that's a highly confident forecast. If it's close to the middle, like 0.51, that's a very uncertain forecast.

During the training phase, that gradual variation in confidence is just what we need. We want the loss to change smoothly, so that we can slide over it with gradient descent. Once we switch from the training phase to the classification phase, however, we don't want the system to beat around the bush anymore. The labels that we use to train the classifier are either 0 or 1, so the classification should also be a straight 0 or 1. To get that unambiguous answer, during the classification phase we can round the result to the nearest integer, like this:

```
def classify(X, w):
    return np.round(forward(X, w))
```

This function could be named predict(), like we used earlier, or classify(). In the case of a classifier, the two words are pretty much synonyms. I opted for classify() to highlight the fact that we're not doing linear regression anymore, because now we're forecasting a binary value.

It seems that we're making great progress toward a classification program... except for a minor difficulty that we're about to face.

## Smoothing It Out

By adding the sigmoid to our program, we introduced a subtle problem: we made gradient descent less reliable. The problem happens when we update the loss() function in our system to use the new classification code:

```
def mse_loss(X, Y, w):
    return np.average((forward(X, w) - Y) ** 2)
```

At first glance, this function is almost identical to the loss() function that we had before: the mean squared error of the predictions compared with the actual labels. The only difference from the previous loss() is that the function that calculates the predicted labels $\hat{y}$ has changed, from predict() to forward().

That change, however, has far-reaching consequence. forward() involves the calculation of a sigmoid, and because of that sigmoid, this loss isn't the same loss that we had before. Here is what the new loss function looks like:

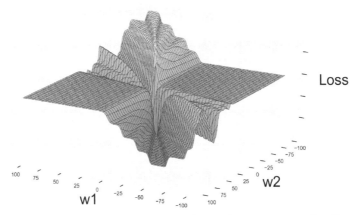

Looks like we have a problem here. See those deep canyons leading straight into holes? We mentioned those holes when we introduced gradient descent—they're the dreaded *local minima*. Remember that the goal of gradient descent is to move downhill? Now consider what happens if GD enters a local minimum: since there is no "downhill" at the bottom of a hole, the algorithm stops there, falsely convinced that it's reached the *global minimum* that it was aiming for.

Here is the conclusion we can take from looking at this diagram: if we use the mean squared error and the sigmoid together, the resulting loss has an uneven surface littered with local minima. Such a surface is hard to navigate with gradient descent. We'd better look for a different loss function with a smoother, more GD-friendly surface.

We can find one such function in statistics textbooks. It's called the *log loss*, because it's based on logarithms:

$$L = -\frac{1}{m} \sum_{i=1}^{m} (y_i \cdot \log(\hat{y}_i) + (1 - y_i) \cdot \log(1 - \hat{y}_i))$$

The log loss formula might look daunting, but don't let it intimidate you. Just know that it behaves like a good loss function: the closer the prediction ŷ is to the ground truth y, the lower the loss. Also, the formula looks more friendly when turned into code:

```
def loss(X, Y, w):
    y_hat = forward(X, w)
    first_term = Y * np.log(y_hat)
    second_term = (1 - Y) * np.log(1 - y_hat)
    return -np.average(first_term + second_term)
```

If you're willing to give it a try, you'll find that the log loss is simpler than it looks. Remember that each label in the matrix Y is either 0 or 1. For labels that are 0, the first_term is multiplied by 0, so it disappears. For labels that are 1, the second_term disappears, because it's multiplied by (1-Y). So each element of Y contributes only one of the two terms.

Let's plot the log loss and see what it looks like:

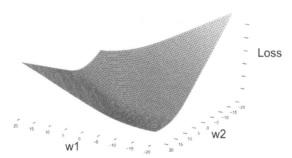

Nice and smooth! No canyons, flat areas, or holes. From now on, this will be our loss function.

## Updating the Gradient

Now that we have a brand-new loss function, let's look up its gradient. Here is the partial derivative of the log loss with respect to the weight, straight from the math textbooks:

$$\frac{\partial L}{\partial w} = \frac{1}{m} \sum_{i=1}^{m} x_i (\hat{y}_i - y_i)$$

If you have good memory, this gradient might look familiar. In fact, it closely resembles the gradient of the mean squared error that we used so far:

$$\frac{\partial MSE}{\partial w} = \frac{2}{m} \sum_{i=1}^{m} x (\hat{y}_i - y_i)$$

See how similar they are? This means that we can take our previous gradient() function…

```
def gradient(X, Y, w):
    return 2 * np.matmul(X.T, (predict(X, w) - Y)) / X.shape[0]
```

…and quickly convert it to the new formula:

```
def gradient(X, Y, w):
    return np.matmul(X.T, (forward(X, w) - Y)) / X.shape[0]
```

With this, we're done converting our system from linear regression to classification. Let's take a moment to see how that change impacted the system's model.

## What Happened to the Model Function?

Back when we did linear regression, our model was a straight line, a plane, or a higher-dimensional hyperplane. In the last few sections, we changed that model by wrapping it in a sigmoid. Let's see what the new model looks like.

To visualize the new model, I wrote a script that trains the classifier on the first column of data in Roberto's file, and then plots the forward() function. Here is the result:

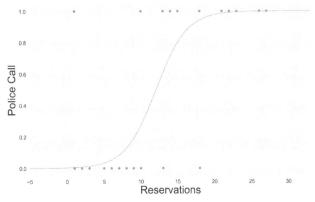

Passing the weighted sum through the sigmoid turned a straight line into something more sigmoid-y. At a glance, you can tell that this curved shape fits the data better than a line ever could. A statistician could also prove mathematically that this model is more stable in the presence of outliers.

We just plotted the output of forward()—the model used by the classifier during training. When it comes time to predict a label, however, the classifier passes that model through the classify() function, resulting in a sharper shape as shown in the next graph:

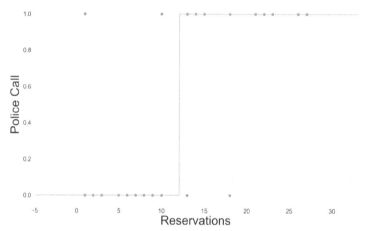

Below a certain threshold, which in this example seems to be around 12, the value of the model is under 0.5, and classify() rounds it to 0. Above that threshold, the value of the model is over 0.5, and classify() rounds it to 1. The result is a stepwise model function. The job of the training phase is to stretch and shift this curve, and ultimately set the threshold where the output switches from 0 to 1.

When you add another input variable, the model function looks similar—but now it's three-dimensional, like the graph on page 73.

Once again, where we used to have a linear surface such as a plane, we now have a curved surface. The value of this surface gets clipped to either 0 or 1 to predict a binary label. If we add more input variables to the data, the same process happens—but the model becomes higher-dimensional, and we cannot visualize it anymore.

To be clear, the diagrams I just showed you have nothing to do with the loss curves that you've seen in Smoothing It Out, on page 69. These plots visualize the model, while the earlier plots visualized the *loss* of the model. Even if these two functions are different, however, they're related. In particular, if the model function contained sudden jumps, so would the loss. In the interest of gradient descent, it's a good thing that the model function looks silky smooth.

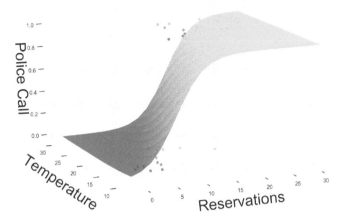

Now that you've seen what the classifier's model looks like, it's time to put it through its paces. Let's run that code.

## Classification in Action

Here's our final binary classification code, in all its glory. It loads Roberto's data file, learns from it, and then comes up with a bunch of classifications:

**05_discerning/classifier.py**
```python
import numpy as np

def sigmoid(z):
    return 1 / (1 + np.exp(-z))

def forward(X, w):
    weighted_sum = np.matmul(X, w)
    return sigmoid(weighted_sum)

def classify(X, w):
    return np.round(forward(X, w))

def loss(X, Y, w):
    y_hat = forward(X, w)
    first_term = Y * np.log(y_hat)
    second_term = (1 - Y) * np.log(1 - y_hat)
    return -np.average(first_term + second_term)

def gradient(X, Y, w):
    return np.matmul(X.T, (forward(X, w) - Y)) / X.shape[0]

def train(X, Y, iterations, lr):
    w = np.zeros((X.shape[1], 1))
    for i in range(iterations):
```

```
        print("Iteration %4d => Loss: %.20f" % (i, loss(X, Y, w)))
        w -= gradient(X, Y, w) * lr
    return w


def test(X, Y, w):
    total_examples = X.shape[0]
    correct_results = np.sum(classify(X, w) == Y)
    success_percent = correct_results * 100 / total_examples
    print("\nSuccess: %d/%d (%.2f%%)" %
          (correct_results, total_examples, success_percent))


# Prepare data
x1, x2, x3, y = np.loadtxt("police.txt", skiprows=1, unpack=True)
X = np.column_stack((np.ones(x1.size), x1, x2, x3))
Y = y.reshape(-1, 1)
w = train(X, Y, iterations=10000, lr=0.001)

# Test it
test(X, Y, w)
```

As we moved from linear regression to classification, most functions in our program had to change. We have a brand-new sigmoid() function. The old predict() split into two separate functions: forward(), which is used during training, and classify(), which is used for classification. We also changed the formula that we use to calculate the loss and its gradient: instead of the mean squared error, we're now using the log loss. As a result, we have brand-new implementations for loss() and gradient().

I also wrote a new test() function that prints the percentage of correct classifications. The instruction np.sum(classify(X, w) == Y) means: first, compare the predicted values to the labels, returning an array that contains True for the elements that match, and False for those that don't; then, count the True elements.

While some code changed since linear regression, the core concepts didn't. The loss() function still tells us how wrong we are. The train() function didn't change at all, and it still finds the weights by descending the loss' gradient. Finally, we still use those weights in classify() (formerly called predict()) to make a classification. Here is what happens when we run this program with 10,000 training iterations:

```
Iteration    0 => Loss: 0.69314718055994495316
Iteration    1 => Loss: 0.68250692927994149883
...
Iteration 9999 => Loss: 0.36572874687292933338

Success: 25/30 (83.33%)
```

The program nailed 25 examples over 30—over 83% of them. Not too shabby!

Check out "The Problem with Accuracy" on ProgML.

(On a side note, the percentage of correctly classified examples is called the *accuracy* of the classifier. Accuracy isn't necessarily the best metric of a classifier's power, but it's a simple and intuitive one—so we'll use it throughout this book. The ProgML[1] site gives you more information about accuracy and a couple of alternative metrics.)

## What You Just Learned

In this chapter we walked through *binary classification*: learning and forecasting data that have a binary label. Linear regression doesn't work well with categorical values, so we introduced a new algorithm, *classification*, to deal with them.

Classification is founded on a function called the *logistic function*, or the *sigmoid* for friends. During training, we used the sigmoid to squeeze any value into the range from 0 to 1. During prediction, we clipped the sigmoid to its nearest binary value—either 0 or 1—to deliver an unambiguous classification.

In linear regression, we used the mean squared error to calculate the loss. Once you add the sigmoid to the recipe, however, the mean squared error's surface becomes bumpy, and hostile to gradient descent. So we switched to an alternative loss function that works well with the sigmoid, called the *log loss*.

The next chapter will be a breakthrough. Now that we know about classification, we're about to apply it to an exciting real-world problem: image recognition. Will our tiny program still work when confronted with *that*?

## Hands On: Weighty Decisions

Change the classification program to print the weights after training. You'll see four weights: the first weight is the bias, and the others map to the input variables in Roberto's examples. You'll see that some weights are larger than others, and some might even be negative.

What do those numbers tell us? Which of the columns in Roberto's file has the biggest impact on the likelihood of a neighbor calling the police?

---

1. https://www.progml.com

# CHAPTER 6

# Getting Real

It's time to make the leap from simple pizza-related examples to the cool stuff: image recognition. We're about to do something magical. Within a few pages, we'll have a program that classifies images.

In this chapter and the next, we'll apply our binary classifier to MNIST, a database of handwritten digits.[1] Just a few years ago, before ML systems could tackle more complex datasets, AI researchers used MNIST as a benchmark for their algorithms. In this chapter, we'll join that esteemed crowd.

### "Not MNIST Again!"

Besides being a common benchmark in the industry, MNIST is a bit like the "Hello, World!" of ML tutorials. In fact, if you had previous exposure to ML, you might roll your eyes at the sight of yet another example based on MNIST. Why couldn't I find a more original dataset for this chapter?

Truth is, I chose MNIST *because* it's common, not in spite of that. While most tutorials crack computer vision with the help of high-level ML libraries, we're going to discuss each and every line of code—so we'd better make things easier for ourselves and use a simple, well-documented dataset. Also, a well-known dataset makes it easier for you to look up and compare alternative examples on the Internet.

This will be our first experience with computer vision, so let's start small. We'll begin by recognizing a single MNIST digit, and leave more general character recognition to the next chapter.

---

1. yann.lecun.com/exdb/mnist

## Data Come First

Before we feed data to our ML system, let's get up close and personal with those data. This section tells you all you need to know about MNIST.

### Getting to Know MNIST

MNIST is a collection of labeled images that's been assembled specifically for supervised learning. Its name stands for "Modified NIST," because it's a remix of earlier data from the National Institute of Standards and Technology. MNIST contains images of handwritten digits, labeled with their numerical values. Here are a few random images, capped by their labels:

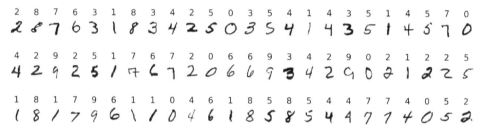

Digits are made up of 28 by 28 grayscale pixels, each represented by one byte. In MNIST's grayscale, 0 stands for "perfect background white," and 255 stands for "perfect foreground black." Here's one digit close up:

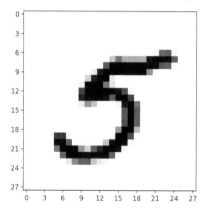

MNIST isn't huge by modern ML standards, but it isn't tiny either. It contains 70,000 examples, neatly partitioned into 7,000 examples for each digit from 0 to 9. Digits have been collected from the wild, so they're quite diverse, as this random assortment of 5s on page 79 proves.

Chalk it up to my age, but I have trouble reading some of these 5s myself. Some look like barely readeable squiggles. If we can write a computer program that recognizes these digits, then we definitely win bragging rights.

Datasets such as MNIST are a godsend to the machine learning community. As cool as ML is, it involves a lot of grindwork to collect, label, clean, and pre-process data. The maintainers of MNIST did that work for us. They collected the images, labeled them, scaled them to the same size, rotated them, centered them, and converted them to the same scale of grays. You can take these digits and feed them straight to a learning program.

MNIST stores images and labels in separate files. There are plenty of libraries that read these data, but the format is simple enough that it makes sense to code our own reader. We'll do that in a few pages.

By the way, you don't have to download the MNIST files: you'll find them among the book's source code, in the data directory. Take a peek, and you'll see that MNIST is made up of four files. Two of them contain 60,000 images and their matching labels, respectively. The other two files contain the remaining 10,000 images and labels that have been reserved for testing.

You might wonder why we don't use the same images and labels for both training and testing. The answer to that question requires a short aside.

## Training vs. Testing

Consider how we have tested our learning programs so far. First, we trained them on labeled examples. Then we used those same examples to calculate an array of predictions, and we compared the predictions to the ground truth. The closer the two arrays, the better the forecast. That approach served us well as we learned the basics, but it would fail in a real-life project. Here is why.

To make my point, let me come up with an extreme example. Imagine that you're at the pub, chattering about MNIST with a friend. After a few beers, your friend proposes a bet: she will code a system that learns MNIST images in a single iteration of training, and then comes up with 100% accurate classifications. How ludicrous! That sounds like an easy win, but your cunning friend can beat you out in this bet easily. Can you imagine how?

Your friend writes a train() function that does nothing, except for storing training examples in a dictionary—a data structure that matches keys to values. (Depending on your coding background, you might call it a "map," a "hashtable," or some other similar name.) In this dictionary, images are keys, and labels are values. Later on, when you ask it to classify an image, the program just looks up that image in the dictionary and returns the matching label. Hey presto, perfectly accurate forecasts in one iteration of training—and without even bothering to implement a machine learning algorithm!

As you pay that beer, you'd be right to grumble that your friend is cheating. Her system didn't really *learn*—it just *memorized* the images and their labels. Confronted with an image that it hasn't seen before, such a system would respond with an awkward silence. Unlike a proper learning system, it wouldn't be able to generalize its knowledge to new data.

Here's a twist: even if nobody is looking to cheat, many ML systems have a built-in tendency to memorize training data. This is a phenomenon known as *overfitting*. You can see that a system is overfitting when it performs better on familiar data than it performs on new data. Such a system could be very accurate at classifying images that it's already seen during training, and then disappoint you when confronted with unfamiliar images.

We'll talk a lot about overfitting in the rest of this book, and we'll even explore a few techniques to reduce its impact. For now, a simple recommendation: *never test a system with the same data that you used to train it.* Otherwise, you might get an unfairly optimistic result, because of overfitting. Before you train the system, set aside a few of your examples for testing, and don't touch them until the training is done.

Now we know how MNIST is organized, and why it's split into separate training and testing set. That's all the knowledge we need. Let's write code that loads MNIST data, and massages those data into a suitable format for our learning program.

## Our Own MNIST Library

Let's recap where we are and where we want to go. In the previous chapters, we built a binary classifier. Now we want to apply that program to MNIST.

As a first step, we need to reshape MNIST's images and labels into an input for our program. Let's see how to do that.

## Preparing the Input Matrices

Our binary classifier program expects its input formatted as two matrices: a set of examples X, and a set of labels Y. Let's start with the matrix of examples X.

X is supposed to have one line per example and one column per input variable, plus a *bias column* full of 1s. (Remember the bias column? We talked about it in Bye Bye, Bias, on page 59.)

To fit MNIST's images to this format, we can reshape each image to a single line of pixels, so that each pixel becomes an input variable. MNIST images are 28 by 28 pixels, so squashing them results in lines of 784 elements. Throw in the bias column, and that makes 785. So that's what X should look like: a matrix of 60,000 lines (the number of examples) and 785 columns (one per pixel, plus the bias). Check out the following graph:

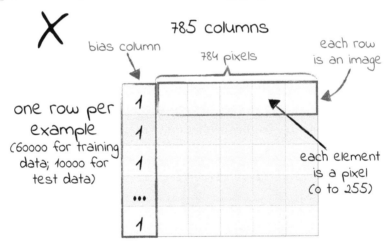

We just graduated from toy examples with three or four input variables to tens of thousands of examples and hundreds of input variables!

Now let's look at Y, the matrix of labels. At first glance, it looks simpler than the matrix of images: it still has one line per example, but only one column, that contains the label. However, we have an additional difficulty here: so far we only built binary classifiers, which expect a label that's either 0 or 1. By contrast, MNIST labels range from 0 to 9. How can we fit ten different values into either 0 or 1?

For now, we can work around that problem by narrowing our scope: let's start by recognizing one specific digit—say, the digit 5. This is a problem of binary classification, because a digit can belong to two classes: "not a 5" and "5."

> ## Leap of Faith
>
> In Preparing the Input Matrices, on page 81, we squash each MNIST image into a row of the X matrix. You might have been scratching your head at this idea. Aren't we destroying the images by flattening them? What's the point of having handwritten digits if we grind them into meaningless rows of pixels?
>
> Indeed, we're performing a leap of faith here: we're trusting in the power of statistics. Even though the geometry of those digits is lost, we're betting that the distribution of their pixels is enough information to identify them. For example, the central pixels in a 7 are likely to be darker than the central pixels in a 0. The brightness of a single pixel might be a very weak hint—but by adding up enough of those weak hints, we hope to get a clue of the digit we're looking at.
>
> This method of looking at individual pixels would likely fail on more complicated data than MNIST. For example, imagine writing a classifier that recognizes the species of an elephant from its picture. When they haven't been wallowing in mud, most elephants look gray—so the classifier would probably need more than the pixels' colors to do its job. Toward the end of this book (in Chapter 19, Beyond Vanilla Networks, on page 247), we'll describe a more powerful image recognition algorithm—one that focuses on shapes composed of multiple pixels.

This means that we should convert all MNIST labels to 0s, except for 5s, which we should convert to 1s. So that's what our Y matrix will look like:

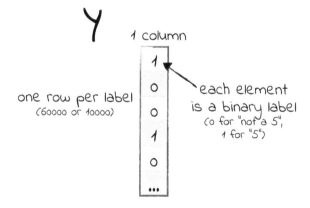

Now we know how to build X and Y. Let's turn this plan into code.

## Cooking Data

The Internet overflows with libraries and code snippets that read MNIST data. But we're developers, so hey, let's write one more! In this section I'll show you code for a tiny library that loads those images and labels, and reshapes them into the X and Y that we've just described.

## Loading Images

Here is code that loads MNIST images into two matrices—one for the training examples, and one for the test examples:

06_real/mnist.py
```python
import numpy as np
import gzip
import struct


def load_images(filename):
    # Open and unzip the file of images:
    with gzip.open(filename, 'rb') as f:
        # Read the header information into a bunch of variables
        _ignored, n_images, columns, rows = struct.unpack('>IIII', f.read(16))
        # Read all the pixels into a NumPy array of bytes:
        all_pixels = np.frombuffer(f.read(), dtype=np.uint8)
        # Reshape the pixels into a matrix where each line is an image:
        return all_pixels.reshape(n_images, columns * rows)


def prepend_bias(X):
    # Insert a column of 1s in the position 0 of X.
    # ("axis=1" stands for: "insert a column, not a row")
    return np.insert(X, 0, 1, axis=1)


# 60000 images, each 785 elements (1 bias + 28 * 28 pixels)
X_train = prepend_bias(load_images("../data/mnist/train-images-idx3-ubyte.gz"))

# 10000 images, each 785 elements, with the same structure as X_train
X_test = prepend_bias(load_images("../data/mnist/t10k-images-idx3-ubyte.gz"))
```

Let's go through this code quickly. load_images() unzips and decodes images from MNIST's binary files. This function is specific to MNIST's binary format, so you don't really need to understand its details. If you're curious to learn them, know that struct.unpack() reads data from a binary file according to a pattern string. In this case, the pattern is '>IIII', which means "four unsigned integers, encoded with the most significant byte first." The code's comments should help you understand the rest of this function.

load_images() returns a matrix that's either (60000, 784), in the case of the training images, or (10000, 784), in the case of the test images. Those matrices can then be passed to the second function, prepend_bias(), to give them an extra column full of 1s for the bias.

Finally, the last few lines in the code store the training and test images into two constants. The idea is that the client of this library doesn't need to call load_images() and prepend_bias(). Instead, it can import the library (with import mnist) and then refer to these constants (with mnist.X_train and mnist.X_test).

And that's it about the images. Now, the labels.

### Loading Labels

This code loads and prepares MNIST's labels:

```
06_real/mnist.py
def load_labels(filename):
    # Open and unzip the file of images:
    with gzip.open(filename, 'rb') as f:
        # Skip the header bytes:
        f.read(8)
        # Read all the labels into a list:
        all_labels = f.read()
        # Reshape the list of labels into a one-column matrix:
        return np.frombuffer(all_labels, dtype=np.uint8).reshape(-1, 1)


def encode_fives(Y):
    # Convert all 5s to 1, and everything else to 0
    return (Y == 5).astype(int)


# 60K labels, each with value 1 if the digit is a five, and 0 otherwise
Y_train = encode_fives(load_labels("../data/mnist/train-labels-idx1-ubyte.gz"))

# 10000 labels, with the same encoding as Y_train
Y_test = encode_fives(load_labels("../data/mnist/t10k-labels-idx1-ubyte.gz"))
```

load_labels() loads MNIST labels into a NumPy array, and then molds that array into a one-column matrix. Once again, you don't have to understand this code, as you're not likely to load MNIST labels that often—but read the comments if you're curious. (A reminder: reshape(-1, 1) means: "Arrange these data into a matrix with one column, and however many rows you need.") The function returns a matrix with shape (60000, 1) or (10000, 1), depending on whether we're loading the training labels or the test labels.

The matrix returned by load_labels() contains labels from 0 to 9. We can pass that matrix to encode_fives() to turn those labels into binary values. We're not going to live with encode_fives() for long, so I didn't bother parameterizing it. I just hard-coded it to encode the digit 5.

The one line in encode_fives() is typical NumPy code—very terse, to the point of being a bit obscure. To clarify it, (Y == 5) means: "create an array that contains True where Y contains a 5, and False where it doesn't." That array is then converted to an array of integers, so that all True values becomes 1, and False values becomes 0. The end result is a new matrix with the same shape as Y, that contains 1 where Y contains a 5, and 0 elsewhere.

After those functions, the final lines in the code define two constants. We can use them to access the training labels and the test labels, respectively.

With that, our MNIST library is complete. Let's save it as a file (mnist.py), and use it to feed our ML program.

## The Real Thing

It's time to reach for our binary classification code (from Classification in Action, on page 73), and run it on MNIST. We do have to adapt it a bit, but the changes are minimal. Indeed, we can use the exact same functions that we used in the previous chapter, as long as we update the main code:

06_real/digit_classifier.py
```
import mnist as data
w = train(data.X_train, data.Y_train, iterations=100, lr=1e-5)
test(data.X_test, data.Y_test, w)
```

One line for training, one for testing. We don't need to load and prepare the data, because our MNIST library library already takes care of that.

And here's the output of our first image classifier:

```
Iteration     0 => Loss: 0.69314718055994528623
Iteration     1 => Loss: 0.80042530259490185518
Iteration     2 => Loss: 0.60370180008019158624
...
Iteration    99 => Loss: 0.11895658384798543650

Success: 9637/10000 (96.37%)
```

Over 96% of the program's forecasts proved accurate. Our program recognizes images!

Now that we've basked in the glory of that number for a moment, I have to play the part of the killjoy. While 96% might seem great, it doesn't necessarily mean that our program is very accurate. Think about it: only 10% of the digits in the MNIST test set are 5s. This means that a naive program that always forecasts 0 (for: "this is not a 5") would hit the mark 90% of the times. Bummer, I know.

To be fair, our program's 96% accuracy is better than that 90% baseline. However, it's hard to gauge how much better it actually is. To get an intuitive sense of this program's accuracy, we have to extend our code to recognize any digit, from 0 to 9. Let's save our victory dance for the next chapter!

> ## Hyperparameter Blues
>
> While writing the "main" code in The Real Thing, on page 85, I had to find values for iterations and lr that work well for this new task. As usual, that search involved some trial and error: I just tweaked those hyperparameters until I was happy with the result.
>
> In this specific case, I found out that lr must be very small. I settled on a value of 0.00001. With a larger lr, the program overflows when calculating the sigmoid and the loss. That overflow is a side effect of using exponentials and logarithms, which can easily churn out enormous numbers. Also, when I tried a slightly larger lr, the program failed to converge—which is a fancy way of saying that gradient descent kept skidding around the minimum loss instead of approaching it.
>
> Later, in Chapter 15, Let's Do Development, on page 177, we'll talk more about tuning hyperparameters. For now, let's just accept that we have to fumble with them whenever we change our algorithm or dataset.

## What You Just Learned

In this chapter we got up close and personal with MNIST. We wrote a little library to import MNIST data and reshape it to X and Y matrices fit for our binary classification code. In the end, we used our program to recognize one of the digits in MNIST, with very encouraging results.

Along the way, you learned a few interesting facts about image recognition. You also learned something about testing ML systems, and how the results of a test can be tricky to interpret because of *overfitting*.

In the next chapter, we'll finally tackle the challenge that we set for ourselves at the beginning of this book: recognizing arbitrary digits. How will our code fare?

## Hands On: Tricky Digits

Our current code recognizes the digit 5. Which digits would you expect to be easier or harder to recognize than a 5? Make a wild guess.

Now, change the code to recognize one of those other digits. Does the experiment confirm your guesses?

# CHAPTER 7

# The Final Challenge

In the previous chapter we achieved our goal of building a computer vision system—but only a basic one. The program we built is a *binary classifier*, as it assigns data to one of two classes: "5" and "not 5." Now we're going to push that program further and tackle the final challenge of Part I of this book: recognize any digit in MNIST.

Instead of binary classification, the problem of recognizing digits involves many classes—and for that reason, it's called a *multiclass classification* problem. Don't fret about multiclass classification, because it's well within our grasp. In fact, here's a simple recipe for multiclass classification: build a binary classifier for each class, and then combine the classifiers from each class into one multiclass classifier. Let's turn that idea into code. Hold on tight: we're tantalizingly close to our goal of building a full-fledged MNIST classifier.

## Going Multiclass

Let's recap where we are and where we want to go. We have a binary classifier that's hardwired to recognize a specific digit, such as 5. It passes images through a weighted sum, and then a sigmoid. The result is a number ranging from 0 to 1. Then we round that number to either 1 or 0, because we want a binary result—a straight "yes, this is a 5" or "no, this isn't a 5," as illustrated in the following picture:

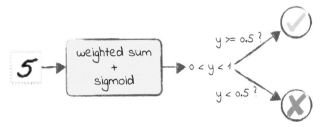

And here is where we want to go: we want a program that takes an image and tells us which digit that image represents, from 0 to 9:

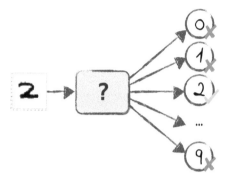

Let's see how we can go from here to there. First, focus on that box right at the center of the first picture—a weighted sum, followed by a sigmoid. There is no common name for this sequence. For short, let's call it WSS, for "Weighted Sum plus Sigmoid." A WSS is just like a binary classifier, minus the last step: instead of returning either 0 or 1, it returns a floating-point number between 0 and 1.

Now imagine building an array of ten WSSs, one per class—from the 0-WSS, that only recognizes zeros, to the 9-WSS that... well, you got the idea. If we run them all, then we get an array of ten numbers like this one:

| "0" | "1" | "2" | "3" | "4" | "5" | "6" | "7" | "8" | "9" |
|---|---|---|---|---|---|---|---|---|---|
| 0.111 | 0.005 | 0.787 | 0.170 | 0.001 | 0.176 | 0.352 | 0.001 | 0.073 | 0.003 |

Each WSS returns a number from 0 to 1, and that number tells us how confident that WSS is. For example, the 2-WSS returns 0.787, which is pretty close to the maximum value 1. This means that the 2-WSS is pretty confident that the image is indeed a 2. By contrast, the other WSSs are less certain of looking at their own digits. For example, the 4-WSS returns a number that's close to 0, so it's pretty sure that the image is *not* a 4. Overall, the 2-WSS is the most confident of the bunch, so this image is probably a 2.

Now we have a more detailed plan for multiclass classification. First, run ten WSSs on the image, each specialized for a different digit. Second, pick the digit that gets the highest confidence from its matching WSS.

We could implement this plan by running the same WSS code ten times, once per class. We could... but we can do better.

## One-Hot Encoding

Remember how we encoded labels in Loading Labels, on page 84? Back then, we only cared about telling apart 5 from other digits. So we encoded the labels by replacing 5 with 1, and other digits with 0:

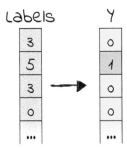

Now that we need to recognize ten digits, we could come up with ten such encoded matrices, one per class. But here is a better way: we can have one big matrix with ten columns, where each column encodes a digit. The result would look like this:

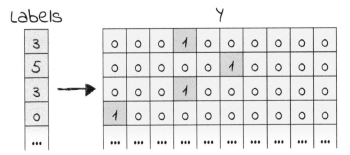

In this example, the first label is a 3, so the fourth cell in the first row of Y is a 1. (It's the fourth cell, not the third, since we're enumerating the digits starting from 0.) Similarly, each row has a 1 in the position matching its original label, and zeros everywhere else.

This way of encoding labels is called *one-hot encoding*, because only one value per row is a hot 1. The rest are cold, cold zeros.

Can you see where this is going? We won't run our code ten times, once per class. Instead, we'll run it once, with one column per class. It's as if each column in the matrix contained the binary encoding for one of the WSSs. This matrix multiplication-based approach works just as well as running a classifier ten times, but it's much faster.

> ### Encoding Non-Numerical Labels
>
> One-hot encoding isn't just for numerical labels, such as those in MNIST. On the contrary, you can one-hot encode any kind of categorical data. If our labels were, say, "duck," "platypus," and "tapir," then we could sort them in an arbitrary (but fixed) order, and encode them as [1, 0, 0], [0, 1, 0], and [0, 0, 1], respectively. In the case of MNIST, the labels happen to be numbers, so it's convenient to sort them in numerical order—but it doesn't have to be that way.
>
> Think of one-hot encoding as a simple dictionary that maps the human-readable label to a fixed-length sequence of zeros containing a single 1.

One-hot encoding is redundant: instead of one number per example, we have as many numbers as we have classes. But that redundancy is usually worth it, as we're about to see in the next section.

## One-Hot Encoding in Action

In Our Own MNIST Library, on page 80, we wrote a library to load and prepare MNIST data. That library encoded the labels with a function called encode_fives(). Let's replace that function with a new one:

07_final/mnist.py
```
def one_hot_encode(Y):
    n_labels = Y.shape[0]
    n_classes = 10
    encoded_Y = np.zeros((n_labels, n_classes))
    for i in range(n_labels):
        label = Y[i]
        encoded_Y[i][label] = 1
    return encoded_Y
```

one_hot_encode() initializes a matrix of zeros with one row per label, and one column per class (Y.shape[0] means "the number of rows in Y"). Then it walks through the matrix, flipping the "hot" values to 1. We can use this function to initialize a one-hot-encoded version of Y_train:

```
# 60K labels, each a single digit from 0 to 9
Y_train_unencoded = load_labels("../data/mnist/train-labels-idx1-ubyte.gz")

# 60K labels, each consisting of 10 one-hot encoded elements
Y_train = one_hot_encode(Y_train_unencoded)

# 10000 labels, each a single digit from 0 to 9
Y_test = load_labels("../data/mnist/t10k-labels-idx1-ubyte.gz")
```

One detail in this code might puzzle you: why do we encode the training data, but not the test data? That's a common source of confusion, so let's clarify that point by looking at the classify() function.

## Decoding the Classifier's Answers

Let's review how classify() works. During the classification phase, the WSSs are going to return arrays of ten numbers from 0 to 1. But when we ask the system to recognize an image, we don't want to see those arrays—we want a human-readable answer such as "3." That means that we must decode the WSSs' answers before returning them.

So far, the classify() function didn't have much to do, apart from calling forward() and rounding its output. Now classify() has a more complex job. It must convert the output of the WSSs back to human-readable labels, like this:

```
07_final/mnist_classifier.py
def classify(X, w):
    y_hat = forward(X, w)
    labels = np.argmax(y_hat, axis=1)
    return labels.reshape(-1, 1)
```

The first line of classify() calculates a matrix of predictions y_hat, with one row per label, and one column per class. Each row in y_hat contains ten numbers between 0 and 1.

The second line uses NumPy's argmax() function to get the index of the maximum value in each row of y_hat—the value that's closer to 1. By default, argmax() finds the maximum over the entire matrix, so this code uses the argument axis=1 to apply it to each row separately. The result is an array of indices, which are also the decoded MNIST labels. (Functions like argmax() take some getting used to, so you might want to play with them in an interactive Python interpreter before you use them. On the other hand, they make for terse, efficient code.)

Finally, the last line of classify() reshapes the labels array to a single-column matrix of digits. Now we finally see why the Y_test matrix isn't one-hot encoded like Y_train. We're going to compare Y_test with the classifier's output, so the two matrices must look the same: a single column of human-readable labels.

We're almost there. We just need one more change to the classifier code.

## We Need More Weights

When we introduced one-hot encoding, we extended the matrix of labels from one to ten columns. Now we need to do the same with the weights.

So far, our matrix of weights had one column, and one row per input variable. We initialized it like this:

```
w = np.zeros((X.shape[1], 1))
```

Now we need ten columns of weights, one per class:

```
w = np.zeros((X_train.shape[1], Y_train.shape[1]))
```

The new w has one row per input variable, and one column per class. This code gets the number of input variables and classes from the number of columns in X and Y, respectively.

At this point, you could well be confused by all those matrix dimensions. I have to confess that I had to pause and double-check them while writing this section. ("Wait, does w have as many rows as X has columns, or is it the other way around?"). Let's take a moment to get a sanity check about all those rows and columns.

## Matrix Dimensions, Reviewed

I have fond memories of my first forays in ML—except for one frustrating, error-prone activity: I never seemed to get those darn matrix dimensions right. After suffering through so many "shapes not aligned" errors, I'd like to spare you that experience. At the risk of being redundant, here's a recap of the dimensions of our matrices.

One note before I dive in: when it comes to matrix dimensions, I find it very useful to sketch them on paper. Try it—it works great for me.

- X is (m, n)—one row per *example*, and one column per *input variable*. The MNIST training set has 60,000 examples, each composed by 784 pixels. Add the bias column, and X becomes (60000, 785).

- Y is a matrix of one-hot-encoded labels. It has one row per *example*, and one column per *class*. If we use k for the number of classes, then Y is (m, k). In our case, that's (60000, 10).

- The matrix of weights w is (n, k)—one row per *input variable*, and one column per *class*. In our case, that's (785, 10). We covered a lot of ground since our first learning program, where w was a single parameter. Now we're training over thousands of parameters!

As a double-check, we can verify that the weighted sum $X \cdot w = Y$ has all the right dimensions. And in fact, it does (see the figure on page 93).

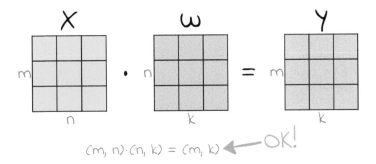

$$(m, n) \cdot (n, k) = (m, k) \longleftarrow \text{OK!}$$

(If you can't remember how the dimensions of matrix multiplication work, review Multiplying Matrices, on page 49.)

One last reminder: the numbers here are the sizes of the matrices during training. The MNIST test set is smaller, and so are the matrices. In particular, X is (10000, 785) during testing. If we classify a single image, then X is a single-row (1, 785) matrix.

After this tedious check through matrix dimensions, you must be eager to review and run the classifier. Let's do it.

## Moment of Truth

This is the time we've been waiting for. We're about to unleash our multiclass classifier on MNIST. Here is the classifier's code, in all its glory:

07_final/mnist_classifier.py
```
import numpy as np

def sigmoid(z):
    return 1 / (1 + np.exp(-z))

def forward(X, w):
    weighted_sum = np.matmul(X, w)
    return sigmoid(weighted_sum)

def classify(X, w):
    y_hat = forward(X, w)
    labels = np.argmax(y_hat, axis=1)
    return labels.reshape(-1, 1)

def loss(X, Y, w):
    y_hat = forward(X, w)
    first_term = Y * np.log(y_hat)
    second_term = (1 - Y) * np.log(1 - y_hat)
    return -np.sum(first_term + second_term) / X.shape[0]
```

```
def gradient(X, Y, w):
    return np.matmul(X.T, (forward(X, w) - Y)) / X.shape[0]

def report(iteration, X_train, Y_train, X_test, Y_test, w):
    matches = np.count_nonzero(classify(X_test, w) == Y_test)
    n_test_examples = Y_test.shape[0]
    matches = matches * 100.0 / n_test_examples
    training_loss = loss(X_train, Y_train, w)
    print("%d - Loss: %.20f, %.2f%%" % (iteration, training_loss, matches))

def train(X_train, Y_train, X_test, Y_test, iterations, lr):
    w = np.zeros((X_train.shape[1], Y_train.shape[1]))
    for i in range(iterations):
        report(i, X_train, Y_train, X_test, Y_test, w)
        w -= gradient(X_train, Y_train, w) * lr
    report(iterations, X_train, Y_train, X_test, Y_test, w)
    return w

import mnist as data
w = train(data.X_train, data.Y_train,
          data.X_test, data.Y_test,
          iterations=200, lr=1e-5)
```

I took this chance to extract a new report() function that logs the percentage of correct results. report() is similar to the test() function that we had before, but it's called once per training iteration, plus once at the very end. This log shows us in detail how well (or badly) our classifier is learning.

## A Tiny Fix

You'd have to be eagle-eyed to spot it, but the final classifier code in Moment of Truth, on page 93 introduces a subtle change into the last line of loss(). So far, that line used NumPy's average() function to calculate the average of (first_term + second_term). However, average() calculates the average over all the *elements* of a matrix, while we want the loss over the examples—which means all the *lines* in the matrix.

So far, that detail didn't matter, because (first_term + second_term) had exactly one element per line. Since we switched to one-hot encoding, however, that matrix has 10 elements per line—so the original code would calculate a loss that's 10 times smaller than the correct one. Even with that bug, the classifier would calculate the same weights, because the minimum of the loss stays in the same position if you divide the loss by 10. However, the printouts of the loss during training would be wrong.

That sneaky bug is further proof that working with matrices is tricky. It even tripped me up, and that mistake almost slipped through this book's code reviews. The new code avoids that problem by calculating the average in the old-fashioned way: it sums all the elements in the matrix, and then divides by the number of lines.

And here's what happens when the program runs:

```
0 - Loss: 6.93147180559945397249, 9.80%
1 - Loss: 8.43445687508333641347, 68.04%
2 - Loss: 5.51204748892387641490, 68.10%
3 - Loss: 2.95687007359365416903, 68.62%
...
200 - Loss: 0.85863196488041293453, 90.32%
```

Let's take a deep breath, because we just built something wonderful. In a few minutes of number-crunching, our little program learned to recognize handwritten digits with over 90% accuracy.

Whitespace excluded, the entire program spans some 35 lines of Python. We could easily squeeze it down to 20 lines if we were willing by sacrificing some readability and logging. Such a short program, and we didn't even use any ML library. There is no rabbit hole of complex code hiding among those lines. We can literally understand the entire thing.

## What You Just Learned

Let's recap our first adventure in machine learning:

- In Chapter 1, How Machine Learning Works, on page 3, we learned what machine learning and *supervised learning* are.

- In Chapter 2, Your First Learning Program, on page 15, we got our first concrete taste of supervised learning: we used *linear regression* to predict one variable from another.

- In Chapter 3, Walking the Gradient, on page 31, we upgraded the learning program with a faster and more efficient algorithm: *gradient descent*.

- In Chapter 4, Hyperspace!, on page 45, we took advantage of gradient descent (and a bit of matrix magic) to implement *multiple linear regression*—like linear regression, only with multiple inputs.

- In Chapter 5, A Discerning Machine, on page 63, we leapt from multiple linear regression to *classification*.

- In Chapter 6, Getting Real, on page 77, we used our binary classifier to recognize a single digit in the *MNIST* dataset.

- Finally, in this chapter we bumped up to *multiclass classification*, recognizing all MNIST characters with over 90% accuracy.

What a journey! Let's do one last exercise. Then, in the next chapter, we'll stop coding for a while and take a bird's-eye view of this thing we've built.

## Hands On: Minesweeper

If you're up for a challenge, here's an optional exercise for you: modify the MNIST classifier to run on the Sonar dataset.[1] The Sonar dataset (also known as the "Mines vs. Rocks" dataset) contains the patterns generated by bouncing sonar signals off two different types of objects: metal cylinders (which could potentially be mines) and rocks. See if you can train the classifier to tell apart mines from rocks.

Don't underestimate this little project. If you're not steeped in Python, it might take you a few hours to write the Sonar equivalent of the mnist.py library, and you'll probably need to browse the documentation of both Python and NumPy. Only tackle this exercise if you like the idea of spending some time on it.

Should you accept the challenge, start by visiting the Sonar dataset's site. Download the examples in sonar.all-data, and read the documentation in sonar.names.

Here are a few hints for you:

- Apart from the hyperparameters, you shouldn't need to change any code in the classifier itself. You should only have to replace the code that loads and prepares data.

- The Sonar dataset includes 208 examples. It will be up to you to split them into a training and a test set. I set aside 48 examples for testing.

- The examples in the Sonar dataset are ordered: all the rocks first, followed by all the mines. You'll have to shuffle them before you split them, if you don't want to end up with a test set that only includes examples of a single class.

- Remember to add a bias column to both X_train and X_test.

- Remember to one-hot encode Y_train, but not Y_test.

- Try a learning rate of 0.01 to begin with, and change it if you aren't happy with the result. A learning rate that's too large can cause errors when calculating the loss, because the logarithms and exponentials generate huge (or tiny) numbers.

- If you train the system for too long, you might find that its accuracy starts *decreasing* instead of increasing. That's an effect of overfitting, the

---

1. https://archive.ics.uci.edu/ml/datasets/Connectionist+Bench+(Sonar,+Mines+vs.+Rocks)

phenomenon we discussed in Training vs. Testing, on page 79. We'll see how to avoid this problem in Part III of this book.

- Finally, note that this is a binary classification problem—so you don't necessarily need the additional complexities of multiclass classification, such as one-hot encoding. However, I ended up one-hot encoding the dataset anyway, so that I could run the same multiclass classifier that we used for MNIST. Alternatively, you can solve this challenge with the binary classifier from Chapter 5, A Discerning Machine, on page 63. In that case, you can use binary-encoded labels that are either 0 or 1, instead of one-hot-encoded labels that are either [1, 0] or [0, 1].

And that's it! See if you can reach 75% accuracy or higher. If you get stuck, check my solution in the 07_final/solution directory.

# CHAPTER 8

# The Perceptron

In the previous chapters we toiled through a lot of nitty-gritties. It's time to take a step back and enjoy the big picture.

In this first part of this book, we built a supervised learning system based on a specific architecture—one that ML pundits would call the *perceptron*. By the end of this chapter, you'll know what a perceptron looks like and what it can do. Crucially, you will also know what it can *not* do, and why we must move forward into more sophisticated algorithms such as neural networks.

Besides wrapping our heads around the perceptron, we're also going to talk about its history. Far from being a boring history lesson, this will be an epic war tale—a clash of ideas that impacted much of what we know about computers.

## Enter the Perceptron

To understand what a perceptron is, let's take a look back at the binary classifier we wrote in Chapter 6, Getting Real, on page 77. That program sorted MNIST characters into two classes: "5" and "not a 5." The following picture shows one way to look at it:

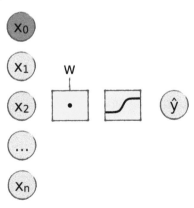

This diagram tracks an MNIST image through the system. The process begins with the *input variables*, from $x_1$ to $x_n$. In the case of MNIST, the input variables are the 784 pixels of an image. To those, we added a bias $x_0$, with a constant value of 1. I colored it a darker shade of gray, to make it stand apart from other input variables.

The next step—that yellow square—is the *weighted sum* of the input variables. It's implemented as a multiplication of matrices, so I marked it with the "dot" sign.

The weighted sum flows through one last function—the light blue square. In general, this is called the *activation function*, and can be different for different learning systems. In our system, we used a sigmoid. The output of the sigmoid is the predicted label $\hat{y}$, ranging from 0 to 1.

During training, the system compares the prediction $\hat{y}$ with the ground truth to calculate the next step of gradient descent. During classification, it snaps the value of $\hat{y}$ to one of its extremes—either 1 or 0, meaning "5" and "not a 5," respectively.

The architecture I just described is the perceptron, the original supervised learning system.

### The Textbook Perceptron

If you look it up on Wikipedia, you'll see that the textbook perceptron is actually simpler than the variant I discuss in this chapter. Instead of gradient descent, the perceptron uses a simpler algorithm, similar to the one we implemented in Chapter 2, Your First Learning Program, on page 15.

Since it doesn't use gradient descent, the vanilla perceptron doesn't need an activation function with a smooth gradient such as the sigmoid. Instead, it can get away with a simple "step" function that snaps the value of the weighted sum to either 1 or 0, depending on whether it's positive or negative.

## Assembling Perceptrons

The perceptron is a great building block for more complex systems. In a sense, we have been assembling multiple perceptrons since the very beginning. Let's see how.

During training, our system reads all the examples together, rather than one example at a time. In a way, that operation is like "stacking" multiple perceptrons, sending one example to each perceptron, and then collecting all the outputs into a matrix, like this:

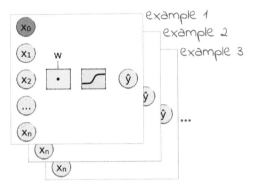

In Chapter 7, The Final Challenge, on page 87, we also assembled perceptrons in a different way. A perceptron is a binary classifier—it classifies things as either 0 or 1. To classify ten digits, we used ten matrix columns, each dedicated to classifying one digit against all the others. Conceptually, that's like using ten perceptrons in parallel as shown here:

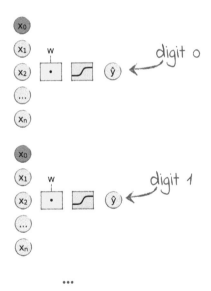

Each parallelized perceptron classifies one class, from 0 to 9. During classification, we pick the class that outputs the most confident prediction.

So we *stacked* perceptrons, and we *parallelized* perceptrons. In both cases, we did it with matrix operations, which was easier and faster than running the same classifier multiple times—once per example, and then once per class.

There is one more way to combine perceptrons: *serialize* them, using the output of one perceptron as input to the next. The result is called a *multilayer perceptron*. We didn't use multilayer perceptrons yet, but we will... a lot. For now, just keep this idea at the back of your mind.

# Where Perceptrons Fail

What's not to love about perceptrons? They're simple, and they can be assembled into larger structures like machine learning construction bricks. However, that simplicity comes with a distressing limitation: perceptrons work well on some datasets, and fail badly on others. More specifically, perceptrons are a good fit for *linearly separable* data. Let's see what "linearly separable" means, and why it matters.

### Linearly Separable Data

Take a look at this two-dimensional dataset:

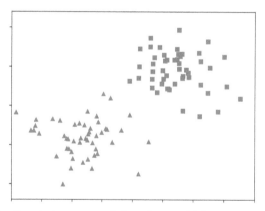

The two classes in the data—green triangles and blue squares—are neatly arranged into distinct clusters. You could even separate them with a line, like this:

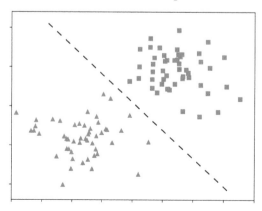

Datasets that can be partitioned with a straight line, like the one we got here, are called "linearly separable" datasets. By contrast, if a dataset can only be partitioned with a curved line, or cannot be partitioned at all, then it's not linearly separable.

Now imagine applying our a classifier to these green and blue points. The classifier would learn how the points are distributed, and then assign arbitrary new points to either the green class or the blue class. Here is the key information I want to give you in this section: our perceptron-based classifier would work pretty well on linearly separable data like these. Later in this book, in Chapter 12, How Classifiers Work, on page 149, we'll see exactly why that's the case. For now, you can take it as a given: train a perceptron on a linearly separable dataset, like the one shown here, and you'll get accurate classifications.

We just saw an example with two-dimensional data. However, the same reasoning applies for data with three or more dimensions—only, instead of a line, you'd have to separate the classes with a higher-dimensional hyperplane. With three dimensions, you'd have to trace a plane; with 785 dimensions, as in the case of MNIST, you'd have to trace a 784-dimensional linear shape. (Good luck with that!) In all of these cases, the intuition stays the same: if you can separate the classes with a "straight" shape, then you're golden: those data are good for a perceptron.

Now let's look at data that's *not* perceptron-friendly.

## Non-Linearly Separable Data

Look at these data:

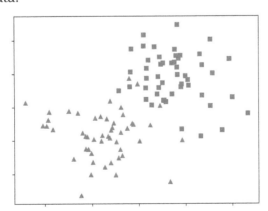

This dataset isn't linearly separable. Whichever line you draw, some data points will fall into the opposite class's camp. In this specific case, a perceptron could still separate most squares from most triangles, and come up with a

### Adding More Classes

In Linearly Separable Data, on page 102, we use a binary classifier to show the meaning of "linearly separable." But what if a dataset has more than two classes, as in the following case?

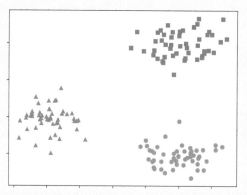

With three classes, we need a *multiclass* (rather than *binary*) classifier, like the one that we built to recognize MNIST digits. However, you might remember that we built that multiclass classifier by combining multiple binary classifiers. We could do the same to classify the dataset here: to recognize those three classes, we'd have three binary classifiers, one per class.

Long story short: even with more than two classes, the concept of linear separability stays pretty much the same. In particular, the data here is linearly separable, because you could trace three straight lines that separate each class from all the other classes. As a result, a perceptron-based classifier would be cool with this dataset.

decent classification. As the data gets more tangled, however, things go south quick, as this last example demonstrates:

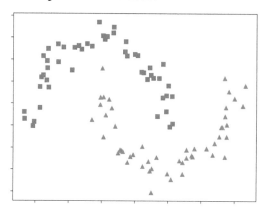

A perceptron would be pretty bad at classifying these points, because there is no way to separate them cleanly with a line. However you trace that line, you end up with at least one partition that contains a mix of squares and triangles.

Granted, most real-life datasets aren't as viciously twisted as the one we just looked at. After all, MNIST is not linearly separable, and we still got a cool 90% accuracy on it. Think about it for a moment, however, and you'll realize that 90% is not that good in practice. One mistake every ten characters is a pretty high error rate for most useful applications.

To make matters worse, that 90% on MNIST is about as far as our perceptron can go. Most real-life datasets are more complex than MNIST, and well beyond the perceptron's reach. There is no way around this: to write useful ML software, we need more than stacked and parallelized perceptrons.

So, that's the perceptron in a nutshell: it's simple, and it only works well on linearly separable data. That's a well understood trade-off today, but that wasn't always the case. In fact, the perceptron was once the center of a grand war of ideas—one that changed the history of computing as we know it. Bear with me for a couple of pages, because that's a story worth telling.

## A Tale of Perceptrons

In the 1950s, the nascent field of artificial intelligence was split into rivaling factions. Two groups competed for academic mindshare: the top dogs were the "symbolists," led by authorities such as Marvin Minsky and John McCarthy; the runners-up were the "connectionists," led by the charismatic Frank Rosenblatt.

The two tribes had very different approaches. The symbolists believed in *programming* an intelligent machine from the ground up. Piece by piece, they planned to build computers that would eventually manipulate concepts faster and better than humans.

This idea might sound overly optimistic today, but it made perfect sense in the 1950s, when people were inventing the first high-level programming languages. Those languages seemed much closer to human thinking than plain old assembly language. Who knew how far that process could go? (In fact, John McCarthy invented one of the first high-level programming languages, LISP, in his quest to code intelligence.)

The opposite faction, the connectionists, chased another dream. Their idea could be summed up as: build a brain, and intelligence will come.

To simplify things, the brain is made of neurons connected through fibers. Each neuron has multiple input fibers, and one output fiber. If the inputs are active in a certain pattern (maybe because they get a signal from the sensory organs), then the output also activates. The connectionist leader Frank Rosenblatt built a machine inspired by that mechanism. By analogy with neurons, he named the machine "perceptron," and its final processing step "activation function."

The first perceptron was a far cry from our tiny Python program. The "Mark 1 perceptron" was a room-sized piece of hardware that looked a bit like a server rack covered by an impenetrable tangle of wires. It had a camera connected to 400 photocells—essentially, very lo-res pixels. The weights were implemented with potentiometers wired to the photocells. During the learning phase, the potentiometers were physically rotated by electric motors.

To overcome the perceptron's limitations, the connectionists also studied *multilayer perceptrons*, which seemed able to tackle non-linearly separable data. Meanwhile, the symbolists were busy writing programs that solved algebra problems and stacked construction blocks with a robot arm.

To be fair, neither faction was making much progress toward intelligent machines. On the other hand, both factions were inclined to ballyhoo and extravagant promises. At one point, Rosenblatt declared that the perceptron was the first step toward machines that would not only be damn smart, but even self-conscious. The popular press bought into it hook, line, and sinker, making symbolists jealous.

The feud went on for years, with the symbolists reaping the lion's share of research funds, and the connectionists playing the part of the popular underdogs. Then, at some point, things really hit the fan.

## The Final Battle

From the 50s to the mid-60s, connectionists had been nibbling at AI research funds. The powerful symbolist leader Marvin Minsky thought that was a waste of money, and decided to set things straight once and for all.

Minsky's plan was simple: he would study the connectionist's ideas, with an eye toward showing their limitations. Together with the like-minded Seymour Papert, he published an entire book on the topic, called *Perceptrons*. The book was essentially Minsky's way to damn perceptrons with faint praise. It focused a lot on what perceptrons could *not* learn—such as non-linearly separable data.

To their credit, Minsky and Papert admitted that multilayer perceptrons could overcome the limitations of regular perceptrons. However, they hasted to add their gut feeling: multilayer perceptrons were probably impossible to train.

In their opinion, the whole idea of building intelligence with perceptrons was little more than a pipe dream.

Bolstered by Minsky's reputation, *Perceptrons* had more impact than the authors themselves intended. Where Minsky and Papert had been nuanced, the scientific community went for the "too long; didn't read" version: "connectionism is a dead end." Within a few months, funding for connectionist research dried up.

The impact of their book didn't stop there. The public had been waiting for a perceptron to stand up and ask for a cup of tea anytime soon. Now one of the major AI eggheads was scoffing at the whole thing. The popular opinion switched, and all of connectionism was filed under "unscientific bollocks."

In the early 70s, Rosenblatt died in a sailboat accident. That seemed like the last nail in the perceptron's coffin.

## The Aftermath

After connectionism was disgraced, it almost disappeared from academic research. Only a handful of researchers over the world, like medieval monks, kept the study of perceptrons alive.

Minsky's parting questions loomed over them like a prophecy of doom. Were multilayer perceptrons really impossible to train? Was the entire idea a dead end? Fifteen years passed before they could answer those questions.

What they found is the subject of the next part of this book.

# Part II

# Neural Networks

*In this part of the book, we'll use what we learned in Part I to build a more sophisticated learning machine: a neural network. Neural networks are leaps and bounds more powerful than perceptrons, but they come with their own set of challenges. We'll spend a few chapters building our first network, and a few more detailing and overcoming those challenges.*

*Here's a mild spoiler: even the first version of our neural network will classify MNIST digits better than the perceptron. But we won't stop there! As you'll see soon, we're going to aim for a target that's way more ambitious: 99% accuracy in character recognition.*

*Fasten your seatbelts... this will be quite the trip.*

# CHAPTER 9

# Designing the Network

Part I of this book was all about the perceptron. Part II is about the perceptron's big brother, and the most important idea in this book: the *neural network*. Neural networks are way more powerful than perceptrons. In Where Perceptrons Fail, on page 102, we learned that perceptrons need simple data that are linearly separable. By contrast, neural networks can deal with gnarly data, like photos of real-world objects.

Even on a simple dataset like MNIST, our perceptron was just scraping by, making almost one mistake every ten characters. With neural networks, we can aim for an order of magnitude better accuracy: in this part of the book, we'd like to build an MNIST classifier that reaches 99% accuracy—one error every 100 characters.

Here's a plan to reach for that lofty goal: over the next few chapters, we'll build and tweak a neural network. Once again, you'll learn by doing, handcrafting code line by line. It will take us three chapters to complete our neural network v1.0:

- In this first chapter we'll design a network that classifies MNIST digits—on paper.

- In the next chapter, Chapter 10, Building the Network, on page 121, we'll write the network's *classification* code.

- In Chapter 11, Training the Network, on page 129, we'll write the network's *training* code.

After these three chapters, we'll have a working neural network. Even then, however, you might struggle to understand how it works. The following chapter, Chapter 12, How Classifiers Work, on page 149, will use our network as a concrete example to answer questions like: "What makes neural networks so powerful?"

After building a neural network and understanding how it works, we'll have some more work to do. The first version of our network won't be very accurate—in fact, it will only be about as accurate as the perceptron. In the remaining three chapters of Part II, we'll unleash the network's power and aim straight for that 99% accuracy.

I won't spoil your fun by telling you whether we'll eventually hit our goal. To find out, you'll have to keep reading. (Or peek at the last pages of Part II... But you wouldn't do that, would you?)

Now that we have a plan for action, let's dive straight into our first task: designing a neural network that classifies MNIST digits.

## Assembling a Neural Network from Perceptrons

Let's see how to build a neural network, starting with the perceptron that we already have. As a reminder, here is that perceptron again—a weighted sum of the inputs, followed by a sigmoid:

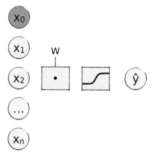

In Part I of this book, we didn't just use the perceptron as is—we also combined perceptrons in two different ways. First, we trained the perceptron with many MNIST images at once; and second, we used ten perceptrons to classify the ten possible digits. In Assembling Perceptrons, on page 100, we compared those two operations to "stacking" and "parallelizing" perceptrons, respectively, as shown in the picture on page 113.

To be clear, we didn't *literally* stack and parallelize perceptrons. Instead, we used matrices to get a similar result. Our perceptron's input was a matrix with one row per image; and our perceptron's output was a matrix with ten columns, one per class. The "stacking" and "parallelizing" metaphors are just convenient shortcuts to describe those matrix-based calculations.

Now we're about to take these extended (stacked and parallelized) perceptrons, and use them as building blocks for a neural network.

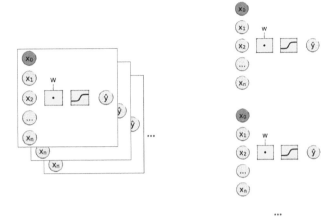

## Chaining Perceptrons

We can build a neural network by *serializing* two perceptrons like this:

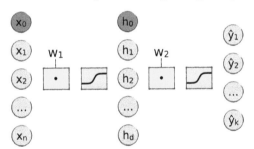

See? Each perceptron has its own weights and its own sigmoid operation, but the outputs of the first perceptron are also the inputs of the second. To avoid confusion, I renamed those values with the letter h, and I used d to indicate their number. h stands for "hidden," because these values are neither part of the network's input, nor the output. (And since I know that you're going to ask: the d stands for nothing in particular. I just took a cue from mathematicians and came up with a random letter.)

Back in the day, a structure like this one was called a *multilayer perceptron*, or an *artificial neural network*. These days, most people simply call it a neural network. The round gray bubbles in the network are called *nodes*, and they're arranged in *layers*, as shown in the picture on page 114.

This network has three layers: an *input layer*, a *hidden layer*, and an *output layer*. You can also concatenate more than two perceptron and end up with more than three layers—but we can save that topic for the next part of this book. For now, we'll focus on three-layered neural networks.

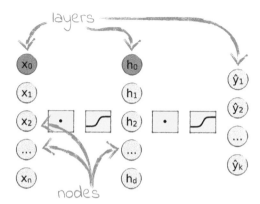

The nodes in the hidden layer are calculated from the nodes in the input layer, except for one node: the bias. When we joined two perceptrons together to create the network, both perceptrons kept their bias node. So now we have a bias node in the input layer, and another in the hidden layer. The values of those nodes are fixed at 1. (If you don't remember why 1, then review Bye Bye, Bias, on page 59.)

Let me be clear on what we mean when we say, for example, "this layer has 10 nodes." That doesn't mean that the neural network represents that layer as an array of 10 elements—it means that the neural network represents that layer as a matrix of 10 columns, and as many rows as it needs. For example, if we're training a network on a dataset of 5,000 examples, then the layer will be represented by a $(5000, 10)$ matrix. Just like the diagram of a perceptron, the diagram of a neural network pretends that the network is always processing one example at the time, for the sake of readability. Remember our "stacking" metaphor: when you look at these diagrams, imagine that there are as many networks as we have training examples, stacked upon each other.

Sometimes, people refer to the nodes in a neural network as *neurons*. To be precise, a neuron isn't just a node. It also includes the components that directly impact its value—the nodes in the previous layer, and the operation in between, as illustrated by the picture on page 115.

Finally, as I mentioned earlier, the functions in between layers are called the *activation functions* of the network. In the network that we're looking at, both activation functions are sigmoids—but that isn't necessarily the case, as we'll find out soon.

With that, we know what a three-layered neural network looks like in general. However, we didn't decide the number of nodes in each layer of our network. Let's do that.

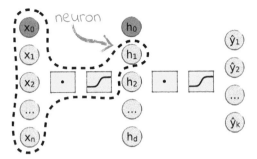

## How Many Nodes?

Let's see how many nodes we need for our network's input, hidden, and output layers.

Let's start with the number of input nodes. Just like a perceptron, our network has an input node for each input variable in the data, plus the bias. We're looking to classify MNIST's 784-pixels images, so that makes 785 input nodes. Our input matrix will have one row per image, and 785 columns—the same as the perceptron.

The number of output nodes is also the same as the perceptron's. There are 10 classes in MNIST, so we need 10 output nodes. The output matrix will have one row per image, and 10 columns.

What about the number of hidden nodes? That one is for us to decide, and in a few chapters we'll see how to take a smart decision. For now, let's go with a simple rule of thumb: the number of hidden nodes is usually somewhere between the number of input and output nodes. So let's set it at 200, that becomes 201 once we add the bias.

You might wonder why I chose an awkward number like 201. After all, the network is likely to perform pretty much the same with one node more or less. So why don't we start with 199 hidden nodes, and end up with a round 200 after adding the bias? Indeed, we could just as well do that. I opted for 201 as a reminder that one of the hidden nodes is special: it has a fixed value of 1, to take care of the bias.

Finally, let's talk about the weights. We built our network by chaining two perceptrons, each with its own matrix of weights. As a result, the neural network has two matrices of weights: one between the input and the hidden layer, and one between the hidden and the output layer. We can get their dimensions with a simple general rule: *each matrix of weights in a neural network has as many rows as its input elements, and as many columns as its output elements.* In other words, w1 is (n, d), and w2 is (d, k). In case you want to check, that rule also applies to the perceptron: the matrix of weights of our perceptron had one row per input variable, and one column per class.

If you find all these matrix dimensions confusing, check them for yourself. Here are the operations in the network:

```
H = sigmoid(X · W1)
Ŷ = sigmoid(H · W2)
```

Remember the rules of matrix multiplication from Multiplying Matrices, on page 49, and also remember that the output of the sigmoid has the same dimensions as its inputs.

Let's sketch the number of nodes and the matrix dimensions on the network diagram. I will use the letter m to indicate the number of inputs, which can vary. It's 60,000 in the MNIST training set, but it can be as little as 1 during classification, if we classify a single image:

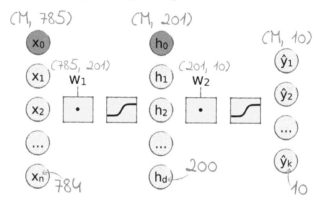

The plan is looking nice. You're probably itching to turn it to code—but first, we have one last change to make.

## Enter the Softmax

Check out the activation functions in our neural network. So far, we took it for granted that both of those functions are sigmoids. However, most neural networks replace the last sigmoid, the one right before the output layer, with another function called the *softmax*.

Let me show you what the softmax looks like, and then we'll see why it's useful. Like the sigmoid, the softmax takes an array of numbers, that in this case are called the *logits*, and returns an array with the same size as the input. Here is the formula of the softmax, in case you want to understand the math behind it:

$$softmax(l_i) = \frac{e^{l_i}}{\sum e^l}$$

You can read this formula as: take the exponential of each logit and divide it by the summed exponentials of all the logits.

You don't need to grok the formula of the softmax, as long as you understand what happens when we use the softmax instead of the sigmoid. Think about the output of the sigmoid in our MNIST classifier, back in Decoding the Classifier's Answers, on page 91. You might remember that for each image in the input, the sigmoid gives us ten numbers between 0 and 1. Those numbers tell us how confident the perceptron is about each classification. For example, if the fourth number is 0.9, that means "this image is probably a 3." If it's close to 0.1, that means "this image is unlikely to be a 3." Among those ten results, we pick the one with the highest confidence.

Like the sigmoid, the softmax returns an array where each element is between 0 and 1. However, the softmax has an additional property: the sum of its outputs is always 1. In mathspeak you would say that the softmax *normalizes* that sum to a value of 1.

That's a nice property, because if the numbers add up to 1, then we can interpret them as probabilities. To give you a concrete example, imagine that we're running a three-class classifier, and the weighted sum after the hidden layer returns these logits:

| logit 1 | logit 2 | logit 3 |
|---------|---------|---------|
| 1.6     | 3.1     | 0.5     |

Judging from these numbers, it seems likely that the item that we're classifying belongs to the second class—but it's hard to gauge *how* likely. Now see what happens if we pass the logits through a softmax:

| softmax 1 | softmax 2 | softmax 3 |
|-----------|-----------|-----------|
| 0.17198205 | 0.77077009 | 0.05724785 |

What's the chance that the item belongs to the second class? Take a glance at these numbers, and you'll know that the answer is 77%. The first class is way less likely, hovering around 17%, while the third is a measly 6%. Add them together, and you get the expected 100%. Thanks to the softmax, we converted vague numbers to human-friendly probabilities. That's a good reason to use softmax as the last activation function in our neural network.

## Here's the Plan

Now that you know about the softmax, let's replace the second sigmoid with a softmax and complete the design of our neural network:

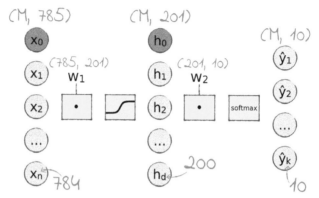

The input layer has 785 columns (one per pixel, plus the bias), and a sigmoid activation function. The hidden layer has 201 columns including the bias, and a softmax activation function. The output layer has 10 columns, matching the 10 classes in MNIST. Finally, the matrices of weights have the right dimensions to make all the matrix multiplications add up. That's all we need to know to get started.

Speaking of code, you must be eager to get down to it. But first, let's recap what we learned in this chapter.

## What You Just Learned

In this chapter we designed an *artificial neural network*—or just a *neural network*, for short—by joining two perceptrons. Because the output of the first perceptron is also the input of the second, the resulting neural network has three *layers*: input, hidden, and output. Each layer is made up of a bunch of *nodes*, or *neurons*.

In between each pair of consecutive layers, there are two operations: a weighted sum of the first layer, and an *activation function*. In our design, we used a sigmoid as the activation function for the input layer, and a *softmax* for the hidden layer. The input and hidden layer also have one bias node each, with a fixed value of 1.

Armed with that knowledge, we designed a network to recognize MNIST characters. In the next chapter we'll turn that design into running code.

### Another Way to Draw Networks

There is no standardized notation for neural networks. This book uses its own simple notation, like the one in Here's the Plan, on page 118. Images of neural networks from other sources are more likely to use a notation that you might call "blobs and lines." It comes in different flavors, but it generally looks something like this:

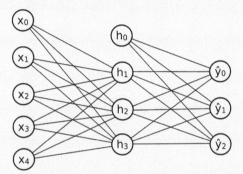

The blobs and lines notation does have a few advantages. For example, all those lines give you a good place to jot down the values of individual weights. If you don't need to do that, however, the lines end up cluttering the diagram and making it harder to sketch.

This book eschews blobs and lines in favor of two other notations. In most of the book, I use a streamlined notation that's good for sketching neural networks. In Chapter 11, Training the Network, on page 129, I use a different notation ("computational graphs") to explain one specific concept. Even if you won't see the blobs and lines notation in these pages, however, you should be aware that it exists. It's useful in some edge cases, and it's common in the wild.

## Hands On: Network Adventures

We didn't write any code in this chapter, so why don't you try writing it yourself? Here's a task for you: set up a timer—maybe thirty minutes, or one hour, depending on your Python coding experience. Then take the perceptron-based code of the MNIST reader from Part I of this book, and try to convert it to the neural network that we designed in this chapter. Take as many shortcuts as you need. For example, feel free to ignore the softmax, and just use a second sigmoid instead. Stop when the timer rings.

Just to be clear, nobody expects that you'll complete the job in one hour. In fact, you might have no code at all when the timer rings. That's okay! The point of this exercise is not to code a neural network. The point is to start thinking about the problem, and also to give yourself a review of the perceptron's code. Once the timer rings, turn the page, and let's code that neural network together.

# CHAPTER 10

# Building the Network

In the previous chapter, we made a plan for building a neural network that classifies MNIST images. We started by concatenating two perceptrons, and we jotted down the number of rows and columns for all the matrices involved. The result was this diagram:

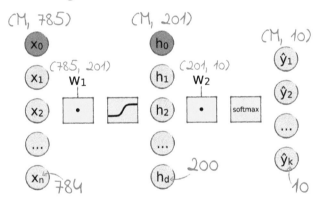

Keep the sketch handy, because we're about to convert it to code. That job will take two chapters. In this one, we'll write the neural network's classification functions—in other words, all the code in the network, except for the training code. In the next chapter, we'll complete the network and unleash it on an unsuspecting MNIST dataset.

Let's get started with the classification functions. For reference, let's start from the functions we already wrote in Part I, to implement the perceptron.

## Coding Forward Propagation

Here is a reprint of forward(), a core function of our perceptron:

```
def forward(X, w):
    weighted_sum = np.matmul(X, w)
    return sigmoid(weighted_sum)
```

forward() implements the operation that we called "forward propagation": it calculates the system's outputs from the system's inputs. In the case of the perceptron, it applies a weighted sum followed by a sigmoid. In the case of a neural network, things become slightly more complicated.

In fact, this is where the name "forward propagation" really comes into its own: passing an MNIST image through a neural network is like propagating data "forward" through the network's layers, from input to hidden to output.

The first step of forward propagation is the same as a regular perceptron's:

```
h = sigmoid(np.matmul(prepend_bias(X), w1))
```

First, we added a bias column to the inputs; second, we computed the weighted sum of the inputs using the first matrix of weights, w1; and third, we passed the result through the sigmoid() function. Look at the sketch that opens this chapter, and you'll see that we just calculated the hidden layer.

Now we can repeat that process and calculate the output layer:

```
y_hat = softmax(np.matmul(prepend_bias(h), w2))
```

We used a different matrix of weights, and we passed the weighted sum through softmax() instead of sigmoid(). (We didn't write softmax() yet, but we will soon.) Apart from those differences, the code that calculates the output layer is similar to the one that calculates the hidden layer: add the bias, compute the weighted sum, and pass it through the activation function.

Let's wrap those two lines of code in a function:

```
def forward(X, w1, w2):
    h = sigmoid(np.matmul(prepend_bias(X), w1))
    y_hat = softmax(np.matmul(prepend_bias(h), w2))
    return y_hat
```

There's one last thing to note in this code. Back when we implemented the perceptron, the prepend_bias() function was part of the code that loaded and prepared the data, right in the mnist.py library. In the neural network, we need to add the bias twice: once in the input layer, and once in the hidden layer. Because of that, we should move prepend_bias() from mnist.py to the main network code, so that we can call it multiple times. Here's that function again:

```
def prepend_bias(X):
    return np.insert(X, 0, 1, axis=1)
```

With that, the outline of forward propagation is done. Now let's fill in the blanks, by writing the softmax() function.

## Writing the Softmax Function

To complete forward propagation, we need to write the softmax() activation function. As it turns out, we can implement softmax() in two lines of code—but those two lines require some attention.

Here is the mathematical formula of the softmax, straight from Enter the Softmax, on page 116:

$$softmax(l_i) = \frac{e^{l_i}}{\sum e^l}$$

And here is that formula converted to code:

```
def softmax(logits):
    exponentials = np.exp(logits)
    return exponentials / np.sum(exponentials, axis=1).reshape(-1, 1)
```

There you have it—more perplexing NumPy code, in case you were missing it. Let's break it down.

Remember, "logits" is the fancy name for the inputs of the softmax. In our case, those inputs are going to be arranged in a matrix that has one row for each MNIST image, and one column per class. For example, if we're training the system with 60,000 images, then softmax() gets a (60000, 10) matrix, and it must return a matrix of the same shape.

The first line in softmax() calculates the exponentials of the logits. The second line divides each exponential by the sum of all the exponentials on the same row. The parameter axis=1 means: "calculate the sum by row, not over the entire matrix." Before doing the division, we must reshape the sums into a one-column matrix—otherwise, NumPy complains that it cannot divide a matrix by a one-dimensional array.

When dealing with NumPy code, the Python interactive interpreter is your friend. Let's fire it up and try out the softmax() function:

```
⇒ output = np.array([[0.3, 0.8, 0.2],
⇒                    [0.1, 0.9, 0.1]])
⇒ softmax(output)
❮ array([[0.28140804, 0.46396343, 0.25462853],
         [0.23665609, 0.52668782, 0.23665609]])
```

We still have one row per image and one column per class, but the softmax rescaled the logits in each row so that they add up to 1.

Now we have the forward() function, and both activation functions—the sigmoid and the softmax. To complete the classifier, however, we still need to take

care of the higher-level classification and testing function: classify() and report().
Let's finish the job.

## Numerical Stability

Our implementations of softmax() and sigmoid() have a problem: they're *numerically unstable*, meaning that they amplify small changes in the inputs. For example, see what happens if we apply softmax() to a small logits and a large logit:

```
⇒ softmax(np.array([[1, 20]]))
❮ array([[   5.60279641e-09,    9.99999994e-01]])
```

softmax() amplified the logits' differences. It returned a tiny value, and a value that's very close to 1. Now let's try two logits that diverge further:

```
⇒ softmax(np.array([[1, 1000]]))
❮ __main__:2: RuntimeWarning: overflow encountered in exp
  __main__:3: RuntimeWarning: invalid value encountered in true_divide
  array([[ 0.,  nan]])
```

Here is what happened. The first element in the output is so small that it *underflows* Python's math libraries, coming back at 0. The second element involves the exponential of 1,000—a huge number that *overflows* Python's math libraries, returning a value of inf (for "infinite"). The softmax() code then tries to divide two infs, resulting in nan (for "not a number"). The first time such an overflow occurs, NumPy generates a warning. We can ignore that warning, but we risk flooding our network with nans and zeros.

Numerically unstable functions such as our softmax() are prone to "blow up" their inputs, resulting in underflows or overflows. To fix this problem, we could write numerically stable implementations of those functions, using alternative formulae that avoid extreme intermediate values. For example, here's a numerically stable variation of the softmax formula:

$$softmax(l_i) = \frac{e^{l_i} + max(e^l)}{\sum e^l + max(e^l)}$$

In a production system, you should always use numerically stable functions. In this book, however, we're going to stick with the plain vanilla formulae. After all, our examples aren't production code—and in Part III, we'll switch from hand-written code to ML libraries, that include numerically stable implementations of all functions right out of the box. Long story short: as you read these chapters, you can ignore overflow warnings, and turn a blind eye to those nans floating around your network.

## Writing the Classification Functions

Back in Decoding the Classifier's Answers, on page 91, we wrote a classify() function that predicted the value of an unlabeled image. Here's that function again, modified for the neural network:

```
def classify(X, w1, w2):
    y_hat = forward(X, w1, w2)
    labels = np.argmax(y_hat, axis=1)
    return labels.reshape(-1, 1)
```

The neural network's classify() is the same as the perceptron's, with the exception that it takes two matrices of weights instead of one. The output of a neural network works like the output of a perceptron: the output layer has one row for each image in X, and one column per class—10 in the case of MNIST. The classify() function uses argmax() to find the most likely prediction in each row, and returns a single-column matrix of predictions.

Our perceptron-based MNIST classifier also comes with a report() function that prints the current loss(), and the percentage of correct classifications over the test set. This function can be called either during the classification phase, or during the training phase, to check how well the system is learning. Here's the report() function, updated for the neural network:

```
def report(iteration, X_train, Y_train, X_test, Y_test, w1, w2):
    y_hat = forward(X_train, w1, w2)
    training_loss = loss(Y_train, y_hat)
    classifications = classify(X_test, w1, w2)
    accuracy = np.average(classifications == Y_test) * 100.0
    print("Iteration: %5d, Loss: %.6f, Accuracy: %.2f%%" %
          (iteration, training_loss, accuracy))
```

With that, we wrote all the code for the classification phase of the neural network. However, since we just mentioned the loss() function, it's worth spending a few more words on it.

## Cross Entropy

So far, we used the *log loss* formula for our binary classifiers. We even used the log loss when we bundled ten binary classifiers in a multiclass classifier (in Chapter 7, The Final Challenge, on page 87). In that case, we added together the losses of the ten classifiers to get a total loss.

While the log loss served us well so far, it's time to switch to a simpler formula —one that's specific to multiclass classifiers. It's called the *cross-entropy loss*, and it looks like this:

$$L = -\frac{1}{m} \sum_{i=1}^{m} y_i \cdot \log(\hat{y}_i)$$

Here's the cross-entropy loss in code form:

```
def loss(Y, y_hat):
    return -np.sum(Y * np.log(y_hat)) / Y.shape[0]
```

If you're curious, you can read how the cross-entropy loss works on the ProgML[1] site. However, you don't need to understand how it works, as long as you remember what it does: like other loss formulae, it measures the distance between the classifier's predictions and the labels. The lower the loss, the better the classifier.

> Check out "Grokking the Cross-Entropy Loss" on ProgML.

Besides its cool name, there is a pragmatic reason to use the cross-entropy loss in our neural network: it's a perfect match for the softmax. More specifically, a softmax followed by a cross-entropy loss makes it easier to code gradient descent. But I'm getting ahead of myself here—that's a topic for the next chapter. For now, just know that the softmax and the cross-entropy loss jive well together, and they'll cap off our neural networks for the rest of this book.

## The Revenge of Local Minima

While we're talking about loss functions, there's a note worth making. Since When Gradient Descent Fails, on page 42, we vetted our loss functions for a major requirement: they had to play well with gradient descent. In particular, the GD algorithm can get stuck in a local minimum—so we picked loss functions that didn't have local minima.

Unfortunately, once you graduate to neural networks, all bets are off: however carefully you select it, the loss of a neural network *can* have local minima. Neural networks have more sophisticated models than perceptrons, that allow them to approximate more complicated functions—but as a downside, the losses of those functions can have "holes" where GD gets stuck.

On the bright side, even though a neural network's loss can have local minima, that doesn't mean that it always does—and even when local minima do exist, they're not necessarily a showstopper. As researchers understand more and more about neural networks, they're finding out that local minima aren't quite as disruptive as we assumed.[a] Most of the times, training a neural network will find a minimum that's good enough, even though we cannot be sure it's *the* best minimum overall.

---

a.     arxiv.org/abs/1412.0233

Finally, let me clear one potential source of confusion. If you look at the code, you might wonder why we bother with the loss in the first place. In fact, we don't even seem to ever use the loss() function, apart from printing its value on the screen.

Indeed, we don't care about the loss as much as the *gradient* of the loss, that we're going to use later during gradient descent. While the loss() function is not really necessary, however, it's still nice to have. We can look at that number to gauge how well the classifier is doing, both during training and during classification. That's the reason why we bothered to code loss() and call it from the report() function.

With the loss() function, our neural network's classification code is done. Let's wrap it up.

## What You Just Learned

In the last few pages, you got acquainted with a new loss function (the *cross-entropy loss*) and a few new concepts, like *numerical stability*. The focus of this chapter, however, was on implementing the neural network that we designed in the previous chapter. Here is all the code that we came up with:

10_building/forward_propagation.py
```
import numpy as np

def sigmoid(z):
    return 1 / (1 + np.exp(-z))

def softmax(logits):
    exponentials = np.exp(logits)
    return exponentials / np.sum(exponentials, axis=1).reshape(-1, 1)

def loss(Y, y_hat):
    return -np.sum(Y * np.log(y_hat)) / Y.shape[0]

def prepend_bias(X):
    return np.insert(X, 0, 1, axis=1)

def forward(X, w1, w2):
    h = sigmoid(np.matmul(prepend_bias(X), w1))
    y_hat = softmax(np.matmul(prepend_bias(h), w2))
    return y_hat

def classify(X, w1, w2):
    y_hat = forward(X, w1, w2)
    labels = np.argmax(y_hat, axis=1)
    return labels.reshape(-1, 1)
```

```
def report(iteration, X_train, Y_train, X_test, Y_test, w1, w2):
    y_hat = forward(X_train, w1, w2)
    training_loss = loss(Y_train, y_hat)
    classifications = classify(X_test, w1, w2)
    accuracy = np.average(classifications == Y_test) * 100.0
    print("Iteration: %5d, Loss: %.6f, Accuracy: %.2f%%" %
          (iteration, training_loss, accuracy))
```

With that, half of our neural network's logic is done—the half that takes care of the classification phase.

This code, however, won't be useful until we've also written the code that trains the network. In the next chapter we'll do that, and we'll test drive the entire thing.

## Hands On: Time Travel Testing

You might be itching to see the neural network running, even though it's incomplete. Right now we have the classification code, that needs pre-calculated weights—but not the training code, that finds the values of those weights. How can we check the first without the second?

We can solve this problem thanks to time travel. Book authors have mastered that elusive skill—and guess what: I just returned from the future, where I have access to the complete neural network code. After training the complete network for a few iterations, I serialized the two matrices of weights to a JSON file named weights.json, that you can find among this chapter's source code.

Go forth, give it a try. Paste this code at the end of forward_propagation.py and run it:

```
import json
with open('weights.json') as f:
    weights = json.load(f)
w1, w2 = (np.array(weights[0]), np.array(weights[1]))

import mnist
report(0, mnist.X_train, mnist.Y_train, mnist.X_test, mnist.Y_test, w1, w2)
```

This code uses Python's json.load() function to deserialize w1 and w2 from the weights.json file. Then it runs a classification on the MNIST test set. If you try it yourself, you should get a bit more than 43% correct matches.

That 43% is nothing to write home about—but remember, these are the weights that I got after just a handful of training iterations. To see how good the neural network gets after some serious training, you'll have to wait for the next chapter. How's that for a cliffhanger?

# CHAPTER 11

# Training the Network

In the previous chapter, we wrote a functioning neural network—or at least half of it. The network's prediction code is done: it passes data through the model, and churns out labels. However, that process also requires a set of weights, and we still didn't write the code that finds those weights. We'll do it in this chapter by implementing the train() function of our neural network.

In the early years of neural networks, training was a tough nut to crack. AI experts even questioned whether they could be trained at all. The answer came in the early 1970s, when researchers found a way to calculate the gradient of a network with an algorithm called *backpropagation*—or "backprop" for friends.

Chances are, you'll never have to implement backpropagation in a real-life project. Modern ML libraries already come with their own ready-made implementations. However, it's still important that you get an intuitive sense of how backpropagation works, so that you're well equipped to deal with its subtle consequences.

In this chapter, we'll see how backpropagation works, and we'll implement it for our neural network. You'll also learn to initialize the network's weights so that they jive well with backprop. At the end of this chapter, we'll put the network through its maiden run. Will it beat the perceptron's accuracy? If so, by how much?

## The Case for Backpropagation

Soon enough, we're going to explain backpropagation from the ground up. But first, let's see why people use backpropagation in the first place.

To begin with, here's a piece of good news: in a sense, you already know how to train a neural network. You train it with gradient descent, like you train

## A Quick Heads Up

I've read backprop tutorials that open with a bold declaration: "backpropagation is easy!" I disagree. Backpropagation is pretty darn hard. It only becomes easy in retrospect, *after* you know how it works.

To work over that initial hump, this chapter focuses on intuition. We'll grok the general workings of backprop, but we'll skip a few details and long-winded calculations.

I strove to keep these explanations as simple as I could, but not simpler. Together with Chapter 4, Hyperspace!, on page 45, this is the most math-heavy chapter in the book. Don't feel frustrated if you don't understand all of it on your first read through. Most people take time to wrap their minds around backpropagation. I know I did!

a perceptron. At each iteration, you calculate the gradient of the loss, then descend that gradient to minimize the loss. (If you need a refresher, review Chapter 3, Walking the Gradient, on page 31.)

Now for the less-than-good news: descending the gradient is the easy part of the job. The tough part is calculating that gradient in the first place.

In the case of the perceptron, we knew how to get the gradient: we calculated the derivatives of the loss with respect to the weights. (Well, we actually looked up those derivatives in a textbook. Still counts.) In the case of a neural network, however, coming up with the equivalent derivatives can be hard. For example, the code that computes the loss in our three-layered network looks something like this:

```
h = sigmoid(matmul(X, w1))
y_hat = softmax(matmul(h, w2))
L = cross_entropy_loss(Y, y_hat)
```

Imagine writing the mathematical equivalent of the previous code, and then taking the derivatives of that formula with respect to $w_1$ and $w_2$. That would be some work, even for someone steeped in calculus.

We could still sweat our way to the gradient of our neural network—but the typical modern network would be much more challenging. Real-world neural networks can be mindbogglingly complicated, with dozens of intricately connected layers and weight matrices. It would be very hard to write down the loss for one of those large networks—let alone calculate its derivatives.

We're facing a dilemma: on one hand, we want to calculate the gradients of the loss for any neural network; on the other, calculating those derivatives is unfeasible, except for the simplest and less powerful networks.

That's where backpropagation enters the picture. Backprop is the way out of that dilemma—an algorithm that calculates the gradients of the loss in any neural network. Once we know those gradients, we can descend them with good old GD.

Let's see how backprop works its magic.

# From the Chain Rule to Backpropagation

Backpropagation is an application of the *chain rule*, one of the fundamental rules of calculus. Let's see how the chain rule works on a couple of network-like structures: a simpler one, and a more complicated one.

## The Chain Rule on a Simple Network

Look at this simple network-like structure:

This one isn't a neural network, because it doesn't have weights. Let's borrow a term from computer science, and call it a *computational graph*. This graph has an input a, followed by two operations: "multiply by two" and "square." The output of the multiplication is called b, and the output of the entire graph is called c.

Now let's say that we want to calculate ∂c/∂a, the gradient of c with respect to a. Intuitively, that gradient represents the impact of a on c: whenever a changes, c also changes, and the gradient measures how much. (If this way of thinking about the gradient sounds perplexing, then maybe review Gradient Descent, on page 33.)

For such a small graph, we could calculate ∂c/∂a in a single shot, by taking the derivative of c with respect to a. As we mentioned earlier, however, that derivation would become impractical for very large graphs. Instead, let's calculate the gradient using the chain rule, that works for graphs of any size.

Here is how the chain rule works. To calculate ∂c/∂a:

1. Walk the graph back from c to a.

2. For each operation along the way, calculate its *local gradient*—the derivative of the operation's output with respect to its input.

3. Multiply all the local gradients together.

Let's see how that process works in practice. In our case, the path back from c to a involves two operations: a square and a multiplication by 2. Let's jot down the local gradients of those two operations:

$$\text{(a)} \xrightarrow{\partial b/\partial a \,=\, 2} \boxed{*2} \xrightarrow[\partial c/\partial b \,=\, 4a]{b \,=\, 2a} \boxed{**2} \xrightarrow{c \,=\, b^2 \,=\, (2a)^2}$$

How do I know that $\partial b/\partial a$ is 2, and $\partial c/\partial b$ is 4a? Well, even though we're using the chain rule, we must still compute the local gradients in the old-fashioned way, taking derivatives by hand. However, don't fret if you don't know how to take derivatives—there are libraries that do that. Just understand how the process works, and you're golden.

Now that we have the local gradients, we can multiply them to get $\partial c/\partial a$:

$$\frac{\partial c}{\partial a} = \frac{\partial c}{\partial b} \cdot \frac{\partial b}{\partial a} = 4a \cdot 2 = 8a$$

So, there's our answer, courtesy of the chain rule: the gradient of c with respect to a is 8a. In other words, if a changes a little, then c changes by 8 times the current value of a.

To recap the chain rule: to calculate the gradient of any node y with respect to any other node x, we multiply the local gradient of all the nodes on the way back from y to x. Thanks to the chain rule, we can calculate a complicated gradient as a multiplication of many simple gradients.

Now let's look at a computational graph that's a bit more similar to a neural network.

---

### Math Deep Dive: The Chain Rule

 If you watched Khan Academy's screencasts on calculus, then you might already have seen the videos on the chain rule.[1] As usual, this material goes deeper than you need for the purposes of reading this chapter—but if you like math, it's definitely worth a watch.

---

## Now For Something More Complicated...

The name "backpropagation" is a shorthand for "calculate the gradients of a neural network's loss with respect to the weights using the chain rule." As an example, check out this second computational graph on page 133.

---

1.   www.khanacademy.org/math/differential-calculus/dc-chain

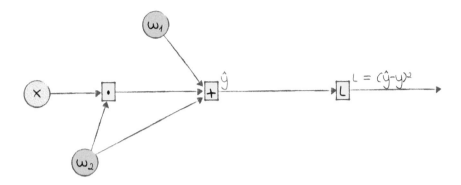

This graph is not going to win any ML competitions. In fact, you might argue that it's not even a neural network. However, it has what it takes to stand for a neural network in this example: an input x, an output ŷ, and a couple of weights. It also has a loss L, calculated as the squared error of the difference between ŷ and the ground truth y.

Imagine freezing this network mid training, right before the next step of gradient descent. Let's say that $w_1$ and $w_2$ are currently 6 and 2. Also, let's say that we only have one training example, that has x = 3 and y = 17. From those numbers, we can calculate the other values in the graph:

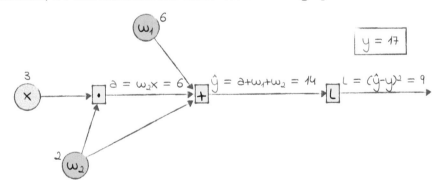

I didn't have a name for the output of the multiplication, so I called it a.

To take a step of GD, we need the gradients of L with respect to $w_1$ and $w_2$. We can compute those gradients with the chain rule. Remember how it works? $\partial L/\partial w_1$ is the product of the local gradients on the way back from L to $w_1$. The same goes for $\partial L/\partial w_2$. Let's get down to business and calculate those local gradients.

Note that this graph has an added difficulty compared with the one from the previous section: some operations have multiple inputs. If an operation has multiple inputs or outputs, then we have to calculate its local gradient for each input–output pair. Taking that fact into account, we need five local gradients. Here they are, complete with their numerical values:

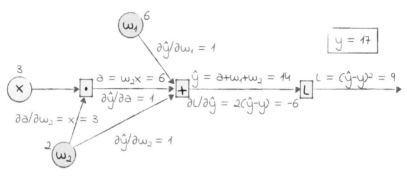

Now we can apply the chain rule. First, let's calculate ∂L/∂w₁. If you wanted to be precise, you could read that gradient as "the gradient of L with respect to w₁"—but because that's a mouthful, machine learning practitioners tend to call it "the gradient of w₁" for short.

To get the gradient of w₁, we multiply all the gradients between L and w₁:

$$\frac{\partial L}{\partial w_1} = \frac{\partial L}{\partial \hat{y}} \cdot \frac{\partial \hat{y}}{\partial w_1} = -6 \cdot 1 = -6$$

There you have it: with the current weights, the gradient of w₁ is -6. To take the next step of GD, we would multiply this gradient by the learning rate, and subtract the result from w₁.

We can follow a similar process to get ∂L/∂w₂, although in this case we have an additional complication: there are two paths leading from w₂ to L—one that passes by the multiplication, and one that doesn't. Whenever we have multiple paths, we have to sum their gradients:

$$\frac{\partial L}{\partial w_2} = \frac{\partial L}{\partial \hat{y}} \cdot \frac{\partial \hat{y}}{\partial w_2} + \frac{\partial L}{\partial \hat{y}} \cdot \frac{\partial \hat{y}}{\partial a} \cdot \frac{\partial a}{\partial w_2} = -6 \cdot 1 + -6 \cdot 1 \cdot 3 = -24$$

∂L/∂w₂ is also negative, but larger than ∂L/∂w₁. Once again, we can multiply this gradient by the learning rate, and subtract the result from w₂.

You can see ∂L/∂w₁ and ∂L/∂w₂ as measures of how much each weight is contributing to the loss. Both weights have a negative contribution, meaning that they must grow so that the loss gets smaller. However, w₂ is contributing more than w₁, because it's involved twice in the calculation of ŷ—once in the multiplication, and once in the sum.

In general, if a weight has a small gradient, that means that it doesn't contribute much to the network's error, so it can change just a little bit. Conversely, a weight with a large gradient is having a big impact on the network's error, and needs to be changed more decisively. Backprop is a way to calculate how much each weight needs to change.

We just applied backpropagation—an algorithm to calculate the gradients of the weights by multiplying the local gradients of individual operations. It's called *back*propagation because, conceptually, it moves in the opposite direction of forward propagation. Forward propagation moves from the inputs to the outputs, and ultimately calculates the loss; backpropagation moves back from the loss to the weights, accumulating local gradients through the chain rule.

Now that we have a grip on backpropagation, let's apply it to our network.

## Applying Backpropagation

Here is our three-layered network, in the form of a computational graph:

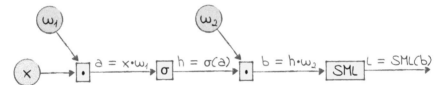

All the variables in the preceding graph are matrices, with the exception of the loss L. The $\sigma$ symbol represents the sigmoid. For reasons that will become clear in a minute, I squashed the softmax and the cross-entropy loss into one operation. I needed a name for that operation, so I temporarily called it SML, for "softmax and loss." Finally, I gave the names a and b to the outputs of the matrix multiplications.

The diagram shown earlier represents the same neural network that we designed and built in the previous two chapters. Follow its operations from left to right: x and $w_1$ get multiplied and passed through the sigmoid, producing the hidden layer h; then, h is multiplied by $w_2$ and passed through the softmax and the loss function, producing the loss L.

Now let's come to the reason we learned backpropagation: we want to calculate the gradients of L with respect to $w_1$ and $w_2$. To apply the chain rule, we need the local gradients on the paths back from L to $w_1$ and $w_2$:

$\sigma'$ and SML' are the derivatives of the sigmoid and the SML operation, respectively. In most of this book I used names such as $\partial\sigma/\partial a$ to indicate derivatives—but if a function has only one variable, as in these cases, then you can indicate its derivative with a simple apostrophe.

Let's roll up our sleeves and calculate those local gradients. Once again, you don't need to be able to take those derivatives on your own. That's what I'm here for! Here are the results:

Back in Cross Entropy, on page 125, I said that the softmax and the cross-entropy loss are a perfect match. Now we can see why. Taken separately, those functions have complicated derivatives—but compose them, and their derivative boils down to a simple formula that's cheap to compute: the network's output minus the ground truth. If you want to see the math behind this derivative, you can find a step-by-step explanation on the ProgML[2] site.

Check out "Killer Combo: Softmax and Cross Entropy" on ProgML.

The derivatives of the matrix multiplications are also short and sweet. If you know how to calculate the derivative of scalar multiplication—well, the derivative of matrix multiplication is the same.

Finally, I looked up the sigmoid's derivative in a math textbook. It's a peculiar one, because it's expressed in terms of the sigmoid itself.

Now that we have the local gradients, we can apply the chain rule to calculate the gradients of the weights. This time, however, we're not going to do it on paper—we're going to write code.

## Staying the Course

We're about to write a backpropagation function that calculates the gradients of the weights in our neural network. Here is a word of warning before we begin: this function is going to be short, but complicated.

We will write code that's a direct application of the chain rule. The chain rule is straightforward when you apply it to scalar gradients, but gets tricky with matrices. In a neural network, you have to "make the multiplications work"

2. https://www.progml.com

by swapping and transposing the operands, so that the dimensions of the matrices involved work well together.

That juggling of matrices is actually easier to do than it is to describe. When you write your own backprop code, you can double-check your calculations in an interpreter, and use the matrix dimensions as a guideline to decide which matrices to transpose, in which order to multiply them, and so on. In written form, however, the reasoning behind those operations takes up more space than we have available in this chapter.

All those things considered, now you have a few options:

- You can read through the rest of this section and see how the backprop code comes together, breezing over the twisty details.

- You can go through the next few pages more carefully, double-checking the matrix operations on your own, either on paper or in a Python interpreter.

- If you're looking for some hard work, you can even write the backpropagation code yourself, peeking at the next pages for hints if you get stuck. This last option is challenging, but it's the best way to wrap your head around all the details of this code, if you're so inclined.

Whichever option you choose, don't get discouraged if you struggle through the corner cases in the next two pages. Those corner cases aren't the point of this chapter. The point is to understand the idea behind backpropagation, and how this code came together.

Preamble done. Let's write the code that calculates the gradient of $w_2$.

## Calculating the Gradient of $w_2$

Here are the local gradients involved in the calculation of $\partial L/\partial w_2$:

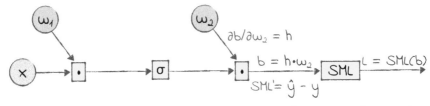

Apply the chain rule with an eye on the previous diagram and you get:

$$\frac{\partial L}{\partial w_2} = \text{SML}' \cdot \frac{\partial b}{\partial w_2} = (\hat{y} - y) \cdot h$$

And here is that formula turned to code:

```
w2_gradient = np.matmul(prepend_bias(h).T, y_hat - Y) / X.shape[0]
```

I had to swap the operands of the multiplication, and transpose one of them—all in the interest of getting a result with the same dimensions as $w_2$. Remember that we're going to multiply this gradient by the learning rate, and subtract it from $w_2$, so the two matrices must have the same shape.

This one-liner contains two more details that you might find baffling. One is the call to `prepend_bias()`. To make sense of it, remember that in the `forward()` function, we add a bias column to h, so we need to do the same during backprop.

The second perplexing detail is the division by X.shape[0] at the end. That's the number of rows in X—that is, the number of examples in the training set. This division is there because the matrix multiplication gives us the accumulated gradient over all the examples. Because we want the *average* gradient, we have to divide the result of the multiplication by the size of the training set.

That was a tightly packed line of code. On to the gradient of $w_1$!

## Calculating the Gradient of $w_1$

Let's look at the local gradients that we need to calculate $\partial L/\partial w_1$:

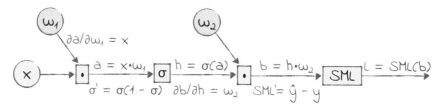

Here comes the chain rule:

$$\frac{\partial L}{\partial w_1} = \text{SML}' \cdot \frac{\partial b}{\partial h} \cdot \sigma' \cdot \frac{\partial a}{\partial w_1} = (\hat{y} - y) \cdot w_2 \cdot \sigma \cdot (1 - \sigma) \cdot x$$

That's a long formula. I split it over two lines of code and a helper function:

```
def sigmoid_gradient(sigmoid):
    return np.multiply(sigmoid, (1 - sigmoid))

a_gradient = np.matmul(y_hat - Y, w2[1:].T) * sigmoid_gradient(h)
w1_gradient = np.matmul(prepend_bias(X).T, a_gradient) / X.shape[0]
```

The next-to-last line calculates $(\hat{y} - y) \cdot w_2 \cdot \sigma'$. There are a few subtleties involved in this calculation. To begin with, this time around we're using h as is, without a bias column. Fact is, the bias column gets added *after* the calculation of h, so its gradient doesn't propagate as far back as the gradient of w1. In other words, that column has no effect on $\partial L/\partial w_1$.

Now, here's a twist: because we ignored the first column of h, we also have to ignore its weights. That's the first *row* of w2, because matrix multiplication matches columns by rows. That's what w2[1:] means: "w2, without the first row."

I have to admit that I got this code wrong the first time. After NumPy complained that my matrix dimensions didn't match, I fixed the code by thinking through the dimensions of all the matrices involved. It was a pretty painful experience.

Moving on with this line of code: the sigmoid_gradient() helper function calculates the sigmoid's gradient from the sigmoid's output. We already know that the sigmoid's output is the hidden layer h, so we can just call sigmoid_gradient(h).

The last line in the code finishes the job, multiplying the previous intermediate result by X. This multiplication involves the same trickery that we experienced when we calculated the gradient of w2: we need to swap the operands, transpose one of the matrices, prepend the bias column to X like we do during forward propagation, and average the final gradient over the training examples.

Phew! I told you that this code was going to be tricky, but we're done now. We can put it all together.

## Distilling the back Function

Here is the backpropagation code, inlined and wrapped into a convenient three-lines function:

```
11_training/neural_network.py
def back(X, Y, y_hat, w2, h):
    w2_gradient = np.matmul(prepend_bias(h).T, (y_hat - Y)) / X.shape[0]
    w1_gradient = np.matmul(prepend_bias(X).T, np.matmul(y_hat - Y, w2[1:].T)
                            * sigmoid_gradient(h)) / X.shape[0]
    return (w1_gradient, w2_gradient)
```

Congratulations! We're done writing the hardest piece of code in this book.

Now that we have the back() function, we're one big step closer to a fully functioning GD algorithm for our neural network. We just need to take care of one last detail: before we start tuning the weights, we have to initialize them. That matter deserves its own section.

### Local Minimum Blues

Neural networks, like perceptrons, are trained with gradient descent. However, there's a difference between GD on a perceptron and GD on a neural network. In the case of perceptrons, we carefully hand-picked the loss surface to be convex—that is, to have no local minima. In the case of a neural network, however, we cannot have that guarantee. The loss function of a neural network is non-convex in general, and it might contain local minima.

In When Gradient Descent Fails, on page 42, you learned that GD is prone to get stuck into a local minimum. In practice, that means that you could train a neural network for a very long time, and you still couldn't be sure that you reached the minimum loss.

How do you cope with local minima in neural networks? The good news is that you don't normally have to. Researchers proved that problematic local minima are pretty rare in practice. Also, people rarely use plain vanilla GD these days. Instead, they use variants that are particularly adept at escaping local minima. (We'll take a look at some of those variants in Chapter 18, Taming Deep Networks, on page 229.) So, while local minima do exist in the loss functions of neural networks, they rarely cause serious problems in practice.

## Initializing the Weights

Let me wax nostalgic about perceptrons for a moment. Back in Part I of this book, weight initialization was a quick job: we just set all the weights to 0. By contrast, weight initialization in a neural network comes with a hard-to-spot pitfall. Let's describe that pitfall, and see how to walk around it.

### Fearful Symmetry

Here is one rule to keep in mind: never initialize all the weights in a neural network with the same value. The reason for that recommendation is subtle, and comes from the matrix multiplications in the network. For example, look at this matrix multiplication:

$$\begin{array}{|c|c|c|}\hline 1 & 2 & 3 \\ \hline 4 & 5 & 6 \\ \hline \end{array} \cdot \begin{array}{|c|c|}\hline 1 & 1 \\ \hline 1 & 1 \\ \hline 1 & 1 \\ \hline \end{array} = \begin{array}{|c|c|}\hline 6 & 6 \\ \hline 15 & 15 \\ \hline \end{array}$$

You don't need to remember the details of matrix multiplication, although you can review Multiplying Matrices, on page 49 if you want to. Here is the interesting detail in this example: even though the numbers in the first matrix are all different, the result has two identical columns, because of the uniformity of the second matrix. In general, if the second matrix in the multiplication has the same value in every cell, the result will have the same values in every row.

Now imagine that the first and second matrices are respectively $x$ and $w_1$—the inputs and the first layer's weights of a neural network. Once the multiplication is done, the resulting matrix passes through a sigmoid to become the hidden layer $h$. Now $h$ has the same values in each row, meaning that all the hidden nodes of the network have the same value. By initializing all the weights with the same value, we forced our network to behave as if it had only one hidden node.

If $w_2$ is also initialized uniformly, this symmetry-preserving effect happens on the second layer as well, and even during backpropagation. In the "Hands On" section at the end of this chapter, we'll get a chance to peek into the network and see how uniform weights cause the network to behave like a one-node network. As you might guess, such a network isn't very accurate. After all, there is a reason why we have all those hidden nodes to begin with.

We don't want to choke our network's power, so we shouldn't initialize its weights to 1, or any other constant value such as 0. Instead, we should initialize the weights to random values. ML practitioners have a cool name for this random initialization: they call it "breaking the symmetry."

To wrap it up, we should initialize the neural network's weights with random values. The next question is: how large or small should those values be? That innocent question opens up yet another can of worms.

## Dead Neurons

We learned that we shouldn't initialize our weights uniformly. However, there is also another rule that we should take to heart: we shouldn't initialize the weights with large values.

There are two reasons for that rule of thumb. One reason is that large weights generate large values inside the network. As we discussed in Numerical Stability, on page 124, large values can cause problems if the network's function are not numerically stable: they can push those functions past the brink, making them overflow.

Even if all the functions in your network are numerically stable, large weights can still cause another subtler problem: they can slow down the network's training, and even halt it completely. To understand why, take a glance at the sigmoid function that sits right at the core of our network, represented in the following graph:

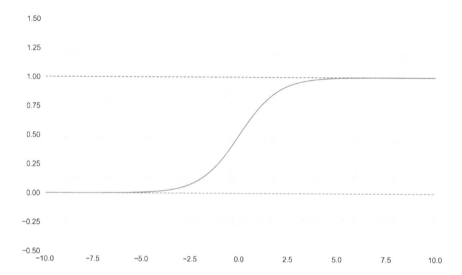

Consider what happens if one of the weights in $w_1$ is very large—either positive or negative. In that case, the sigmoid gets a large input. With a large input, the sigmoid becomes a very flat function, with a gradient close to 0. In technical terms, the sigmoid gets *saturated*: it's pushed outside of its ideal range of operation, to a place where its gradient becomes tiny.

During backpropagation, that tiny gradient gets multiplied by all the other gradients in the chain, resulting in a small overall gradient. In turn, that small gradient forces gradient descent to take very tiny steps.

To summarize this dismaying chain of cause and effect: the larger the weight, the flatter the sigmoid; the flatter the sigmoid, the smaller the gradient; the smaller the gradient, the slower GD; and the slower GD, the less the weight changes. A handful of large weights are enough to slow the entire training to a crawl.

If the numbers in the network get even larger, things go south fast. Imagine that the network has an input with a value of 10, and a weight that's around 1000. See what happens when those weight and input are multiplied and fed to the sigmoid:

```
⇒  import neural_network as nn
⇒  weighted_sum = 1000 * 10
⇒  nn.sigmoid(weighted_sum)
‹  1.0
```

The sigmoid saturated: it got so close to 1, that it underflowed and just returned 1. Even worse, its gradient underflowed to 0:

```
⇒  nn.sigmoid_gradient(nn.sigmoid(weighted_sum))
❰  0.0
```

Remember the chain rule? During backpropagation, this gradient of 0 gets multiplied by the other local gradients, causing the entire gradient to become 0. With a gradient of 0, gradient descent has nowhere to go. This weight is never going to change again, no matter how long we train the network. In machine learning lingo, the node associated with this weight has become a *dead neuron.*

In the first page of this chapter, I mentioned that backpropagation comes with a few subtle consequences. Dead neurons are one of them. A dead neuron is stuck to the same value forever. It never learns, and doesn't contribute to GD. If too many neurons die, the network loses power—and worse, you might not even notice.

So, how do we prevent dead neurons?

## Weight Initialization Done Right

Let's wrap up what we said in the previous sections. We should initialize weights with values that are:

- *Random* (to break symmetry)
- *Small* (to speed up training and avoid dead neurons)

It's hard to gauge how small exactly the weights should be. In Part III of this book, we'll look at a few popular formulae to initialize weights. For now, we can use an empirical rule of thumb. We'll make each weight range from 0 to something around the following value, where r is the number of rows in the weight matrix:

$$w \approx \pm\sqrt{\frac{1}{r}}$$

Read it as: the absolute value of each weight shouldn't be much bigger than the square root of the inverse of rows. That idea makes more sense if you think that all weights add something to the network's output—so, as the weight matrix gets bigger, individual weights should become smaller.

Here is a function that initializes the weights with the previous formula:

11_training/neural_network.py

```
def initialize_weights(n_input_variables, n_hidden_nodes, n_classes):
    w1_rows = n_input_variables + 1
    w1 = np.random.randn(w1_rows, n_hidden_nodes) * np.sqrt(1 / w1_rows)

    w2_rows = n_hidden_nodes + 1
    w2 = np.random.randn(w2_rows, n_classes) * np.sqrt(1 / w2_rows)

    return (w1, w2)
```

NumPy's random.randn() function returns a matrix of random numbers taken from what is called the *standard normal distribution*. In practice, that means that the random numbers are small: they might be positive or negative, but unlikely to stray far from 0. The code creates two such matrices of weights, and then scales them by the range suggested by our rule-of-thumb formula.

---

**Math Deep Dive: The Standard Normal Distribution**

 You might be curious about the standard normal distribution. What does it look like, and why does it generate numbers that are close to zero? To wrap your mind around it, check out Khan Academy's lessons on modeling data distributions.[3]

---

If you're confused by the dimensions of the two matrices, remember the rule that we mentioned in How Many Nodes?, on page 115: each matrix of weights in a neural network has as many rows as its input elements, and as many columns as its output elements.

Did you hear that "click" sound? That was the last piece of our neural network's code falling into place. We're finally about to run this thing!

**Getting Used to Randomness**

If you initialize a neural network with random weights, then you should expect a slightly different loss every time you train it. If you wish, you can avoid that randomess by seeding NumPy's random number generator with np.random.seed(a_known_seed).

During my first ML experiences, I always seeded the random generator. I strove for deterministic code that gave the same result every time. Over time, I learned that a good classifier stays good no matter how you initialize its weights, as long as you use small enough values. Like most ML practitioners, I learned to stop worrying and embrace the randomness.

## The Finished Network

Here is the complete code of our neural network:

---

3. www.khanacademy.org/math/statistics-probability/modeling-distributions-of-data#normal-distributions-library

```python
import numpy as np


def sigmoid(z):
    return 1 / (1 + np.exp(-z))


def softmax(logits):
    exponentials = np.exp(logits)
    return exponentials / np.sum(exponentials, axis=1).reshape(-1, 1)


def sigmoid_gradient(sigmoid):
    return np.multiply(sigmoid, (1 - sigmoid))


def loss(Y, y_hat):
    return -np.sum(Y * np.log(y_hat)) / Y.shape[0]


def prepend_bias(X):
    return np.insert(X, 0, 1, axis=1)


def forward(X, w1, w2):
    h = sigmoid(np.matmul(prepend_bias(X), w1))
    y_hat = softmax(np.matmul(prepend_bias(h), w2))
    return (y_hat, h)


def back(X, Y, y_hat, w2, h):
    w2_gradient = np.matmul(prepend_bias(h).T, (y_hat - Y)) / X.shape[0]
    w1_gradient = np.matmul(prepend_bias(X).T, np.matmul(y_hat - Y, w2[1:].T)
                            * sigmoid_gradient(h)) / X.shape[0]
    return (w1_gradient, w2_gradient)


def classify(X, w1, w2):
    y_hat, _ = forward(X, w1, w2)
    labels = np.argmax(y_hat, axis=1)
    return labels.reshape(-1, 1)


def initialize_weights(n_input_variables, n_hidden_nodes, n_classes):
    w1_rows = n_input_variables + 1
    w1 = np.random.randn(w1_rows, n_hidden_nodes) * np.sqrt(1 / w1_rows)

    w2_rows = n_hidden_nodes + 1
    w2 = np.random.randn(w2_rows, n_classes) * np.sqrt(1 / w2_rows)

    return (w1, w2)


def report(iteration, X_train, Y_train, X_test, Y_test, w1, w2):
    y_hat, _ = forward(X_train, w1, w2)
    training_loss = loss(Y_train, y_hat)
    classifications = classify(X_test, w1, w2)
    accuracy = np.average(classifications == Y_test) * 100.0
    print("Iteration: %5d, Loss: %.8f, Accuracy: %.2f%%" %
          (iteration, training_loss, accuracy))
```

```python
def train(X_train, Y_train, X_test, Y_test, n_hidden_nodes, iterations, lr):
    n_input_variables = X_train.shape[1]
    n_classes = Y_train.shape[1]
    w1, w2 = initialize_weights(n_input_variables, n_hidden_nodes, n_classes)
    for iteration in range(iterations):
        y_hat, h = forward(X_train, w1, w2)
        w1_gradient, w2_gradient = back(X_train, Y_train, y_hat, w2, h)
        w1 = w1 - (w1_gradient * lr)
        w2 = w2 - (w2_gradient * lr)
        report(iteration, X_train, Y_train, X_test, Y_test, w1, w2)
    return (w1, w2)

import mnist
w1, w2 = train(mnist.X_train, mnist.Y_train,
               mnist.X_test, mnist.Y_test,
               n_hidden_nodes=200, iterations=10000, lr=0.01)
```

To write the very last line here, I had to set values for the hyperparameters. The number of hidden nodes was easy: we'd already decided to have 200 hidden nodes—plus the bias, that's added automatically by the network. By contrast, it took me some time to find a good value for lr: I had to try a few different learning rates, and pick the one that resulted in the lowest loss. Near the end of Part II, we'll look at a more systematic way to choose hyperparameter values.

And at long last, here are the results of running the network:

```
Iteration:     0, Loss: 2.38746031, Accuracy: 13.61%
Iteration:     1, Loss: 2.34527197, Accuracy: 15.00%
...
Iteration:  9999, Loss: 0.14668400, Accuracy: 93.25%
```

The perceptron that we built in Chapter 7, The Final Challenge, on page 87 couldn't reach 93% accuracy, no matter how long you trained it. The neural network has to do more calculations than a perceptron, so it takes a bit longer to pass 90% accuracy—but after that, it just keeps going. After a few hours of number crunching, the network has reached over 93% accuracy in character recognition on MNIST. Pretty good, although still far from our lofty goal of 99% accuracy.

In case you think that my enthusiasm for that 1% improvement is unwarranted, look at it from the opposite point of view: the perceptron makes a classification mistake over 8% of the times, while the network gets it wrong less than 7% of the times. In a production system, that improvement might already make a difference—and that is only the beginning. Over the next few chapters, we'll push that accuracy much higher.

Let's recap what we learned in this long chapter.

## What You Just Learned

In this chapter, you learned *backpropagation*—an algorithm to calculate the gradients of the weights in a neural network. Those gradients represent the impact of each weight on the overall loss.

Each training iteration in a neural network ping-pongs between two steps:

1. *Forward propagation*: the network calculates each layer from the previous one, from the input layer to the output $\hat{y}$.

2. *Backpropagation*: the network bounces its way back from the output layer to the weights, using the *chain rule* to calculate their gradients. Then it descends those gradients, pushing the loss down, and $\hat{y}$ closer to the ground truth y.

You also learned that neural networks don't train well if all the weights have the same value. Instead, you should *break their symmetry* by initializing the weights with random values. Those initial values should also be small to avoid problems like *overflows* and *dead neurons*.

With that, we can cap off this three-chapters miniseries on putting together a neural network. We deserve a little rest after all this detail-oriented work. In the next chapter, we'll consider the big picture. In particular, we'll ask ourselves a question that we haven't really answered so far: how the heck do neural networks work?

## Hands On: Starting Off Wrong

In Fearful Symmetry, on page 140, we learned that we shouldn't initialize all the neural network's weights to the same value. See for youself what happens if we ignore that advice.

You can use NumPy's zeros() function to initialize all the weights to 0. For example, here is how you get a matrix of zeros with two rows and three columns:

```
⇒ np.zeros((2, 3))
❮ array([[ 0.,   0.,   0.],
         [ 0.,   0.,   0.]])
```

The parameter to zeros() has its own parentheses, because it's a tuple—an immutable collection of values. (For more about tuples, read Collections, on page 280.) In this case, the tuple has two values, that are the rows and columns of the matrix, respectively.

After you initialize the weights to zero, run the network for a few iterations, and see what happens. Compare its results to the results of the randomly initialized network. How does it fare? Also try modifying the zero-initialized network to give it fewer hidden nodes. Do you see a significant difference in accuracy?

Finally, peek into the zero-initialized network as it trains. For example, here is how you can print ten rows from around the middle of $w_1$ and $w_2$:

```
print(w1[120:130])
print(w2[120:130])
```

What do you see?

# CHAPTER 12

# How Classifiers Work

We spent most of this book building classifiers—first a perceptron, and now, in the last few chapters, a full-fledged neural network. And yet, you might struggle to grasp intuitively what makes classifiers tick. Why do perceptrons work well on some datasets, and not on others? What do neural networks have that perceptrons don't? It's hard to answer these questions, because it's hard to paint a mental image of a classifier doing its thing.

The next few pages are all about that mental image. A new concept, called the *decision boundary*, will help us visualize how perceptrons and neural networks see the world. This insight is not only going to nourish your intellect—it will also make it easier for you to build and tune neural networks in the future.

Let's start with a look back at the perceptron.

## Tracing a Boundary

If we hope to understand classification intuitively, then we need a dataset that we can visualize easily. MNIST, with its mind-boggling hundreds of dimensions, is way too complex for that. Instead, we'll use a simpler, brain-friendly dataset:

```
12_classifiers/linearly_separable.txt
Input_A            Input_B           Label
-0.470680718301    -1.905835436960   1
0.9952553595720    1.4019246363100   0
-0.903484238413    -1.233058043620   1
-1.775876322450    -0.436802254656   1
```

Those are just the first few lines. The file contains 300 examples in total, each with two input variables and a binary label. I wrote a program to plot these data, that you can find in the book's source code as usual. (It's called plot_data.py.) It uses the two input variables as coordinates, and marks each point based on its label—blue squares for 0 and green triangles for 1, as shown in the following graph:

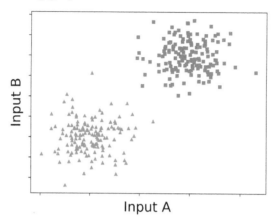

Those are two neatly partitioned classes. We could even trace a straight line between the blue squares and the green triangles. Back in Chapter 8, The Perceptron, on page 99, we gave a name to datasets that can be partitioned with a line: we called them "linearly separable" datasets. We also said that perceptrons are good at learning linearly separable data. Let's put that notion to the test by brushing up the perceptron from Part I of this book.

**Browsing this Chapter's Code**

This chapter is chock-full of diagrams. The code that I used to generate them is in the 12_classifiers directory of this book's downloadable source code. Among other things, that directory includes:

- Two datasets, as text files: linearly_separable.txt and non_linearly_separable.txt.

- The code for our classifiers: the perceptron (perceptron.py) and the neural network (neural_network.py).

- Four programs that load the datasets, train the classifiers, and print out their decision boundaries (plot_perceptron_boundary.py and plot_neural_network_boundary.py) and their model functions (plot_perceptron_model.py and plot_neural_network_model.py).

Remember, you can download the code for all the examples from https://pragprog.com/titles/pplearn/source_code. Happy hacking!

## The Perceptron on Its Home Turf

Let's run the perceptron on the linearly_separable.txt dataset. To begin with, here is the code that loads and formats the data:

```
12_classifiers/plot_perceptron_boundary.py
import numpy as np
x1, x2, y = np.loadtxt('linearly_separable.txt', skiprows=1, unpack=True)
X_train = X_test = prepend_bias(np.column_stack((x1, x2)))
Y_train_unencoded = Y_test = y.astype(int).reshape(-1, 1)
Y_train = one_hot_encode(Y_train_unencoded)
```

In Training vs. Testing, on page 79, you learned that real-life ML systems should separate training data from test data. This is not a real-life system, however, so I assigned the same examples to both the training and the test sets. Apart from that detail, the previous code prepares the data pretty much like we did for MNIST: it prepends a bias column to the examples, converts the labels to integers (because loadtxt() returns them as floats), and one-hot encodes them.

Now we can let the perceptron loose on the data:

```
import perceptron
w = perceptron.train(X_train, Y_train,
                     X_test, Y_test,
                     iterations=10000, lr=0.1)
```

And here's what we get:

```
0 - Loss: 1.38629436111989057245, 50.00%
1 - Loss: 1.29274511217352139347, 100.00%
...
9999 - Loss: 0.00702079217010578415, 100.00%
```

As you can see, 1,000 iterations were overkill: it took just one of them for the perceptron to reach perfect accuracy on these data. As we expected, perceptrons eat linearly separable data for breakfast. Let's try to visualize why.

## Grokking Classification

You might remember that back in What Happened to the Model Function?, on page 71, we visualized the model function of a binary classifier. Now let's do the same for the specific classifier that we just used. The graph on page 152 shows what the model function looks like at the end of the training phase.

Let me recap the meaning of this diagram. The sigmoid-shaped surface is the model function of the classifier. The perceptron generated this surface during the training phase, tweaking the model's parameters to approximate the data points. If you squint a little, you can see the blue squares and green triangles that the model is trying to approximate.

During the prediction phase, the classifier applies this model to an arbitrary point—that is, an arbitrary value of Input A and Input B. For that point, the

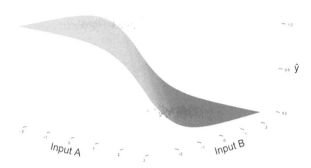

model yields a value of $\hat{y}$ between 0 and 1. The classifier then rounds this value to the nearest integer. The values below 0.5 are rounded to 0, and classified as blue squares. The values above 0.5 are rounded to 1, and classified as green triangles.

Now consider the invisible boundary that separates the two classes—the points where the value of $\hat{y}$ is exactly 0.5. That's called the *decision boundary*, because a point is classified as a blue square or a green triangle depending on which side of the boundary it falls, as shown in this graph:

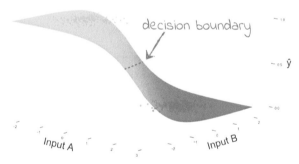

In a sense, you could say that the classifier's work is all about the decision boundary. During training, the classifier finds a boundary to separate the blue squares from the green triangles. During classification, it uses that boundary to decide whether a data point is a blue square or green triangle.

Some things are better shown in two dimensions, so on page 153 is a flattened version of the previous diagram. It shows the areas that are classified as blue or green, and the boundary in between.

This diagram shows that the decision boundary separates the two classes perfectly: all the blue squares are in the blue area, and all the green triangles are in the green area. That means that if we ask the perceptron to classify

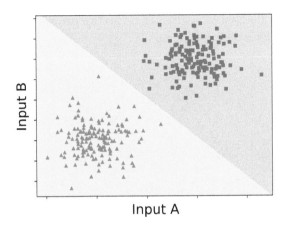

any of those points, it will return the correct label. If the perceptron had less than 100% accuracy, then we'd see some blue squares over the green area, or the other way around.

I already gave you a lot of information and showed you quite a few diagrams—but that was all a build-up to the first crucial piece of information in this chapter. Here it is: no matter how much you change a perceptron's weights, its decision boundary will always be a straight line. Perceptrons don't do curves.

To be clear, I'm talking about a "straight line" because the datasets in these examples have two input variables. If they had more, then the boundary would be the higher-dimensional equivalent of a line, like a three-dimensional plane, or a 785-dimensional hyperplane. However, we can just agree to be informal and say a perceptron's decision boundary is a "straight line" for all those cases.

As we discussed in Chapter 8, The Perceptron, on page 99, perceptrons work well on linearly separable data. That fact is a direct consequence of their straight decision boundary. After all, that's the definition of "linearly separable": data that can be separated by a straight line.

Now let's see what happens when we train a perceptron on data that's *not* linearly separable.

## A Line Is Not Enough

Here are a few lines from a second file of data:

```
12_classifiers/non_linearly_separable.txt
Input_A                Input_B                Label
0.185872557346525      0.567645715301291      0
0.284770005578376      0.458145376240974      1
0.150041107877389      0.453290078176759      0
```

...and so on. This dataset looks the same as the previous one. When we plot it, however, it sings a different song:

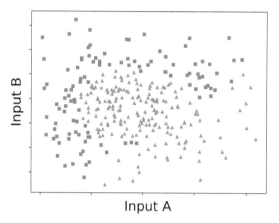

There is no way to divide blue squares and green triangles with a straight line. Train the perceptron on these examples, and it will struggle:

```
0 - Loss: 1.38629436111989057245, 36.00%
1 - Loss: 1.38092065346487014033, 64.00%
…
9999 - Loss: 1.09745315956710487448, 73.33%
```

I tried with more iterations and different values of lr, to no avail: I never got anything as high as 80% accuracy. The reason for that weak performance becomes obvious if we plot the perceptron's decision boundary:

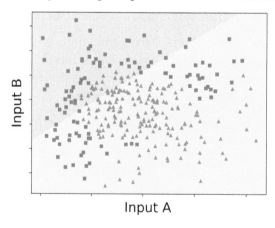

See? The perceptron made a brave attempt at cutting off a slice of blue squares. However, plenty of blue squares are still misclassified as green triangles.

So far, this chapter has been a slightly different take on a fact that you already knew: perceptrons only jive well with linearly separable data. But we're not stuck with perceptrons, are we? Fast-forward to our latest and greatest classifier: the neural network.

## Bending the Boundary

Let's switch from the perceptron to the neural network. What does its decision boundary look like?

If you bother to try the neural network on the linearly separable dataset, you'll find that it gets the same perfect accuracy as the perceptron, and a similarly straight decision boundary. On the second dataset, however, things get interesting.

Here's the code that trains the neural network on the non-linearly separable dataset:

```
12_classifiers/plot_neural_network_boundary.py
import numpy as np
import neural_network as nn
x1, x2, y = np.loadtxt('non_linearly_separable.txt', skiprows=1, unpack=True)
X_train = X_test = np.column_stack((x1, x2))
Y_train_unencoded = Y_test = y.astype(int).reshape(-1, 1)
Y_train = one_hot_encode(Y_train_unencoded)
w1, w2 = nn.train(X_train, Y_train,
                  X_test, Y_test,
                  n_hidden_nodes=10, iterations=100000, lr=0.3)
```

That's pretty much the same code that we used to train the perceptron, with a few minor differences. Note that it doesn't add a bias column to the data, as the network's code takes care of that. As ever, I tried a few different values for the hyperparameters n_hidden_nodes, iterations, and lr. I ended up with the values here, which seem like a good compromise between training time and accuracy.

Here are the results:

```
Iteration:      0, Loss: 0.65876824, Accuracy: 64.00%
Iteration:      1, Loss: 0.65505330, Accuracy: 64.00%
...
Iteration: 99999, Loss: 0.05917079, Accuracy: 97.00%
```

Now we're talking! The reason for that increased accuracy becomes evident if you visualize the neural network's model on page 156.

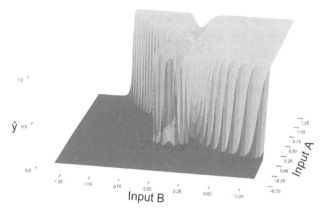

And here is a similar diagram in two dimensions, showing the neural network's decision boundary:

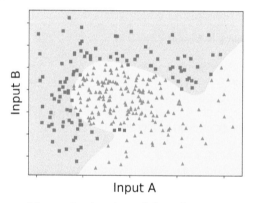

We came to the second important point of this chapter: a neural network can bend its model and decision boundary in ways that a perceptron can't. In the case that we're looking at, the network did a decent job of bending the boundary to separate blue squares and green triangles, leaving just a handful of misclassified points.

Intuitively, a neural network's boundary-twisting powers come from its multiple layers. The perceptron boils down to a simple weighted sum followed by a sigmoid—and that means that its model always ends up looking like a sigmoid. By chaining additional perceptrons, the neural network gets rid of that limitation. If you want a more formal explanation of why multiple layers allow the network to create bumpy models, you'll find one on the ProgML[1] site.

Check out "The Math of Multiple Layers" on ProgML.

---

1. https://www.progml.com

Now you know, having seen it with your own eyes, why neural networks leave perceptrons in the dust.

## What You Just Learned

In this chapter you learned about a powerful concept: the *decision boundary* of a classifier. During the training phase, a classifier shapes the decision boundary to separate the classes in the dataset. Thereafter, it classifies data points based on which side of the boundary they fall.

Now that you know about the decision boundary, you also understand why a neural network is generally more powerful than a perceptron. A perceptron can only draw a straight decision boundary, so it only works well with linearly separable data. A neural network is happy to bend its decision boundary around pretzeled data.

Now that you have a better appreciation for neural networks and how they work, you might wonder: if neural networks are so powerful, why didn't our network outshine the perceptron when it came to classifying MNIST? Fear not, because in the next three chapters we're going to tweak and tune the neural network, unleashing its full potential.

## Hands On: Data from Hell

In this chapter's source directory you can find an additional dataset named circles.txt. Edit the plot_data.py file so that it loads this dataset, and run it to take a look at the data. Spoiler alert: circles.txt is about as non-linearly separable as they get.

Edit plot_perceptron_boundary.py to load circles.txt and run it. What does the perceptron's boundary look like? Do the same with plot_neural_network_boundary.py and plot_neural_network_model.py. How does the neural network fare on these data?

# CHAPTER 13

# Batchin' Up

By now, we're familiar enough with gradient descent. This chapter introduces a souped-up variant of GD: *mini-batch gradient descent.*

Mini-batch gradient descent is slightly more complicated than plain vanilla GD—but as we're about to see, it also tends to *converge faster.* In simpler terms, mini-batch GD is faster at approaching the minimum loss, speeding up the network's training. As a bonus, it takes less memory, and sometimes it even finds a better loss than regular GD. In fact, after this chapter, you might never use regular GD again!

You might wonder why we're focusing on training speed, when we have more pressing concerns to deal with. In particular, the accuracy of our neural network is still disappointing—better than a perceptron, yes, but well below our target 99% on MNIST. Shouldn't we make the network more accurate first, and faster later? After all, as Donald Knuth has said, "premature optimization is the root of all evil"![1]

However, there's a reason to speed up training straight away. Within a couple of chapters, we're going to inch toward that 99% goal by tuning the network iteratively: we'll tweak the hyperparameters, train the network... and then do it all over again, until we're happy with the result. Each of those iterations could take hours. We'd better find a way to speed them up—otherwise, the tuning process might take days.

You might also wonder why we're looking for an alternative algorithm, instead of speeding up the algorithm that we already have. Here's the answer: soon enough, we'll stop writing our own backpropagation code, and we'll switch to highly optimized ML libraries. Instead of optimizing code that we're going to

---

1.   en.wikiquote.org/wiki/Donald_Knuth

throw away soon, we'd better focus on techniques that will stay valid even after we switch to libraries.

Mini-batch gradient descent is one of those techniques. Let's see what it's about. But first, let's review what happens when we train a neural network.

## Learning, Visualized

To accelerate training, we need to understand in more detail how it works. Let's take a deeper look at how the neural network's loss and accuracy change during training.

We know that during training, the loss goes down, and the accuracy goes up. Staring at those numbers, however, doesn't tell the whole story. To visualize the loss and accuracy, I hacked the neural network to return two lists—the histories of the loss and the accuracy, stored at each iteration. I trained the network to collect the two histories, and then plotted them over 30 iterations, as illustrated in the following graphs (if you want to run the code yourself, you can find it in the code download in batching/plot_loss.py):

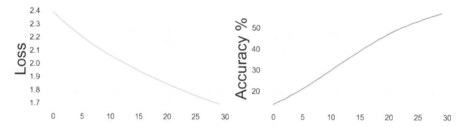

These diagrams show what we expect: as we train the network, the loss decreases, and the accuracy increases. However, even looking at the diagrams doesn't really tell us how well the network is doing. For example, we can see that the accuracy is still below 60% after 30 iterations. Is that an early sign of failure, or just the first step toward success? We don't really know until we train longer.

This time, let's train the system for 1,000 iterations. We'd better grab something to eat first—on my laptop, this training session takes almost half an hour. Here are the results:

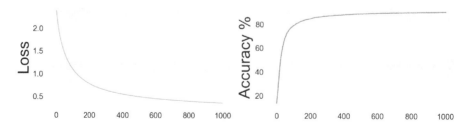

## Loss vs. Accuracy

If you look closely at the loss and the accuracy of a training neural network, you might notice one detail. The loss is *strictly decreasing*—it always drops from one iteration to the next. By contrast, the accuracy increases over time, but not necessarily at each iteration. Sometimes it stays the same, and it might even take the occasional turn downwards. Here is why.

The loss decreases at each step because that's what gradient descent does: it steps down the loss's gradient, finding a lower value at each step. In a future chapter, we'll see that the wrong configuration could cause GD to step on a higher loss than it started from—but that's a relatively rare corner case. In general, if we ever see the loss increasing, then we should hasten to change the network's hyperparameters, or debug our GD code.

While the loss is a continuous quantity, the network's accuracy is discrete, because it depends on how many test examples are classified correctly. After the first few minutes of training, that number might stay flat for a long time, while the network fiddles with the weights trying to nail one more example. The accuracy might even drop temporarily, maybe because the network is trading a higher error on a single example with lower errors on many others. For these reasons, while the network's accuracy does increase in the long term, in the short term it might flatten, or even skid up and down a bit.

To wrap it all up: in gradient descent, the loss normally drops at each and every step. On the other hand, the accuracy climbs—but not necessarily at each and every step.

All that being said, those rules are only valid for plain vanilla GD, and they don't necessarily apply to the GD variants that we're about to discuss. In particular, we're about to abandon the idea that the loss always decreases from one step to the next.

These diagrams are much more informative than the previous ones. It seems that the loss is *asymptotic*: it drops quickly in the first few iterations, and then approaches an ideal minimum value, without ever quite reaching it. The network's accuracy has a similar shape, only it's pointing upward.

Look closer, and you'll see that the accuracy is never going to reach that target 99%, no matter how long we train this network. In fact, at the end of Chapter 11, Training the Network, on page 129, we trained it for 10,000 iterations, and the final accuracy still hovered around 93%. Armed with the previous diagrams, we could have guessed that value even after the first thousand iterations.

To achieve that elusive 99%, we need to tune the network's hyperparameters—and that's where we face the dilemma I mentioned at the beginning of this chapter. On one hand, we must train the network for quite some time just to gauge how well it's doing. On the other hand, we must train it multiple times, so that we can tune it. "Slow" and "frequent" don't mix. It would be nice if the network could give us earlier feedback. Then we could quickly see where that accuracy is headed, and stop the training if it's not going anywhere.

Can we have our cake, and eat it too? As luck would have it, we can—with a different approach to gradient descent.

# Batch by Batch

The style of gradient descent that we used so far is also called *batch gradient descent*, because it clusters all the training examples into one big batch, and calculates the gradient of the loss over the entire batch. A common alternative is called *mini-batch gradient descent*. Maybe you already guessed what it does: it segments the training set into smaller batches, and then takes a step of gradient descent for each batch.

You might wonder how small batches help speed up training. Stick with me for a moment: let's implement mini-batch GD and give it a test drive.

## Implementing Batches

In most cases, we should shuffle a dataset before we split it into batches. That way, we're sure that each batch contains a nice mix of examples—as opposed to having all the examples of a certain type clustered in the same batch. However, MNIST already comes pre-shuffled, so we can just take the training set and split it into batches straight away. This function does the job:

```
def prepare_batches(X_train, Y_train, batch_size):
    x_batches = []
    y_batches = []
    n_examples = X_train.shape[0]
    for batch in range(0, n_examples, batch_size):
        batch_end = batch + batch_size
        x_batches.append(X_train[batch:batch_end])
        y_batches.append(Y_train[batch:batch_end])
    return x_batches, y_batches
```

This code loops from 0 to the number of training examples, with a step equal to the batch size. Then it slices X_train to get a batch of examples, and it appends the batch to a list. It does the same with Y_train. The results are two lists that contain the training set split into batches, where each batch is itself a list.

In case you're wondering, the last batch in the list can be smaller than batch_size. If we called the function with a training set of 103 elements and a batch_size of 10, then it would happily return two lists of eleven batches, the last of which only contains three elements. That's okay—mini-batch GD doesn't care whether the batches are all the same size.

Now that we have prepare_batches(), we can update the neural network's report() and train() functions to do mini-batch GD. As usual, look for the arrows in the left margin to spot changes:

13_batching/neural_network.py

```
➤   def report(epoch, batch, X_train, Y_train, X_test, Y_test, w1, w2):
        y_hat, _ = forward(X_train, w1, w2)
        training_loss = loss(Y_train, y_hat)
        classifications = classify(X_test, w1, w2)
        accuracy = np.average(classifications == Y_test) * 100.0
➤       print("%5d-%d > Loss: %.8f, Accuracy: %.2f%%" %
➤             (epoch, batch, training_loss, accuracy))

➤   def train(X_train, Y_train, X_test, Y_test, n_hidden_nodes,
➤             epochs, batch_size, lr):
        n_input_variables = X_train.shape[1]
        n_classes = Y_train.shape[1]

        w1, w2 = initialize_weights(n_input_variables, n_hidden_nodes, n_classes)
        x_batches, y_batches = prepare_batches(X_train, Y_train, batch_size)
➤       for epoch in range(epochs):
➤           for batch in range(len(x_batches)):
➤               y_hat, h = forward(x_batches[batch], w1, w2)
➤               w1_gradient, w2_gradient = back(x_batches[batch], y_batches[batch],
➤                                               y_hat, w2, h)
                w1 = w1 - (w1_gradient * lr)
                w2 = w2 - (w2_gradient * lr)
➤               report(epoch, batch, X_train, Y_train, X_test, Y_test, w1, w2)
        return (w1, w2)
```

There are now two nested loops in train(). The inner loop is a step of gradient descent on a single batch. The outer loop is called an *epoch*, and it goes through all the batches in the training set. Instead of a single hyperpameter named iterations, this version of train() has two: epochs and batch_size.

As a smoke test, let's train the network for two epochs with a batch size of 20,000:

```
if __name__ == "__main__":
    import mnist as data
    w1, w2 = train(data.X_train, data.Y_train,
                   data.X_test, data.Y_test,
                   n_hidden_nodes=200, epochs=2, batch_size=20000, lr=0.01)
```

The first line in the previous code (the one that opens with an if) is a common Python idiom. It means: "only execute the following code if someone runs the file as a program"; for example, by typing python3 neural_network.py. By contrast, if this file is loaded like a library, with the import keyword, this code is not executed. Some of the files in this chapter's code import this file like that, and that's why I fenced the training code behind this if idiom. You can read more about Python's _main_ idiom in The main Idiom, on page 287.

Here is the result of training the neural network in batches:

```
0-0 > Loss: 2.38777852, Accuracy: 13.56%
0-1 > Loss: 2.34556340, Accuracy: 14.99%
0-2 > Loss: 2.30576333, Accuracy: 16.17%
1-0 > Loss: 2.26975858, Accuracy: 17.95%
1-1 > Loss: 2.23549849, Accuracy: 19.46%
1-2 > Loss: 2.20197211, Accuracy: 21.11%
```

The MNIST training set contains 60,000 examples, so each epoch spans three batches.

In practice, people often train neural networks with smaller batches—as small as 16 or 32 elements. Let's see what happens when we use smaller batch sizes.

## Training with Batches

We're about to perform an experiment, training the neural network on MNIST with two different configurations: plain old batch GD, and mini-batch GD with a batch size of 256. We'll run each training for 20 minutes, and then compare the training history for the two configurations.

To compare the two trainings, we could use either the history of the loss, or the history of the accuracy. Accuracy is what we really care about, but the loss is a more reliable measure, as I discussed in Loss vs. Accuracy, on page 161. That's why people traditionally use the loss for this kind of comparison. We'll do the same.

Here is a diagram of the loss for the two training runs:

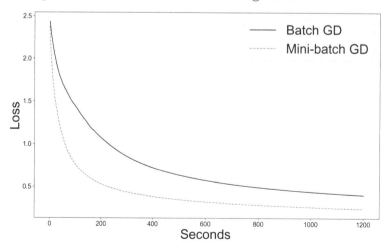

Glance at the diagram, and you'll see that mini-batch GD is beating batch GD hands down. Right off the bat, mini-batch GD blazes down the gradient, while batch GD huffs behind. After the first 200 seconds or so, the loss of mini-batch GD is already starting to flatten out, while the loss of batch GD is still decreasing. After 20 minutes, batch GD is still lagging behind mini-batch GD.

Let me make one thing clear: while mini-batch GD easily wins the speed race, it wouldn't necessarily win the marathon. If we keep the experiment running for hours, then batch GD might eventually catch up. In the short term, however, mini-batch GD is giving us quicker feedback, and that's what we care about while we're tuning the network. With mini-batch GD, it takes a handful of minutes to see how well our network is doing. With batch GD, it takes multiple times as much.

So now you know that mini-batch GD gives us faster feedback. But why?

## Understanding Batches

Mini-batch GD feels counter-intuitive. Why do smaller batches result in faster training? The answer is that they don't: if anything, mini-batch GD is generally *slower* than batch GD at processing the whole training set because it calculates the gradient for each batch, rather than once for all the examples.

Even if mini-batch GD is slower, it tends to *converge* faster during the first iterations of training. In other words, mini-batch GD is slower at processing the training set, but it moves quicker toward the target, giving us that fast feedback we need. Let's see how.

### Twist That Path

To see why mini-batches converge faster, I visualized gradient descent on a small two-dimensional training set. As usual, you'll find the programs that generate these diagrams among this chapter's source code.

The diagram on page 166 illustrates the path of plain-vanilla batch GD on the loss surface during the first few dozens of iterations.

You might remember a similar diagram from back when I introduced gradient descent. At each iteration, the system calculates the gradient of the loss over the entire training set, and steps in the opposite direction as the gradient, rolling steadily toward the minimum.

Now let's repeat the training using batches. In fact, let's use the smallest possible batch size: a batch size of 1. This extreme variant of mini-batch GD

is often called *stochastic gradient descent*, where "stochastic" is statistics lingo for "randomly distributed." The idea of stochastic gradient descent is that you select one random example per iteration, and take a step of GD based on that one example. In our case, we don't even need to select a random example at each iteration because the MNIST dataset has already been shuffled. We can just pick the examples in order, one at a time.

This diagram illustrates the result of training the neural network with stochastic GD:

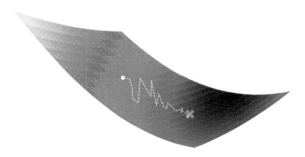

Now that's an interesting picture. Instead of taking bold steps in the direction of the minimum, stochastic GD staggers toward it like a drunk algorithm, sometimes moving in the *opposite* direction. What's happening?

Here is the reason of that erratic motion: when it comes to calculating the loss, a single example might or might not be representative of the entire training set. For "more typical" examples, the loss surface is similar to the one of the entire dataset, and a step of GD tends to aim straight toward the minimum. On the other hand "less typical" examples result in a pretty different loss surface, that might send GD off in the wrong direction. Because of that uncertain stagger, the global loss does not necessarily decrease at each step, as it does in batch GD.

Even though stochastic GD proceeds in a meandering motion, most steps move toward the general direction of the minimum, and each step happens quickly because it involves a single example. As a result, the algorithm tends to converge quickly, even though it takes a long time to process all the examples.

Now let's see what happens if we calculate the loss over more than one example at each step.

## Batches Large and Small

This time, we'll train the network for half an hour with four different batch sizes:

- 1 (stochastic GD)
- 32 (mini-batch GD with smaller batches)
- 128 (mini-batch GD with larger batches)
- 60000 (batch GD—one batch for the entire MNIST training set)

I'll spare you the wait. Here are the results:

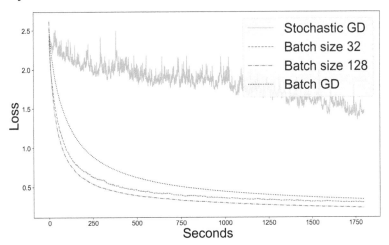

We can see one thing straight away: stochastic GD might work well for some other problems, but not our particular problem and network configuration.

In our case, it results in a loss that hops around like an over-caffeinated grasshopper, and doesn't seem to drop much over time.

As the batch size increases, the loss gets smoother. That happens because the more examples you have, the more likely that their average loss approximates the average loss of the entire training set. As a result, each step of gradient descent is more likely to end up closer to the goal, rather than further away from it.

Smoother, however, is not necessarily better. Batch GD is silky smooth, but it doesn't give us the fastest feedback, nor the best final loss. A batch size of 32 gives us faster feedback in the first few iterations, and a lower loss at the end of the experiment—even though batch GD seems likely to catch up in the long term. A batch size of 128 does even better, with great short-term feedback, and a very low final loss. We don't know what happens after 10 or 100 hours of training, but a batch size of 128 looks like a safe bet so far.

And that's what happens when we use different batch sizes on our specific problem. Now let's get the big picture on batches in general.

## Batches: The Good and the Bad

I introduced mini-batch GD because it tends to converge faster than batch GD. That benefit, however, is not its only selling point, or even its most important one. Let's go through the other reasons to use batches—and a few reason not to.

Here is the most important benefit of batches: while batch GD forces you to keep the entire training set in memory, mini-batch GD can load data batch by batch, leaving most data offline. If that frugality doesn't sound compelling, consider the astounding size of today's training sets. You can keep MNIST in memory, but you cannot do that with the multi-terabyte training sets that Google and Facebook are using these days. Not only mini-batch GD allows you to load batches one at a time—it also allows you to process those batches in parallel, on multiple cores or servers. Bottom line: as you graduate from small experiments to large systems, mini-batches become your only option.

Mini-batch GD comes with another subtle and important advantage over batch GD. All the way back in When Gradient Descent Fails, on page 42, I mentioned that gradient descent can get stuck into "holes" while stepping over the gradient surface. I called those holes "local minima," as opposed to the "global minimum"—the lowest point of the loss surface overall.

Just like batch GD, mini-batch GD can fall into a local minimum—but its random fluctuations may get it un-stuck, and back on its way to the global minimum. That's the reason why this variants of GD sometimes results in a lower loss than batch GD, even in the long term. A lower loss generally means more accurate classification, so that's a big deal.

As cool as mini-batch GD is, it does come with a few drawbacks. As we've seen, it requires a bit more code than batch GD. It also introduces batch_size, that is yet another hyperparameter that we have to tune. Also, mini-batch GD causes the loss to flutter up and down. If you happen to stop your experiment when the loss is relatively high, then you might lose some accuracy because of sheer bad luck. And finally, very small batch sizes (as in the case of stochastic GD) might be too much of a good thing, and fail to converge, as we've seen in our experiment on MNIST.

Overall, the benefits of mini-batch GD trump its drawbacks. In the next chapters, we'll forget about regular GD and just use batches all the time. If you wish, you can revert to regular GD at any time by setting batch_size to the size of the training set.

## What You Just Learned

Since I introduced gradient descent, we've been training all of our ML systems the same way: for each step of gradient descent, we calculated the gradient of the loss over the entire training set. That flavor of gradient descent is called *batch gradient descent*.

In this chapter, I introduced a different way to do gradient descent: *mini-batch gradient descent*. In mini-batch GD, we take the loss over a *subset* of examples at each step. We also tried an extreme variant of mini-batch GD: *stochastic gradient descent*, where we take the loss on a single example at a time.

Mini-batch GD often converges faster than batch GD. As a result, it gives us early feedback on the training. It's also perfect for large training sets that don't fit in memory, and it gives you the option to parallelize training on multiple machines. Finally, mini-batch GD tends to be good at escaping "holes" in the loss, so it can yield a lower loss than batch GD.

Now that you know about mini-batch GD, we're one step closer to tuning our neural network and making it really accurate. We only have one last wrinkle to take care of—and we'll smooth it out in the next chapter.

## Hands On: The Smallest Batch

In Batches Large and Small, on page 167, we found out that stochastic GD doesn't work well for our specific problem and neural network configuration. On the other hand, mini-batch GD with a batch size of 32 seems to do okay.

What's the smallest batch size that gives us better early feedback than plain old batch GD? Find out for yourself by changing the batch sizes in compare_batch_sizes.py, from the 13_batching directory in the book's source code.

It is also possible that stochastic GD would work better on our problem if we used different hyperparameters. For example, try it with a smaller learning rate. Do you get a smoother loss?

# CHAPTER 14

# The Zen of Testing

Soon enough, we'll get to tune our neural network and make it as accurate as we can. Before we do that, however, we need a reliable test to measure that accuracy. As it turns out, ML testing comes with a subtly counterintuitive hurdle that can easily trip you up.

It's hard to explain that hurdle in a few lines—so give me a few pages instead. This short chapter tells you where that testing trapdoor is, and how to step around it.

## The Threat of Overfitting

Since Part I of this book, we've been using two separate sets of examples—one for training our algorithms, and one for testing them. Let's refresh our memory: why don't we use the same examples for both training and testing?

I'll use a metaphor to answer that question. Imagine this: you're teaching basic math to a class of young kids. You already prepared 60 multiple-answer multiplication quizzes. You plan to assign most of those quizzes as homework. You also plan to select 10 quizzes for a final test, to check how well the kids are learning.

To recap, you want to split the quizzes in two groups: "homework" and "test." Here are two options: either you assign all 60 quizzes to "homework," and then re-use 10 of them in "test"; or you split the quizzes, assigning 50 of them to "homework," and the remaining 10 to "test." Which option would you pick?

I'd probably go for the second option, for one reason: I don't want the kids to *memorize* multiplications—I want them to *understand the rules* of multiplications. For that reason, I'd rather test their knowledge on quizzes that they haven't seen before. Otherwise, they might cross the right answers just because they happen to remember those answers from their exercises.

The same reasoning applies when we train a supervised learning system. If we train a network to recognize photos of beagles, we want it to recognize *any* beagle picture—not just the specific ones it encountered in training. That's easier said than done. Supervised learning systems, like people, have a tendency to memorize their training examples instead of generalizing from them. Back in Training vs. Testing, on page 79, we called this problem "overfitting."

To counter overfitting, we introduced the idea of a test set. Just like the teacher in our story, we train our neural networks on one set of examples, and test them on a different set of examples. That's how we get a realistic estimate of a network's performance in production, where it will be faced with data that it's never seen before.

Because of overfitting, the network tends to be more accurate on familiar training data, and less accurate on unfamiliar test data. Conversely, the network's loss tends to be lower on the training data, and higher on the test data.

Let's put those expectations to the test. I hacked together a version of our neural network that tracks the loss and accuracy on both the training and the test set, iteration by iteration. Then I ran this hacked network for 10,000 iterations, with batch GD (that is, putting all the examples in one large batch), n_hidden_nodes=200, and lr=0.01:

```
0 > Training loss: 2.43321 - Test loss: 2.42661
1 > Training loss: 2.38746 - Test loss: 2.38024
...
9999 > Training loss: 0.14669 - Test loss: 0.22979
Training accuracy: 96.13%, Test accuracy: 93.25%
```

This chart shows how the two losses change during training:

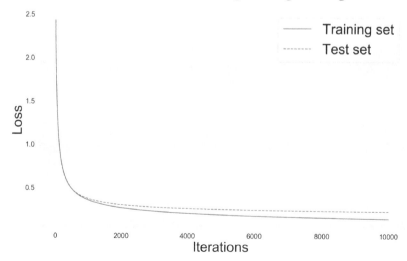

The losses start on even ground, but they diverge soon. As the network churns through the training set, its loss on that set decreases faster than the loss on the test set. A lower loss generally means higher accuracy—and indeed, at the end of training the network nails 96% of the training examples, but only 93% of the test examples. If we didn't have a test set, then we'd harbor the illusion that our error rate is below 4%, when in truth it's closer to 7%. That large difference is the effect of overfitting: the network is more accurate on training data, just because—well—those are the data it trained on.

Here is the takeaway lesson—we'll call it "the Blind Test Rule," and capitalize its name to underline that it's important: *test your system on data that it hasn't seen before.* Stick to this rule, and you won't get disappointed by a neural network that's less accurate on real-world data than it was on test data.

"Fair enough," you might say. "We already respect the Blind Test Rule—so, problem solved." Unfortunately, it's easy to violate the rule by mistake. In fact, as we're about to find out, we already did.

## A Testing Conundrum

To see where the testing hurdle is, consider that we're going to tune our neural network with an iterative process. That process is going to work like this:

1. Tune the network's hyperparameters.
2. Train the network on the training set.
3. Test the network on the test set.
4. Repeat until we're happy with the network's accuracy.

This process is pretty much the ML equivalent of software development, so we can simply call it like that: "the development cycle."

We already went through a few iterations of development in the previous chapter, when we measured the network's performance with different batch sizes. However, we overlooked a distressing fact: the development cycle violates the Blind Test Rule. Here is why.

During development, we tune the neural network's hyperparameters while looking at the network's accuracy on the test set. By doing that, we implicitly custom-taylor the hyperparameters to get a good result on that set. In the end, our hyperparameters are optimized for the test set, and are unlikely to be equally good on never-before seen production data. In a sense, our own brain violates the Blind Test Rule, by leaking information about the test examples into the network. We threw overfitting out of the door, and it sneaked back in through the window.

If you find it hard to understand how the development cycle can cause over-fitting, think of a similar example from software development. People commonly use standardized benchmarks to measure the performance of hardware such as graphics cards. Every now and then, a hardware maker is caught "optimizing for the benchmark"—that is, engineering a product to get great results on a particular benchmark, even though those results don't translate as well to real-world problems. The development cycle can easily mislead us into the same kind of "cheating" behavior, where a machine learning algorithm gets unrealistic results on the test set. Call it "unintended optimization," if you wish. To avoid unintended optimization, we shouldn't use the test set during tuning.

Unintended optimization is a sneaky issue. As long as we're aware of it, however, we can avoid it with a low-cost approach: instead of two sets of examples, we can have three—one for training, one for testing, and a third one that we can use during the development cycle. This third set is usually called the *validation set*. If we use the validation set during development, then we can safely use the test set at the very end of the process, to get a realistic estimate of the system's accuracy.

Let me recap how this strategy works:

1. *The setup:* we put the test set aside. We'll never look at it until the very end.

2. *The development cycle:* we train the network on the training set as usual, but we use the *validation* set to gauge its performance.

3. *The final test:* after we've tweaked and tuned our hyperparameters, we test the network on the *test* set, which gives us an objective idea of how it will perform in production.

The key idea in this strategy is worth repeating: put the test set under a stone, and forget about it until the very end of the process. We shouldn't cave in to the temptation of using the test set during the development process. As soon as we do, we'll violate the Blind Test Rule, and risk unrealistic measures of the system's accuracy.

How many examples should we set aside for the validation and test sets? That depends on the specific problem. Some people recommend setting aside 20% of the examples for the validation set, and just as many for the test set. That's called the "60/20/20" split.

In MNIST, however, we have plenty of examples—70,000 in total. It feels like a waste to set aside almost 30,000 examples for testing. Instead, we can take the 10,000 examples from the current test set, and split them in two groups of 5,000—one for the validation set, and one for the new test set. Here's the updated code that does that:

**14_testing/mnist_three_sets.py**

```python
# X_train/X_validation/X_test: 60K/5K/5K images
# Each image has 784 elements (28 * 28 pixels)
X_train = load_images("../data/mnist/train-images-idx3-ubyte.gz")
X_test_all = load_images("../data/mnist/t10k-images-idx3-ubyte.gz")
X_validation, X_test = np.split(X_test_all, 2)

# 60K labels, each a single digit from 0 to 9
Y_train_unencoded = load_labels("../data/mnist/train-labels-idx1-ubyte.gz")

# Y_train: 60K labels, each consisting of 10 one-hot-encoded elements
Y_train = one_hot_encode(Y_train_unencoded)

# Y_validation/Y_test: 5K/5K labels, each a single digit from 0 to 9
Y_test_all = load_labels("../data/mnist/t10k-labels-idx1-ubyte.gz")
Y_validation, Y_test = np.split(Y_test_all, 2)
```

There you have it—a training set, a validation set, and a test set.

> ## Model Selection
>
> In A Testing Conundrum, on page 173, I tell you that the development cycle is all about grabbing a neural network and tuning its hyperparameters. However, that definition is a bit limiting. While this book focuses on neural networks, a real-world project might decide to use a different algorithm instead. For example, maybe a particular problem is better solved with a quick linear regression, instead of a slow and cumbersome neural network.
>
> The process of comparing different algorithms and selecting the right one for the job is called *model selection*. Like hyperparameter tuning, model selection is guided by the validation set: you try different algorithms, and pick the one that gives you the best validation accuracy. That fact only makes the validation set even more important: it doesn't just help you tune hyperparameters—it also guides you toward the right algorithm.

## What You Just Learned

So far, we split our examples in a *training set* and a *test set*. This approach, however, tends to break down once we start tuning our system's hyperparameters, because it sneakily leads us to optimize the system for the specific examples in the test set.

In this chapter, we switched to a more sophisticated approach, splitting the test set in two: a smaller test set, and a brand-new *validation set*. We'll use the validation set for development, and the test set only once, for our final benchmark. During the final benchmark, the network comes in contact with the test set for the first time, so it should give us a reliable idea of the network's accuracy on future production data.

One word of warning before we move on: this three-sets strategy helps us measure our system's accuracy correctly, but it doesn't eliminate overfitting. Our network is still going to yield unrealistically good results on the training and the validation set—we just decided not to trust those results, and look at the results on the test set instead.

In other words, we worked around overfitting, but we didn't vanquish it. In fact, overfitting is this book's recurring villain, and it will rear its ugly head again. We'll have a final confrontation with overfitting in Chapter 17, Defeating Overfitting, on page 211. For the time being, we'll have to live with it, and neutralize its effects by applying the Blind Test Rule.

Armed with that sound testing strategy, we can finally roll up our sleeves and dive into development.

## Hands On: Thinking About Testing

This exercise isn't literally "hands on." Instead, it asks you to stop for a moment, and think about what could go wrong as you split a dataset.

Imagine that you receive a large dataset of handwritten characters—kinda like MNIST, only for letters from A to Z. You want to build a classifier for this dataset, so you need training, validation, and test sets. Let's say that the entire dataset is made up of 1,000,000 characters, and you plan to reserve 50,000 characters for the validation set, and 50,000 more for the test set. Here's the code that does that:

```
data_train, data_validation, data_test = np.split(data_all, [900_000, 950_000])
```

This line splits data_all at the two given indexes. The result is that data_train contains 900,000 characters, data_validation contains 50,000, and the rest are left for data_test.

The code here seems innocuous enough, but it contains a sneaky problem that might easily trip you up—or not, depending on the specific dataset. Here's the question that I ask you to ponder: can you imagine what that problem is, and what's the specific thing that makes this splitting strategy potentially wrong? How would you counter the problem if it happens?

Try to answer yourself, then read my answer in the 14_testing/solution folder.

# CHAPTER 15

# Let's Do Development

We spent a few chapters building a neural network, and a few more investigating its finer points. In this chapter, we'll come down to the wire and shoot for 99% accuracy on MNIST. To get there, we'll follow an iterative process that is the ML equivalent of software development. In fact, you can call it just that: development.

Like software development, ML development is too broad an activity to fit in this chapter—or this book. It involves people with different skills, from mathematicians to engineers. Even the engineering part of the job is vaster than just "build a neural network and tune it": real-life ML systems are often complicated pipelines composed of multiple algorithms and services. To make things harder, ML development is often an art as well as a science: it requires plenty of experience, educated guesses, and plain old luck.

As the saying goes, however, "the harder you practice, the luckier you get"—so, let's start practicing. We'll look at ML development in a nutshell, focusing on three activities:

1. We already decided to crack our problem with a neural network. We'll start by preparing our dataset for that network. For example, we'll rescale the input variables to make them more network-friendly.

2. Then we'll move into the development cycle. At each step, we'll improve the network's accuracy by tuning its hyperparameters: lr, the batch size, and so on.

3. At the end of the process, we'll put the network to a final test.

Along the way, remember the testing strategy from Chapter 14, The Zen of Testing, on page 171. We have three sets of examples: training, validation, and test. We'll put the test set under a rock right now and ignore it until the final test at the end of the process. Instead, during the development cycle, we'll use the *validation* set to measure the network's performance. In fact, the validation set is sometimes called the *dev set*, because it's used during development.

Now we have a plan. Let's jump in and see how close we can get to that 99%.

# Preparing Data

You might think that an ML engineer spends her time dreaming up and training sophisticated algorithms. Just like programming, however, the job comes with a less glamorous and more time-consuming side. In the case of ML, that grindwork usually involves preparing data.

If you're not convinced that preparing data is a big time sink, think of the effort that went into MNIST. Somebody had to collect and scan 60,000 handwritten digits. They probably hand-checked all those digits to remove the examples that were not representative of real-life digits, maybe because they were too garbled. They also had to center, crop, and scale those images to the same resolution, taking care to avoid graphical artifacts such as jagged edges. I'd wager that they also processed all digits to give them uniform lightness and contrast, from clear-white to pitch-black. Last but not least, they labeled each example, and double-checked the labels to sieve out mistakes.

In the case of MNIST, we don't have to do all that work—somebody did it for us. However, we can still massage MNIST a bit further, to make it more friendly to our network.

Preparing data is a complex activity in itself. Here, we're going to scratch its surface by looking at a couple of common techniques, and we'll get an intuitive understanding of what those techniques are for.

## Checking the Range of Input Variables

Before you feed data to a neural network, it's a good idea to check that all input variables span similar ranges. Imagine what happens if one input variable ranges from 0 to 10, and another from 1,000 to 2,000. The two variables might be equally important to predict the label, but the second one would contribute more to the loss, just because it's bigger. As a result, the network would focus on minimizing the loss of the larger variable, and mostly ignore the smaller one.

To avoid that problem, you can rescale the variables to a similar range. That operation is called *feature scaling*, where *feature* is just another name for "input variable." In our case, we don't need to bother with feature scaling, because all the variables in MNIST are 1-byte pixels—so they never drop below 0 or raise over 255.

However, even if your input variables span a similar range, you don't want that range to extend to large numbers. The problem with feeding large numbers to the network is that they tend to cause large numbers *inside* the network. As we learned in Dead Neurons, on page 141, neural networks work better when they process values that are close to zero, because that's where sigmoids give their best.

Bottom line: if your input variables are spread out (for example, from -10,000 to +10,000), or off-center (for example, from 10,000 to 10,100), then you should shift them and scale them to make them small and centered around zero. Let's see a common technique to do that.

## Standardizing Input Variables

To keep input variables close to zero, ML practitioners often *standardize* them. "Standardization" means slightly different things to different people, but its most common meaning is this: "rescale the inputs so that their average is 0 and their standard deviation is 1."

In case you don't know, the *standard deviation* measures how "spread out" a variable is. If the standard deviation is low, that means that the values tend to stay close to their average. For example, the height of humans has a relatively low standard deviation because nobody is hundreds of times taller than anyone else. On the other hand, the height of plants has a high standard deviation because a plant can be as short as moss, or as tall as a redwood.

A quick way to standardize a bunch of inputs is to to subtract their average, and divide them by their standard deviation:

```
standardized_inputs = (inputs - np.average(inputs)) / np.std(inputs)
```

This operation gives us the kind of data we want: data that are centered around zero, and never stray too far from it.

Here's an updated version of mnist.py that standardizes the dataset:

15_development/mnist_standardized.py

```
def standardize(training_set, test_set):
    average = np.average(training_set)
    standard_deviation = np.std(training_set)
    training_set_standardized = (training_set - average) / standard_deviation
    test_set_standardized = (test_set - average) / standard_deviation
    return (training_set_standardized, test_set_standardized)


# X_train/X_validation/X_test: 60K/5K/5K images
# Each image has 784 elements (28 * 28 pixels)
X_train_raw = load_images("../data/mnist/train-images-idx3-ubyte.gz")
X_test_raw = load_images("../data/mnist/t10k-images-idx3-ubyte.gz")
X_train, X_test_all = standardize(X_train_raw, X_test_raw)
X_validation, X_test = np.split(X_test_all, 2)
```

We could standardize each input variable separately, or all of them together. The input variables in MNIST all have comparable sizes, so the preceding function standardizes them together. It uses NumPy to calculate the average and standard deviation of the training set, and then applies the formula:

standardized-values = (original-values - average) / standard_deviation

The last four lines load the two MNIST datasets, standardize them, and split the test data into a validation set and a test set, like we did in the previous chapter. Let me spell out what the standardize() function does, because this process is a common cause of rookie mistakes:

1.  The function calculates the average and the standard deviation on the training set alone, because that's the only information that we want to train on. If we involve the validation and test set in those calculation, we'll leak information from those sets into the neural network's training.

2.  On the other hand, after calculating those parameters, the function uses them to standardize all three sets: the training, the validation, and the test set. That's because we want the three sets to be similar—otherwise, the network would fail once it moves from training to testing. If we ever deployed our network to production, we'd also have to standardize production data with the same average and standard deviation.

So, calculate the average and the standard deviation on the training set alone, then use them to standardize the entire dataset. I know that process is confusing, because it tripped me up a few times as a beginner.

So, we just standardized MNIST. Let's check whether it was worth it.

## Standardization in Practice

Let's check the effect of standardization on our neural network's accuracy. The following code runs the network twice, once with regular MNIST and once with standardized MNIST. Each configuration runs for two epochs, with a batch size of 60. The MNIST training set contains 60,000 examples, so that's 1,000 iterations per epoch:

15_development/mnist_vs_standardized_mnist.py
```
import neural_network as nn
import mnist as normal
import mnist_standardized as standardized

print("Regular MNIST:")
nn.train(normal.X_train, normal.Y_train,
         normal.X_validation, normal.Y_validation,
         n_hidden_nodes=200, epochs=2, batch_size=60, lr=0.1)

print("Standardized MNIST:")
nn.train(standardized.X_train, standardized.Y_train,
         standardized.X_validation, standardized.Y_validation,
         n_hidden_nodes=200, epochs=2, batch_size=60, lr=0.1)
```

Here are the results after a few tens of minutes of number crunching:

```
Regular MNIST:
    0-0 > Loss: 2.28073164, Accuracy: 18.90%
    …
    RuntimeWarning: overflow encountered in exp
    …
    1-999 > Loss: 0.41537869, Accuracy: 84.60%
Standardized MNIST:
    0-0 > Loss: 2.26244033, Accuracy: 17.96%
    …
    1-999 > Loss: 0.21364970, Accuracy: 91.80%
```

We don't know what would happen if we kept training the system for days, but this short test gives us pretty compelling numbers. The network is way more accurate when we train it on standardized MNIST than regular MNIST. Also, while regular MNIST causes an overflow during training, standardized MNIST doesn't. It seems that having smaller input variables makes the network more numerically stable, just as the theory goes.

All in all, the verdict is clear: from now on, we'll use the standardized version of MNIST. And now that we have data we trust, let's move into the heart of the development cycle.

# Tuning Hyperparameters

We built a neural network and prepared its input data, but that was only the beginning. The same algorithm running on the same data can yield wildly different results, depending on hyperparameters such as the learning rate and the number of hidden nodes.

ML development is mostly about finding good values for those hyperparameters. Compared to software development, that task can look like a form of black magic: there is no hard-and-fast rule that tells you how to set those hyperparameters. In fact, I chickened out of the issue whenever it came up, offering vague advice like: "try different values for the hyperparameters, and see which ones work better."

In this section, I'll give you some more concrete guidelines. Here's the first: don't change multiple hyperparameters at the same time. Otherwise, you won't know which changes affected the network's accuracy. Instead, let's tune those hyperparameters one at a time, starting with the easy one.

## Picking the Number of Epochs

epochs is arguably the easiest hyperparameter to tune. We already know that the longer you train a system, the more accurate it becomes—up to a point. After a certain number of epochs, the accuracy gets as high as it can, and training for longer becomes a waste of time. Overtraining a system might even become counterproductive, and *decrease* its accuracy—a case that we'll explore in Chapter 17, Defeating Overfitting, on page 211.

Long story short: you should train a network long enough to reach its maximum accuracy, but not any longer. So, here's the common approach to picking the number of epochs: start with a very high number, and take note of the number of epochs where the accuracy seems to level off. That's the "right" number of epochs.

## Tuning the Number of Hidden Nodes

Another crucial hyperparameter is the one that we called h—the number of hidden nodes. Here is an experiment that proves how important this hyperparameter is. I trained our network on a simple two-dimensional dataset—the same one that we used in Bending the Boundary, on page 155. Then I plotted the network's decision boundaries for 1, 2, 10, and 20 hidden nodes. The charts on page 183 illustrate the results.

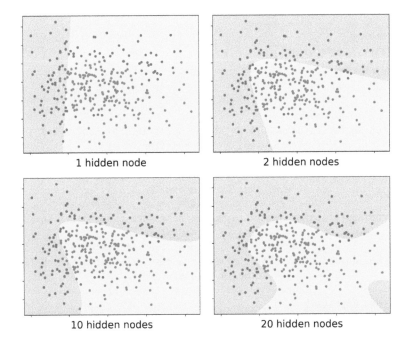

1 hidden node   2 hidden nodes

10 hidden nodes   20 hidden nodes

These charts show that, in general, a network with more hidden nodes can draw a more complicated boundary. With a single hidden node, the neural network behaves like a perceptron, with a straight decision boundary. As the number of hidden nodes increases, the network gets better at twisting the boundary and follow the contour of the data.

That doesn't mean we should go wild and use thousands of hidden nodes. First of all, more hidden nodes slow down training. Second, too many hidden nodes can make the network too smart for its own good, leading it to overfit the training data, as I described in The Threat of Overfitting, on page 171. As ever, we've got to find the sweet spot between too few and too many hidden nodes.

Some practitioners use a simple rule of thumb to find a number of hidden nodes that's good enough: they make it the average between the number of input and output nodes. Let's call that the "average rule." Our network has 785 input nodes and 10 output nodes, so the average rule would suggest something around 400 hidden nodes.

Let's test the average rule on our case. We'll use the compare.py utility, which you can read about in Using compare.py, on page 185. The following code tries a few values of h, both above and below 400:

**15_development/compare_hidden_nodes.py**

```
import compare
import mnist_standardized

DATA = mnist_standardized
BATCH = 128
LR = 0.1
TIME = 60 * 10
compare.configuration(data=DATA, n_hidden_nodes=10, batch_size=BATCH,
                      lr=LR, time_in_seconds=TIME,
                      label="h=10", color='orange', linestyle='-')
compare.configuration(data=DATA, n_hidden_nodes=100, batch_size=BATCH,
                      lr=LR, time_in_seconds=TIME,
                      label="h=100", color='green', linestyle='--')
compare.configuration(data=DATA, n_hidden_nodes=400, batch_size=BATCH,
                      lr=LR, time_in_seconds=TIME,
                      label="h=400", color='blue', linestyle='-.')
compare.configuration(data=DATA, n_hidden_nodes=1000, batch_size=BATCH,
                      lr=LR, time_in_seconds=TIME,
                      label="h=1000", color='black', linestyle=':')
compare.show_results()
```

Here are the results:

```
Training: h=10
  Loss: 0.35488827 (4 epochs completed, 1932 total steps)
Training: h=100
  Loss: 0.24496126 (2 epochs completed, 1312 total steps)
Training: h=400
  Loss: 0.32815639 (1 epochs completed, 503 total steps)
Training: h=1000
  Loss: 0.39487844 (0 epochs completed, 243 total steps)
```

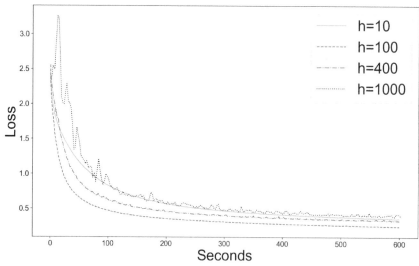

Too many hidden nodes seem to make the training unstable, with the loss jigging about a lot. More importantly, 100 hidden nodes result in a lower loss, at least after 10 minutes of training. Ten minutes aren't much, so we might want to review the decision later—but for now, let's settle on 100 hidden nodes.

Number of hidden nodes: checked. Let's move on to the most familiar hyperparameter of them all.

### Using compare.py

To compare network configurations throughout this section, I wrote a a simple utility library called compare.py. You use it by calling two functions: configuration() and show_results(). configuration() trains the neural network for a specified time, using specific hyperparameter values. After you've called configuration() a few times, you call show_results() to plot and compare the training histories for all the configurations you've run. You can see a concrete example in Tuning the Number of Hidden Nodes, on page 182.

Be careful when you interpret the results of compare.py. If you train two configurations for a few minutes, and the first yields a better loss, that doesn't mean that it's going to be better in the long term. Good things come to those who wait, and some configurations might simply be slower at pushing down the loss—but once they do, they might push it lower than their speedier competitors. Rather than just look at the final value of the loss, check out the chart plotted by show_results() to get a better idea of what's happening during training. As we said in the beginning of this chapter, configuring a neural network is not an exact science.

## Tuning the Learning Rate

Hello, lr, old buddy. This hyperparameter has been with us since almost the beginning of this book. Chances are, you already had a fling at tuning it, maybe by trying a few random values. It's time to be a tad more precise about lr tuning.

To understand the trade-off of different learning rates, let's go back to the basics and visualize gradient descent. The following diagrams show a few steps of GD along a one-dimensional loss curve, with three different values of lr. The red cross marks the starting point, and the green cross marks the minimum:

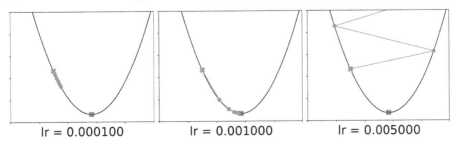

lr = 0.000100          lr = 0.001000          lr = 0.005000

Remember what lr does: the bigger it is, the larger each step of GD is. The first diagram uses a small lr, so the algorithm takes tiny steps towards the minimum. The second example uses a larger lr, which result in bolder steps and a faster descent.

However, we cannot just set a very large lr and blaze towards the minimum at ludicrous speed, as the third diagram proves. In this case, lr is so large that each step of gradient descent lands farther away from the goal than it started. Not only this training process fails to find the minimum, it fails to converge, *increasing* the loss at every step instead of decreasing it. In fact, if you have a smooth loss function with a single minimum, you could prove mathematically that batch gradient descent always finds that minimum—*as long as* lr is sufficiently small. With a large lr, all bets are off.

Now we've seen that a very small lr can slow down GD, and a very large lr can derail GD completely. As ever, we need to strike a balance. Armed with that information, let's brush up compare.py and try a few values of lr:

```
15_development/compare_lr.py
import compare
import mnist_standardized

DATA = mnist_standardized
HIDDEN = 100
BATCH = 128
TIME = 60 * 10
compare.configuration(data=DATA, n_hidden_nodes=HIDDEN, batch_size=BATCH,
                      lr=0.001, time_in_seconds=TIME,
                      label="lr=0.001", color='orange', linestyle=':')
compare.configuration(data=DATA, n_hidden_nodes=HIDDEN, batch_size=BATCH,
                      lr=0.01, time_in_seconds=TIME,
                      label="lr=0.01", color='green', linestyle='-.')
compare.configuration(data=DATA, n_hidden_nodes=HIDDEN, batch_size=BATCH,
                      lr=0.1, time_in_seconds=TIME,
                      label="lr=0.1", color='blue', linestyle='--')
compare.configuration(data=DATA, n_hidden_nodes=HIDDEN, batch_size=BATCH,
                      lr=1, time_in_seconds=TIME,
                      label="lr=1", color='black', linestyle='-')
compare.show_results()
```

lr has a wide range of reasonable values, so it doesn't make sense to try values on a linear scale, such as 0.1, 0.2, and 0.3. Instead, the previous code tries an exponential scale: 0.001, 0.01, 0.1, and 1. In some cases we might have to hunt for even bigger or, more frequently, smaller values of lr. In our case, it seems that these values span a big enough range:

```
Training: lr=0.001
  Loss: 1.64907297 (3 epochs completed, 1543 total steps)
Training: lr=0.01
  Loss: 0.53636065 (3 epochs completed, 1600 total steps)
Training: lr=0.1
  Loss: 0.23230808 (3 epochs completed, 1552 total steps)
Training: lr=1
  Loss: 0.07311269 (3 epochs completed, 1572 total steps)
```

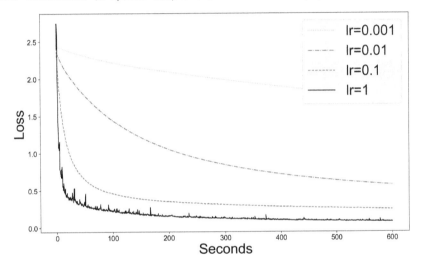

See those spikes with lr=1? It seems that this value is slightly too large, causing some steps of GD to land further from the minimum than they started from. On the other hand, it isn't large enough to derail the algorithm entirely, and it yields a lower loss than the other values we tried. Also, after a few minutes of training, it seems that the instability fades away, probably because each step of GD becomes so small that even a large lr isn't enough to make it diverge.

In the long term, it seems that an lr of 1 pays back for its negative effects. We'll stick with this value, and move on to the next hyperparameter.

## Tuning the Batch Size

We already compared the effects of different batch sizes in Batches Large and Small, on page 167. Back then, we found that batches can speed up training and shorten the development cycle. Now that we're nearing the end of that cycle and have set all the other hyperparameters, let's have another shot at comparing batch sizes:

15_development/compare_batch_sizes.py

```
import compare
import mnist_standardized

DATA = mnist_standardized
HIDDEN = 100
LR = 1
TIME = 60 * 5
compare.configuration(data=DATA, n_hidden_nodes=HIDDEN, batch_size=60000,
                      lr=LR, time_in_seconds=TIME,
                      label="batch_size=60000", color='orange', linestyle=':')
compare.configuration(data=DATA, n_hidden_nodes=HIDDEN, batch_size=256,
                      lr=LR, time_in_seconds=TIME,
                      label="batch_size=256", color='green', linestyle='-.')
compare.configuration(data=DATA, n_hidden_nodes=HIDDEN, batch_size=128,
                      lr=LR, time_in_seconds=TIME,
                      label="batch_size=128", color='blue', linestyle='--')
compare.configuration(data=DATA, n_hidden_nodes=HIDDEN, batch_size=64,
                      lr=LR, time_in_seconds=TIME,
                      label="batch_size=64", color='black', linestyle='-')
compare.show_results()
```

This time, I skipped the test on stochastic GD—that is, a batch size of 1. Last time we tried it, stochastic GD added a lot of noise to our diagram, and it didn't go anywhere in terms of performance. Instead, I focused on three more promising batch sizes: 64, 128, 256, and batch GD—that is, all the examples in one batch. Here is the resulting diagram:

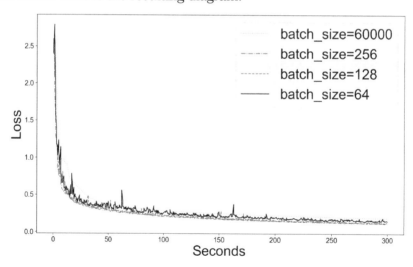

The losses are so close together that it's hard to make out which batch size is doing better. Instead of squinting at the diagram, let's look at the exact numbers:

```
Training: batch_size=60000
  Loss: 0.18655365 (241 epochs completed, 241 total steps)
Training: batch_size=256
  Loss: 0.11773560 (2 epochs completed, 678 total steps)
Training: batch_size=128
  Loss: 0.12600472 (1 epochs completed, 668 total steps)
Training: batch_size=64
  Loss: 0.14859866 (0 epochs completed, 656 total steps)
```

The numbers show that after 5 minutes of training, a batch size of 256 results in a lower loss than the 128 that we used so far. Let's switch to 256 from now on.

That's it. We went through each and every hyperparameter in our neural network, and now we have good values for all of them. Mind you, that doesn't mean that we must stick with those values forever. We could probably shave a few more decimal points off the loss by cycling through the hyperparameters a second or a third time. That being said, we did make a lot of progress on tuning our network—so we can call it a day for now.

Let's wrap up our short adventure in ML development, and distill all this hard work into one number: our neural network's accuracy.

## The Final Test

It's been a while since we reviewed the code of the neural network. Here it is—all of it, for the last time:

15_development/neural_network.py
```python
import numpy as np


def sigmoid(z):
    return 1 / (1 + np.exp(-z))


def softmax(logits):
    exponentials = np.exp(logits)
    return exponentials / np.sum(exponentials, axis=1).reshape(-1, 1)


def sigmoid_gradient(sigmoid):
    return np.multiply(sigmoid, (1 - sigmoid))


def loss(Y, y_hat):
    return -np.sum(Y * np.log(y_hat)) / Y.shape[0]


def prepend_bias(X):
    return np.insert(X, 0, 1, axis=1)
```

```
def forward(X, w1, w2):
    h = sigmoid(np.matmul(prepend_bias(X), w1))
    y_hat = softmax(np.matmul(prepend_bias(h), w2))
    return (y_hat, h)


def back(X, Y, y_hat, w2, h):
    w2_gradient = np.matmul(prepend_bias(h).T, (y_hat - Y)) / X.shape[0]
    w1_gradient = np.matmul(prepend_bias(X).T, np.matmul(y_hat - Y, w2[1:].T)
                            * sigmoid_gradient(h)) / X.shape[0]
    return (w1_gradient, w2_gradient)


def classify(X, w1, w2):
    y_hat, _ = forward(X, w1, w2)
    labels = np.argmax(y_hat, axis=1)
    return labels.reshape(-1, 1)


def initialize_weights(n_input_variables, n_hidden_nodes, n_classes):
    w1_rows = n_input_variables + 1
    w1 = np.random.randn(w1_rows, n_hidden_nodes) * np.sqrt(1 / w1_rows)

    w2_rows = n_hidden_nodes + 1
    w2 = np.random.randn(w2_rows, n_classes) * np.sqrt(1 / w2_rows)

    return (w1, w2)


def prepare_batches(X_train, Y_train, batch_size):
    x_batches = []
    y_batches = []
    n_examples = X_train.shape[0]
    for batch in range(0, n_examples, batch_size):
        batch_end = batch + batch_size
        x_batches.append(X_train[batch:batch_end])
        y_batches.append(Y_train[batch:batch_end])
    return x_batches, y_batches


def report(epoch, batch, X_train, Y_train, X_test, Y_test, w1, w2):
    y_hat, _ = forward(X_train, w1, w2)
    training_loss = loss(Y_train, y_hat)
    classifications = classify(X_test, w1, w2)
    accuracy = np.average(classifications == Y_test) * 100.0
    print("%5d-%d > Loss: %.8f, Accuracy: %.2f%%" %
          (epoch, batch, training_loss, accuracy))


def train(X_train, Y_train, X_test, Y_test, n_hidden_nodes,
          epochs, batch_size, lr):
    n_input_variables = X_train.shape[1]
    n_classes = Y_train.shape[1]

    w1, w2 = initialize_weights(n_input_variables, n_hidden_nodes, n_classes)
    x_batches, y_batches = prepare_batches(X_train, Y_train, batch_size)
```

```
for epoch in range(epochs):
    for batch in range(len(x_batches)):
        y_hat, h = forward(x_batches[batch], w1, w2)
        w1_gradient, w2_gradient = back(x_batches[batch], y_batches[batch],
                                        y_hat, w2, h)
        w1 = w1 - (w1_gradient * lr)
        w2 = w2 - (w2_gradient * lr)
        report(epoch, batch, X_train, Y_train, X_test, Y_test, w1, w2)
return (w1, w2)
```

Let's put this thing through its final test.

### Stretching for 99%

Throughout this chapter, we've been training our network on the training set and measuring its performance on the validation set. As we planned earlier in Chapter 14, The Zen of Testing, on page 171, the time has come to recover the test set that we've been willfully ignoring all this time. We'll classify the entire test set using the hyperparameters we've found in the last few pages:

15_development/final_test.py
```
import neural_network as nn
import mnist_standardized as data

nn.train(data.X_train, data.Y_train, data.X_test, data.Y_test,
         n_hidden_nodes=100, epochs=10, batch_size=256, lr=1)
```

You must be eager to see the results. Here they are:

```
0-0 > Loss: 2.22356892, Accuracy: 26.70%
0-1 > Loss: 2.38862271, Accuracy: 35.50%
0-2 > Loss: 2.08208522, Accuracy: 39.94%
...
9-234 > Loss: 0.04350713, Accuracy: 98.24%
```

After a handful of seconds, the accuracy of the neural network breezes past 90%—and then it just keeps going. On my machine, the network takes a few hours to pass the 98% mark. If you let it run for even longer, it gets up to around 98.6% before leveling up for good. That's not quite the 99% that we aimed for, but it's still very impressive for less than 100 lines of code!

## Hands On: Achieving 99%

In the beginning of Part II, we set a target for ourselves: 99% accuracy on MNIST. We just got so close, reaching 98.6%. That last 0.4%? That's up to you.

I told you that configuring a network can be more art than science, and this Hands On is proof of that. Here's my suggestion: to find better hyperparameters than the ones we have now, drop compare.py. Instead, use neural_network_quieter.py, an alternative version of the network that logs accuracy only once every 10 epochs—it's much faster. Here are a few things that you can try:

- The standardized version of MNIST generally works better. There's no reason not to use it.

- Sometimes, it pays off to be patient and wait for more epochs before giving up. However, if 20 or 30 epochs go by without the accuracy increasing at all, then it may be time to try another configuration.

- More hidden nodes slow down the training, but they make the network smarter when dealing with gnarly data. Don't be afraid to push that number higher.

- The smaller the learning rate, the slower the training, but those small steps help the network reach closer to the minimum loss. Try a slightly smaller value of lr than the one we settled on.

- We talked a lot about the pros and cons of small batches in the past. All that being said, in this specific case I had more luck with very large batch sizes.

Hitting that 99% with our neural network is entirely possible. Happy hunting! Check out the 15_development/solution directory if you want to compare your hyperparameters to the ones that I found.

## What You Just Learned… and the Road Ahead

Let's consider what we've achieved in this second part of the book. We built a neural network from scratch, we understood how and why it works, and we even worked through advanced details such as mini-batch gradient descent and testing. In this last chapter, we pushed the network as far as we managed, by *standardizing* its input data and tuning its hyperparameters.

Real-world ML development is more complicated than we described in these few pages, just like real-world coding is more complicated than the toy problems in programming books. However, now you have an idea of how to reach the goal that we set for ourselves at the beginning of Part II: get accurate classifications from a neural network. Remember when we thought that 90% accuracy on MNIST was cool? Now we're the proud coders of a 99% accurate network. High five!

We had to work hard to reach that goal, but we never doubted that we would eventually make it. After all, training a neural network sounds like a reasonable task these days. That wasn't always the case, as you might remember from A Tale of Perceptrons, on page 105.

In the 1980s and the 1990s, the battle of ideas between symbolists and connectionists was over, and the symbolists had won. Neural networks were mostly considered a dead end, and only a few researchers were still studying them. Eventually, those researchers implemented backpropagation, and proved the skeptics wrong: it *was* in fact possible to train neural networks! The connectionists had reason to rejoice...and yet, history still seemed to work against them.

You see, neural networks were cool, but also limited. The network that we built in this book is an example of those limitations. Sure, that 1% error rate is impressive—but it cannot compare to the accuracy of a human being, that can identify MNIST characters with close to 99.9% accuracy. What good is a neural network if a human can do the same job ten times more accurately?

The connectionists believed that neural networks could eventually beat humans—if only they could have more than just three layers. They experimented with so-called "deep" neural networks, that had four, five, or even more layers. The results of those experiments were mixed. Deep networks were indeed more accurate than "shallow" three-layered networks, but they were also unstable, finicky, and very hard to train.

Then, in the early 2000s, things changed radically.

In the last part of the book, we'll talk about those changes. Be prepared: if Part I was like crash-landing on an unknown planet, and Part II felt like a space adventure...well, Part III will be like that final sequence in *2001: A Space Odyssey*. Let's take a deep breath, and enter deep learning.

# Part III

# Deep Learning

*Deep learning is a set of complex technologies, but they all spring from a simple idea: neural networks become more powerful if they have many layers. Those "deep" networks pose more challenges than the "shallow" three-layered networks that we built so far. In the next few chapters, we'll describe and overcome those challenges.*

*Adding layers is just the beginning. In the last few years, the original concept of deep learning branched out into many innovative—and sometimes wonder-ful—ideas. We'll take a look at some of those.*

*In Parts I and II, we used MNIST as our benchmark. MNIST will also be our starting point in the first chapters of Part III—but eventually we'll outgrow it, and tackle more complex datasets. Brace yourself!*

# CHAPTER 16

# A Deeper Kind of Network

The third part of this book is all about *deep learning*, the major breakthrough in modern artificial intelligence. "Deep learning" means a few different things, but first and foremost, it stands for "neural networks with many layers." Deeper networks have more sophisticated models than shallow networks—so they're able to generate more complicated functions to approximate data.

Later on, you'll see that there is more to deep learning than adding layers. Deep learning is actually a set of interconnected techniques with intimidating names such as "convolutions," "recurrent neural networks," and "generational adversarial networks." By the end of this book, you'll have a better idea of those techniques, and you'll be well equipped to explore them on your own.

To begin, we'll start from that basic concept: adding layers to a neural network. In this chapter, we'll create two networks—a shallow one with three layers, and a slightly deeper one with four. We'll run both networks on the same dataset, and we'll compare their results.

In the first two parts of this book, we proudly wrote our code from scratch, line by line. As you move into deep learning, however, that do-it-yourself approach takes up more and more time. It also becomes less compelling, because you already have a solid grasp of the fundamentals, and don't need to linger on every little detail. Long story short: from this chapter onward, we'll write our neural networks with Keras, a popular ML library. We'll focus on the big picture, and Keras will take care of the nitty-gritties.

Let's recap what you can expect from this chapter:

- We'll see how to build a neural network with Keras.
- We'll write a three-layered network and run it on a simple dataset.
- We'll add a layer to the network and see how its performance changes.

Before we get into building networks, however, let's prepare a dataset to run them on.

## The Echidna Dataset

Do you remember the concept of a decision boundary, introduced back in *Tracing a Boundary*, on page 149? Soon enough, you'll see how a neural network's decision boundary changes as you add a fourth layer. For that purpose, I prepared a dataset that's twisty, but also easy to visualize. Here it is:

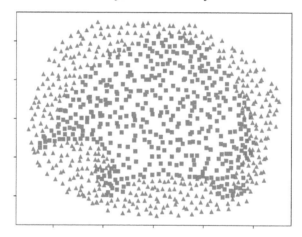

This dataset has two input variables and two classes, visualized here as squares and triangles. If you happen to be a fan of marsupials, you might notice that the dataset happens to be shaped like an echidna:[1]

---

1. https://en.wikipedia.org/wiki/Echidna

My wife and I still remember an unexpected encounter with a wild echidna on a trip to Australia. Let's not mince words: echidnas are cool.

I saved the Echidna dataset to a file named echidna.txt. I also wrote an echidna.py file that does the same job as the mnist.py file from earlier chapters. It loads the data and the labels into two variables named X and Y, and also splits it into training, validation, and test sets:

```
⇒ import echidna as data
⇒ data.X.shape
❮ (855, 2)
⇒ data.X[0:3]
❮ array([[ 0.01653543,  0.42533333],
         [ 0.14566929, -0.332     ],
         [ 0.19133858, -0.47866667]])
⇒ data.Y[0:3]
❮ array([[0],
         [1],
         [1]])
⇒ data.X_train.shape
❮ (285, 2)
⇒ data.Y_train.shape
❮ (285, 1)
```

We won't use the test set in this chapter, but the training and validation sets will become useful soon.

Now let's build a neural network that learns the Echidna dataset.

## Building a Neural Network with Keras

Python boasts a few large ML libraries such as PyTorch[2] and TensorFlow.[3] They're complex, and they tend to evolve fast. I won't use them in this book, or even talk about them. If I did, my code examples and explanations would likely be obsolete by the time you read these pages.

Instead, I'll use a slimmer and more stable library named Keras.[4] Keras is a thin layer that sits on top of the "big" libraries and hides them behind a nice, clean programming interface. Keras started out as a tool for prototyping, but it quickly became one of the most popular ways to build neural networks in Python—it was even adopted by TensorFlow as an official interface. With Keras, we can use the heavyweight libraries without getting bogged down by their complexities.

---

2. pytorch.org
3. www.tensorflow.org
4. keras.io

There are different ways to install Keras, depending on your operating system, your CPU and GPU, and so on. On most systems, you can install it like other libraries: either globally via *pip*, or inside a Conda environment. To install it globally:

```
pip3 install keras==2.3.1
```

Alternatively, here's how you install Keras 2.3.1 in the machinelearning Conda environment:

```
conda activate machinelearning
conda install keras=2.3.1
```

When you install Keras 2.3.1, you also get TensorFlow—so you can start building neural networks straight away. As usual, if this installation doesn't work for you, check out the updated installation instructions on ProgML.[5]

## A Plan and a Piece of Code

Let's build a neural network for the Echidna dataset. As a starting point, we can use the MNIST network that we designed back in Chapter 9, Designing the Network, on page 111. Here it is:

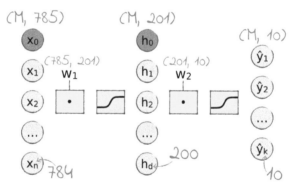

As a reminder, M is the number of examples in the training set, and 784 is the number of input variables in MNIST. Here is how we can modify this network to learn the Echidna dataset instead:

1.  The Echidna dataset has two input variables, so we only need two input nodes.

2.  The Echidna dataset has two classes, so we only need two output nodes instead of 10.

3.  The number of hidden nodes is a hyperparameter that we can change later. To begin with, let's go with 100 hidden nodes.

---

5.  www.progml.com

4.  Finally, the MNIST network is complicated by the bias nodes $x_0$ and $h_0$. We have good news here: Keras takes care of the bias under the hood, so we can forget about the bias nodes altogether.

After applying those changes, here is the plan for our new network:

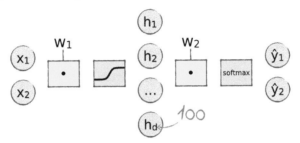

Now I'm going to show you how you can implement this network with Keras. I'm about to drop the entire neural network code right in your lap. Don't worry if it looks confusing—we'll step through it in a minute. Here is the whole thing:

16_deeper/network_shallow.py

```python
from keras.models import Sequential
from keras.layers import Dense
from keras.optimizers import RMSprop
from keras.utils import to_categorical
import echidna as data

X_train = data.X_train
X_validation = data.X_validation
Y_train = to_categorical(data.Y_train)
Y_validation = to_categorical(data.Y_validation)

model = Sequential()
model.add(Dense(100, activation='sigmoid'))
model.add(Dense(2, activation='softmax'))

model.compile(loss='categorical_crossentropy',
              optimizer=RMSprop(lr=0.001),
              metrics=['accuracy'])

model.fit(X_train, Y_train,
          validation_data=(X_validation, Y_validation),
          epochs=30000, batch_size=25)

boundary.show(model, data.X_train, data.Y_train)
```

That isn't much code, considering it's building the network, training it, and even checking its accuracy on the validation set. Let's step through this program line by line.

## Loading the Data

The first few lines in the Keras neural network focus on preparing the training set and the validation set:

```
from keras.utils import to_categorical
import echidna as data

X_train = data.X_train
X_validation = data.X_validation
Y_train = to_categorical(data.Y_train)
Y_validation = to_categorical(data.Y_validation)
```

X_train and X_validation are the same as in echidna.py—the previous code just renames them for consistency. On the other hand, the labels require some more processing because echidna.py doesn't one-hot encode them. The last two lines one-hot encode the labels with Keras's to_categorical() function, which behaves the same as the one_hot_encode() function we wrote ourselves in Part I. In other words, to_categorical() converts the labels from this...

```
⇒ data.Y_train[0:3]
❮ array([[0],
         [1],
         [1]])
```

...to this:

```
⇒ to_categorical(data.Y_train[0:3])
❮ array([[1., 0.],
         [0., 1.],
         [0., 1.]], dtype=float32)
```

The data is in—now let's assemble the network.

## Creating the Model

The next few lines define the shape of the neural network:

```
model = Sequential()
model.add(Dense(100, activation='sigmoid'))
model.add(Dense(2, activation='softmax'))
```

This code uses the object-oriented features of Python. (If you know nothing about objects and classes, then maybe read Creating and Using Objects, on page 290 to get up to speed. It will only take you a few minutes.)

The first line in the code creates a "sequential model," so called because it assembles a neural network as a sequence of layers. Keras comes with a few options for building a neural network, but in this book we'll always use the sequential model.

The second and third line create the hidden layer and the output layer, and add them to the network. There is no need to create an input layer, because Keras takes care of that automatically: as soon as we start feeding data to the network, Keras will look at the shape of the data and create an input layer with a matching number of nodes, which in our case is two. As I mentioned earlier, Keras will also add a bias node to the input and the hidden layer, so we don't need to worry about the bias either.

The model and the layers are Python objects: the model is an object of class Sequential, and the layers are objects of class Dense. A layer is *dense* when each of its nodes is connected to all the nodes in a neighboring layer. We'll look at other types of layers in the next chapters. For the time being, dense layers will be the only layers we deal with.

To create a Dense layer, Keras needs two arguments: the number of nodes, and the name of an activation function. Keras supports all the popular activation functions, including the two that we need in this network: the sigmoid and the softmax. Note that for each layer, we specify the activation function that comes *before* the layer, not after it.

We have a neural network. That was quick! Now let's configure it.

## Compiling the Model

The next statement configures the neural network—or, in the lingo of Keras, "compiles" it:

```
model.compile(loss='categorical_crossentropy',
              optimizer=RMSprop(lr=0.001),
              metrics=['accuracy'])
```

First, this statement tells Keras which formula to use for the loss. We want the same formula we used for the MNIST network in Part II: the cross-entropy loss, which Keras calls categorical_crossentropy.

Second, this statement tells Keras which algorithm it should use to minimize the loss during training. Keras comes with multiple flavors of gradient descent—in fact, I cheated a bit here: instead of plain vanilla GD (which Keras calls SGD), this code uses a souped-up version of GD called RMSprop. RMSprop is generally better and faster than SGD, and that extra speed will be welcome when we start experimenting with this network. I'll go into the details of RMSprop in *Chapter 18, Making It Better.*

When we create the RMSprop object, we also pass it the parameters that this particular algorithm needs. RMSprop only needs one parameter: the learning rate lr.

Finally, the last parameter to compile() tells Keras which metrics to report during training. By default, Keras only prints one metric on the terminal: the loss. In this case, we tell it that we also want to track the accuracy.

Networking configuration: check. Let's move on to the training phase.

## Training the Network

The next statement trains the network—or "fits" it, as Keras prefers to say:

```
model.fit(X_train, Y_train,
          validation_data=(X_validation, Y_validation),
          epochs=30000, batch_size=25)
```

Besides the training set, fit() takes an optional parameter with the validation set. If you pass it the validation set, as in the previous code, Keras will print out your validation loss and accuracy at the end of each epoch, together with the training loss and accuracy. The call to fit() is also where we specify the remaining two hyperparameters: epochs and batch_size.

We're almost done with the neural network's code. We just have one last line to go through.

### The Dialects of Machine Learning

One of the challenges of learning a new ML library is getting used to its vocabulary. For example, in these pages, we say that Keras uses the expression "compile the network" to mean "configure the network," and it prefers the term "fitting" to the term "training."

Some of those vocabulary preferences can be quite confusing. For example, Keras uses the name "stochastic gradient descent" (SGD) to mean "GD with batches." By contrast, many people—us included—use that name to mean "GD with a batch size of 1," specifically.

We'll have to live with these slightly confusing names. As you learned by now, the vocabulary of machine learning varies a lot from person to person.

## Drawing the Boundary

The last line in the program prints out the neural network's decision boundary. That's not a Keras feature—it's a little utility I wrote called boundary.py that you can find in this chapter's source code. The boundary.show() function takes a trained neural network and a bi-dimensional dataset, and prints out the network's decision boundary over the dataset:

```
import boundary
```

```
boundary.show(model, data.X_train, data.Y_train)
```

Note that boundary.show() takes the labels *without* one-hot encoding.

With that, we have all it takes to run this neural network on the Echidna dataset, measure its accuracy on the training and the validation set, and check out its decision boundary. Let's run this thing!

## Keras in Action

Training the neural network took me a few minutes on my laptop. Here's the output, stripped down to the essential information:

```
Using TensorFlow backend.
Train on 285 samples, validate on 285 samples
Epoch 1 - loss: 0.7222 - acc: 0.5088 - val_loss: 0.6928 - val_acc: 0.4807
Epoch 2 - loss: 0.6966 - acc: 0.5018 - val_loss: 0.6904 - val_acc: 0.5193
...
Epoch 30000 - loss: 0.1623 - acc: 0.9193 - val_loss: 0.1975 - val_acc: 0.9018
```

The accuracy on the training set gets up to 0.9193—that is, 91.93%. However, we know from Training vs. Testing, on page 79 that the training accuracy could be polluted by overfitting. Instead, we should look at the validation accuracy: 90.18%.

Now let's check out the network's decision boundary:

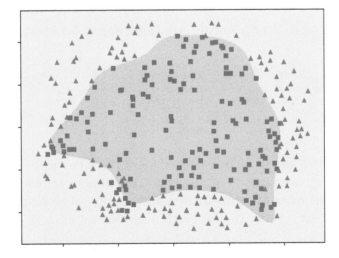

The network did a decent job of finding a boundary that separates the data points inside and outside the echidna shape. However, it doesn't seem very good at contouring small details like the echidna's nose and claws. That lack of finesse in the boundary explains why the neural network misclassifies about one point in ten.

Maybe a deeper network might do better on those small details? After all, that's the selling point of deep learning: just like a shallow neural network tracks the twists in a dataset better than a perceptron, a deep neural network should do even better.

Let's find out for ourselves, by adding a layer to our neural network.

**TensorFlow Warnings**

When I run Keras-based code, I usually get a bunch of warnings from the TensorFlow back end. Most are inconsequential issues with specific versions of the two libraries —such as Keras using a deprecated feature of TensorFlow. One of those warnings, however, commands more attention: it tells me that my TensorFlow version and configuration are suboptimal because they don't leverage all the features in my CPU.

I could probably recompile TensorFlow to squeeze some extra performance out of it, but I decided not to. My laptop is never going to be a speed demon anyway, so I'd rather ignore those warnings, and just rent a GPU in the cloud whenever I need serious speed. If you get those warnings as well, you might decide to recompile TensorFlow and gain some speed—but be aware that compiling TensorFlow is a bit of a rabbit hole, so don't expect to be done in a few minutes.

## Making It Deep

Let's add one more layer to our three-layered neural network:

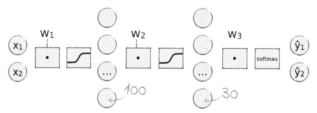

Each of the four layers in this deeper network comes with its own set of weights and its own activation function. The number of nodes in the new layer is yet one more hyperparameter, and we should be ready to tune it if we want the best results. To begin with, I set this value at 30.

Let's turn this plan into code. That's where using Keras really pays off, as adding this layer is a matter of adding one line of code to the model:

```
16_deeper/network_deep.py
model = Sequential()
model.add(Dense(100, activation='sigmoid'))
```

```
➤  model.add(Dense(30, activation='sigmoid'))
   model.add(Dense(2, activation='softmax'))
```

That's all we need. Let's run this deeper network and see whether it fares better than the three-layered network we used before:

```
Using TensorFlow backend.
Train on 285 samples, validate on 285 samples
Epoch 1 - loss: 0.7111 - acc: 0.4947 - val_loss: 0.6967 - val_acc: 0.4807
...
Epoch 30000 - loss: 0.0056 - acc: 1.0000 - val_loss: 0.7029 - val_acc: 0.8982
```

And here is the neural network's decision boundary:

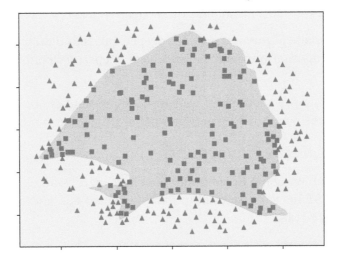

Take a moment to look at the numbers and the previous diagram. What do you think of them? Do you notice anything specifically?

At a glance, you might think that this network is amazingly successful. Its decision boundary is exceptionally good at tracking the fine details of the Echidna training set, contouring even the tiniest details to separate squares and triangles with uncanny precision. As a result, the network sports a perfect accuracy of 1 on the training set—which means that it nails the label on 100% of the training examples.

Do a double take, however, and you'll notice something distressing: while this network is perfectly accurate on the training set, it doesn't even come close to that perfection on the validation set. In fact, with 89.92% accuracy, this deep network does *worse* than its shallow counterpart on the validation set!

Let's take a deep breath and consider what we learned from this little experiment.

## What You Just Learned

In this chapter, we used the Keras ML library to write a quick three-layered neural network, and train it on a simple dataset. That shallow network gave us decent results, but it seemed to have trouble dealing with fine details in the data.

We expected that a deeper network would do better, so we added a fourth layer to the network. The results were disappointing. While the deeper network proved 100% accurate on the training set, it got nowhere near that accuracy on the all-important validation set. In fact, the deeper network did worse on the validation set than the shallow three-layered network.

To recap, we made our neural network deeper, but that didn't make it better. In fact, it seems that once our network gets deeper, its performance hits a brick wall.

Now, here come the good news: we can do something about that problem, and unleash the power of deep networks. That's the topic of the next chapter.

## Hands On: Keras Playground

Now that you have some Keras under your belt, here is an exercise for you: take the MNIST network we built in Part II of this book and rewrite it from scratch using Keras.

Keras already comes with a few common datasets, MNIST included—so you don't have to use our mnist.py library. Instead, you can load MNIST and one-hot encode its labels with this piece of code:

```
from keras.datasets import mnist
from keras.utils import to_categorical

(X_train_raw, Y_train_raw), (X_test_raw, Y_test_raw) = mnist.load_data()
X_train = X_train_raw.reshape(X_train_raw.shape[0], -1) / 255
X_test = X_test_raw.reshape(X_test_raw.shape[0], -1) / 255
Y_train = to_categorical(Y_train_raw)
Y_test = to_categorical(Y_test_raw)
```

The first time you run this code, Keras will download MNIST all by itself.

Note that MNIST doesn't have a validation set out of the box. You can either bend the rules and use the test set to validate the network, or split the test set into a validation set and a smaller test set, like we did before.

Note that this code doesn't standardize the inputs as accurately as we did in our earlier implementations: it just divides all the input pixels by 255 so they'll range from 0 to 1. Feel free to use the more sophisticated standardization method we used in Standardization in Practice, on page 181. When I tried that method, I found it didn't make a difference for my network—so I chose not to use it.

I showed you the code to load the data, but writing the network is up to you. When it comes time to call model.compile(), you can decide which algorithm to use—either SGD (that is, standard gradient descent) or the more advanced RMSProp that we used earlier in this chapter. If you wish, try both and compare the training speed and final accuracy on the training and the test set.

Don't expect that the Keras MNIST network will work well with the same hyperparameters we found in Chapter 15, Let's Do Development, on page 177. You have a different implementation, so you'll probably need to find new values for those hyperparameters. Aim for 99% accuracy or better. If you want to take a peek, you'll find my solution in the 16_deeper/solution directory, as usual.

One last thing: you should notice that the Keras-based neural network is faster than the one we wrote from scratch. That's no surprise—after all, Keras has been carefully optimized, and our code hasn't. However, most of the CPU power during the training of a neural network is spent multiplying matrices, and our earlier code delegated that operation to the highly optimized NumPy. Bottom line: you should expect the Keras version of the neural network to be faster than the old bespoke version, but not *crazy* faster.

Happy coding!

# CHAPTER 17

# Defeating Overfitting

Overfitting has been our nemesis throughout the book. In this chapter, we'll finally confront this archenemy.

To refresh your memory, a system that overfits is like a student who learns by rote memory. She might be good at solving familiar problems from textbooks, but she'll struggle when confronted with new problems. Likewise, an overfitting system could be okay at classifying its training data, and then fail when classifying data it hasn't seen before.

In earlier chapters, you learned a strategy to work around overfitting: split your data into training, validation, and test sets. Use the training set to train the system, the validation set to tune its performance, and the test set for a final check-up. That way, you can test the system on previously unseen data, and get a reliable, overfitting-free measure.

That testing strategy works, but it's a stopgap. It doesn't eliminate overfitting—it just prevents overfitting from polluting our metrics. Unfortunately, overfitting has worse consequences than imprecise metrics. Like that sloppy student I mentioned earlier, an overfitting system is good at *memorizing*, but bad at *generalizing*. We experienced that problem when we built a deep network at the end of the previous chapter. That network reached perfect accuracy on the training set, bit it did worse than its shallow counterpart on the validation set.

In the next few pages, we'll investigate the causes of overfitting and its subtler consequences. Later on, we'll apply a few methods to nip overfitting in the bud—the so-called *regularization* techniques. With those techniques under our belt, we'll finally unleash the power of our deep neural network.

## Overfitting Explained

Before we talk about reducing overfitting, let's get to know our enemy better. In this section, we'll dig into the causes of overfitting. What's happening under the hood of an overfitting neural network?

To fully grok overfitting, you should also understand its opposite: *underfitting*. In this section, we'll take a look at underfitting as well.

Let's start by investigating the causes of overfitting.

### The Causes of Overfitting

So far, I explained overfitting with vague metaphors like "a student memorizing the textbooks." It's time to take a glimpse under the hood of supervised learning and understand how overfitting really happens.

Imagine that we want to predict the number of customers at a hot dog stand, starting from a bunch of historical samples. As usual, we split the samples into training, validation, and test sets. For example, the following graph charts a slice of training data that spans the first three weeks of January. The horizontal axis is the day, and the vertical axis is the average number of customers per hour:

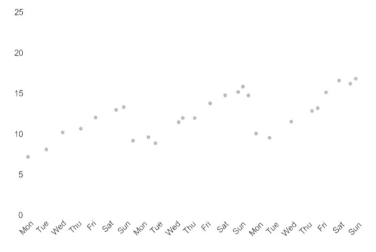

Now consider what happens when we train a neural network with these data. We know from the beginning of this book that supervised learning approximates training data with a model function, like the graph on page 213.

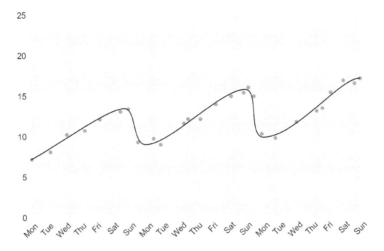

Once the network has found this model, it can use it to forecast future customers. However, here's a catch. If a neural network is powerful enough, it might find a model that fits the data very closely, like this:

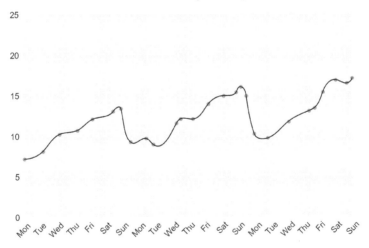

What do you think of this model function? I'd call it too precise for its own good. It tracks every tiny fluctuation in the data, including those that are probably *statistical noise*—irrelevant random variations. For example, our data show an uptick on the second Monday of January. However, we don't expect that the hot dog stand gets extra customers every year on that particular day. It seems more likely that the uptick depended on factors that are irrelevant or unknown. Maybe the weather happened to be especially nice that Monday, so more people were in the streets buying hot dogs.

We just came to the root cause of overfitting: it literally means "fitting too well." A powerful neural network can be so eager to fit the data that it ends up fitting the noise in it ("Yo, there's an uptick on the second Monday of the year") rather than focus on the meaningful patterns ("Hey, customers tend to grow from Sunday to Saturday").

Now imagine measuring the loss of the two models—the smoother one, and the overfitting one. The overfitting model tracks the data better than the smoother model, so it has a lower loss. That low loss, however, is custom-tailored to the training data. Apply both models to validation data, and the music changes. Here is the smooth model...

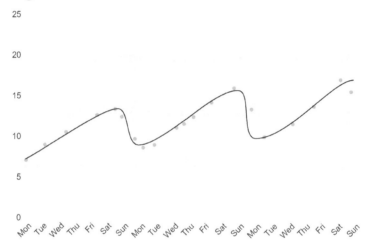

...and here is the overfitting model:

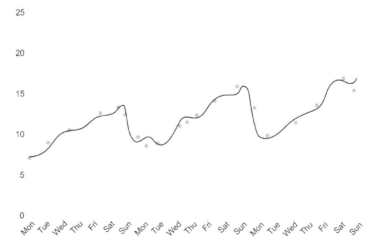

With all those pointless nooks and crannies, the overfitting model fits validation data *worse* than the smooth model! That's what overfitting does: at best,
it gives you overly optimistic results on training data; at worst, it damages
the network's performance on non-training data.

Note that the longer you train this neural network, the more tightly the
overfitting model approximates the training data—and the worse it approximates the validation data. As a result, overfitting can lead to a situation where
training becomes counterproductive: more training results in a less accurate
network.

I gave you an example based on one-dimensional data and numerical labels,
but the same phenomenon happens with higher-dimensional data, or data
with categorical labels. All supervised learning systems fit a model to data,
so they're all prone to memorize noise. For example, a system that recognizes
images of dogs might focus on irrelevant details in the training data ("Look,
a yellow pillow!") and lose sight of the important commonalities ("Gee, dogs
are hairy"). As it gets better at tracking the noise in the training images, this
system gets worse at generalizing to new data.

Now you know that powerful neural networks tend to overfit their training
data. That's also the reason why I waited until Part III of this book to discuss
the details of overfitting. The simple three-layered networks from Part II could
hardly overfit complicated datasets like images. On the other hand, the
deeper networks that we're building now can overfit even complicated datasets.
Once you step into deep learning, that's when overfitting graduates from
"minor nuisance" to "pain in the neck."

To wrap it all up, overfitting can cause three related problems:

- It confuses our metrics, because it yields an accuracy on the training set
  that isn't representative of the system's accuracy on new data.

- It actively reduces a system's accuracy on new data.

- After a certain number of training epochs, it can make additional training
  counterproductive: the more you train the system, the worse it becomes.

## Overfitting vs. Underfitting

You just learned that a powerful system is more likely to overfit its training
data. So, what if the system isn't very powerful at all? As an example, consider
what happens if you feed the hot dog data to a linear regression program. In
that case, the model function might look like the graph shown on page 216.

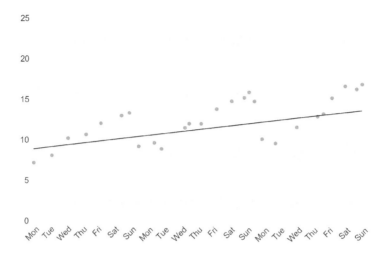

This model is too simplistic for the data at hand, so it isn't going to make accurate predictions. You can say that the system is *underfitting.* Just as "overfitting" means "fitting too well," "underfitting" means "not fitting well enough."

In most real-life cases, the data and the model are multidimensional, so you cannot plot them like we did in the previous diagrams. However, you can still tell whether your system is overfitting or underfitting by looking at the metrics of loss and accuracy: an overfitting system is good at classifying training data and less good at classifying test data; an underfitting system is bad at both.

To wrap it up, powerful supervised learning systems tend to overfit, and simpler systems tend to underfit. People sometimes refer to that notion as the *bias-variance trade-off,* where "bias" and "variance" are alternative terms for "underfitting" and "overfitting" (see Bias and Variance, on page 217).

That being said, overfitting and underfitting aren't mutually exclusive, and you might encounter a neural network that does a bit of both. In a few pages, we'll see an example of a system that is both underfitting, because it has low accuracy on the training data, *and* overfitting, because it has even lower accuracy on the validation data.

In this section, we stumbled upon one of the major challenges of supervised learning: striking a balance between too much overfitting and too much underfitting. When you build a supervised learning system, you've got to find a middle ground between those two annoying phenomena.

Let's see how to do that, going back to our deep network—and to the Echidna dataset.

> **Bias and Variance**
>
> ML practitioners use the terms "overfitting" and "underfitting" all the time, but statisticians have their own terms for those phenomena. Instead of saying that a model overfits the data, they say that a system has "high variance"; and instead of saying that it underfits the data, they say that it has "high bias."
>
> We won't use the terms "variance" and "bias" in this book, but you might encounter them elsewhere. Just remember that "high variance" stands for "overfitting," and "high bias" stands for "underfitting," and you'll be swell.

# Regularizing the Model

You learned three important concepts in the previous section:

- Powerful neural networks tend to *overfit*.
- Simple neural networks tend to *underfit*.
- You should strike a balance between the two.

Here is a general strategy to strike that balance: start with an overfitting model function that tracks tiny fluctuations in the data, and progressively make it smoother until you hit a good middle ground. That idea of smoothing out the model function is called "regularization," and is the subject of this section.

In the previous chapter, we took the first step of the process I just described: we created a deep neural network that overfits the data at hand. Let's take a closer look at that network's model, and afterwards we'll see how to make it smoother.

## Reviewing the Deep Network

To gain more insight into overfitting, I made a few changes to our deep neural network from the previous chapter. Here's the updated training code. The rest of the code didn't change, so I skipped it:

```
17_overfitting/network_deep.py
import losses

history = model.fit(X_train, Y_train,
                    validation_data=(X_validation, Y_validation),
                    epochs=30000, batch_size=25)

boundary.show(model, data.X_train, data.Y_train,
              title="Training set")
boundary.show(model, data.X_validation, data.Y_validation,
              title="Validation set")
losses.plot(history)
```

The original network visualized the decision boundary superimposed over the validation set. I added a second diagram that shows the same boundary over the training set. Besides, I also plotted the history of the losses during training. Conveniently, Keras's model.fit() already returns an object that contains that history—so I just had to write a utility to visualize it, that I called losses.py.

After adding this instrumentation, I trained the deep network again, with these results:

```
loss: 0.0059 - acc: 1.0000 - val_loss: 0.6656 - val_acc: 0.9053
```

Because the weights in the neural network's are initialized randomly, these numbers aren't exactly the same that we got in the previous chapter—but they're in the same ballpark. Once again, we have perfect accuracy on the training set, while the accuracy on the validation set is about 10% lower.

Good thing that we have that validation set! Imagine what could happen without it. Basking in the glory of that illusory 100% accuracy, we'd deploy the network to production... and only then we'd find out that it's way less accurate than we thought.

### Data Distribution

In this book, we're often confronted with a difference between a neural network's accuracy on the training data and on other data (like the validation set, or production data). In all those cases, we explain that difference as an effect of overfitting. However, there might be a simpler reason why a neural network does better on the training set than it does elsewhere. Maybe the examples in the training set are fundamentally different than other data.

For example, consider this scenario: we're building a neural network that recognizes vocal commands, and we train it with thousands of examples recorded by professional speakers. In production, however, the system is confronted with the voices of regular people speaking in noisy environments. The network will have a lower accuracy in production than it had on the training set, but that doesn't happen because of over-fitting. It happens because we cheated on your network: we trained it on one kind of data, and ran it on different data. A statistician would say that the training set has a different *distribution* than the production data.

Preparing datasets for a supervised learning system is an advanced topic that is outside the scope of this book. You will have plenty of time to build up that experience once you start working on real-life projects. Here, we will just take it for granted that the training, validation, and test sets all have the same distribution as the production data.

Those numbers are telling, but the diagrams that follow are even more insightful. Here's the history of the losses during training:

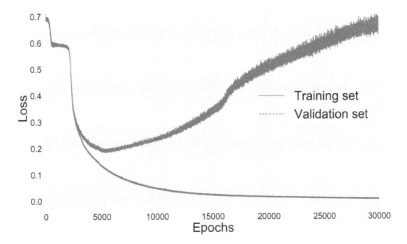

The network starts learning fast, then slows down, then accelerates again—and throughout this process, the losses on the training and the validation set decrease in lockstep. That's until overfitting kicks in, and the two losses part ways. While the training loss keeps happily decreasing, the validation loss skyrockets. That's an obnoxious consequence of overfitting: the longer we train this network, the worse it becomes at classifying new data.

Next, let's check out the network's decision boundary. The following diagram shows it printed over the training set:

## Training set

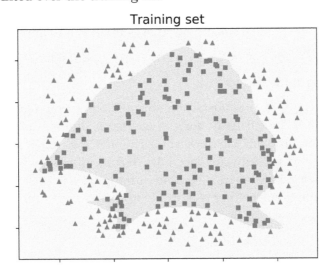

This decision boundary expertly contours the training data without missing a single point. When we overlay the boundary on the validation set, however, its limitations become apparent, as shown in this diagram:

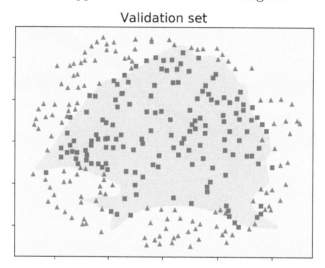

Validation set

Now we see why the network is so inaccurate on the validation set. The ornate convolutions of its decision boundary do more harm than good. This boundary contours the training data closely, but it misclassifies a lot of points in the validation data. In a sense, our deep network is a victim of its own cleverness. A simpler, less baroque boundary would probably do a better job at generalizing to new data points.

We've seen first hand that overfitting may make a network look better, but perform worse. It's time to smooth out that boundary, and improve the neural network's accuracy.

## L1 and L2 Regularization

L1 and L2 are two of the most common methods to regularize a decision boundary—the technical name for the operation that we informally called "smoothing out." L1 and L2 work similarly, and they have mostly similar effects. Once you get into advanced ML territory, you may want to look deeper into their relative merits—but for our purposes in this book, I suggest you follow a simple rule: either pick randomly between L1 and L2, or try both and see which one works better.

Let's see how L1 and L2 work.

## How L1 and L2 Work

L1 and L2 rely on the same idea: add a regularization term to the neural network's loss. For example, here's the loss augmented by L1 regularization:

$$L_{regularized} = L_{non-regularized} + \lambda \sum |w|$$

In the case of our neural network, the non-regularized loss is the cross-entropy loss. To that original loss, L1 adds the sum of the absolute values of all the weights in the network, multiplied by a constant called "lambda" (or $\lambda$ in symbols).

Lambda is a new hyperparameter that we can use to tune the amount of regularization in the network. The greater lambda, the higher the impact of the regularization term. If lambda is 0, then the entire regularization term becomes 0, and we fall back to a non-regularized neural network.

To understand what the regularization term does to the network, remember that the entire point of training is to minimize the loss. Now that we added that term, the absolute value of the weights has become part of the loss. That means that the gradient descent algorithm will automatically try to keep the weights small, so that the loss can also stay small.

What do small weights have to do with regularization? To answer that question, consider what the weights do: the values in the first layer of the network are multiplied by some of the weights, and then combined together. That process happens again in the second layer, in the third layer, and so on, until the last layer. By consequence, if the weights are big, then a small change of the inputs tends to result in a large change of the outputs. Conversely, if the weights are small, then a small change in the inputs tends to result in a small change of the outputs. In other words, small weights cause the model function to change slowly, instead of jerking up and down.

Bottom line: L1 works by keeping the weights small, and small weights have a regularizing effect on the model function. Bingo! The L2 method uses the same exact approach, with a minor difference: instead of the absolute values of the weights, it uses their squared values.

Here's a wrap-up of L1 and L2 regularization:

- These techniques roll the weights into the neural network's loss.
- To minimize the loss, GD tends to keeps the weights small.
- Smaller weights tend to result in a smoother model.

Let's try one of these techniques in our testbed neural network.

## L1 in Action

Most ML libraries come with ready-to-use L1 and L2 regularization. We have to pick one, so let's go with L1 regularization. To use L1 in our Keras neural network, we need a new import:

```
from keras.regularizers import l1
```

Then we add a new parameter to the network's inner layers:

17_overfitting/network_regularized.py
```
model = Sequential()
model.add(Dense(100, activation='sigmoid', activity_regularizer=l1(0.0004)))
model.add(Dense(30, activation='sigmoid', activity_regularizer=l1(0.0004)))
model.add(Dense(2, activation='softmax'))
```

Keras allows you to set up L1 for each layer independently. After a few experiments, I regularized both inner layers with $\lambda = 0.0004$, which seems to strike a good balance between overfitting and underfitting. If we wanted to squeeze every last drop of accuracy out of the network, we could tune each layer's lambda separately.

Remember that the non-regularized network gave us about 100% accuracy on the training set, and about 90% on the validation set. By contrast, here's a run of the regularized network:

```
loss: 0.1684 - acc: 0.9509 - val_loss: 0.2278 - val_acc: 0.9263
```

The network's accuracy on the validation set increased from 90% to well above 92%—which means about one fourth fewer errors. That's pretty good! We gave up a 5% of cheap training accuracy for an extra 2% of that precious validation accuracy.

Not only is this network better than the earlier, non-regularized version—it's also better than its shallow counterpart from the previous chapter, that was stuck around 90%. Thanks to regularization, we finally reaped the benefit of having a four-layers network instead of a three-layered network. All this talking about deep learning is starting to win us some concrete progress.

The reason for the neural network's increased performance becomes clear if you look at its decision boundary, shown in the diagrams on page 223.

That's a very smooth echidna. This regularized boundary isn't as cleverly convoluted as the one we had before—but it's all the better for that. It doesn't fit the training data quite as well, but it's a better fit for the validation data.

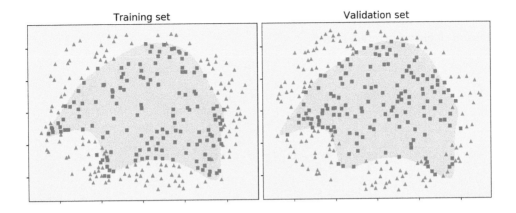

Finally, this graph shows the history of the training loss and the validation loss:

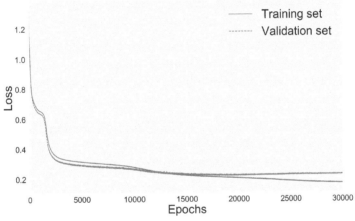

The two losses stay much closer together than before, which means that there is very little overfitting going on.

### Too Much of a Good Thing

Can't we push lambda higher and decrease overfitting even more? We might, but then we could fall out of the frying pan of overfitting and into the fire of underfitting. For example, here is what I got when I bumped up the lambda of the first hidden layer fivefold, from 0.0004 to 0.002:

```
loss: 0.2392 - acc: 0.9123 - val_loss: 0.2486 - val_acc: 0.9053
```

Our network's accuracy slided back to 90%—no better than it was without regularization, and as much as a shallow, three-layered neural network. This time, however, the accuracy on the training set took a hit as well. That's a hint that we're now underfitting, not overfitting, the training data.

Take a look at the network's decision boundary, and you'll see where that loss of accuracy comes from:

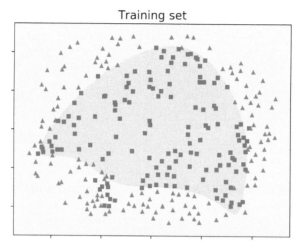

See? A smoother decision boundary is all well and good, but if you overdo it, the network will lose much of its ability to shape the boundary, and it will underfit the data. That lambda of 0.0004 seems like a good trade-off between overfitting and underfitting for this network and dataset.

With that, we're done talking about L1 and L2 regularization. However, these are far from the only regularization methods we have at our disposal. Let's review a few more before wrapping up this chapter.

## A Regularization Toolbox

Just like tuning hyperparameters, reducing overfitting is more art than science. Besides L1 and L2, there are many other regularization methods you can use. Here's an overview of some of them.

The most fundamental regularization technique is also the first one you should reach for: make the overfitting network smaller. After all, overfitting happens because the system is too clever for the data it's learning. Smaller networks are not as clever as big networks. Try reducing the number of hidden nodes, or even removing a few layers. You'll have a go at this approach in the chapter's closing exercise.

Instead of simplifying the model, you can also reduce overfitting by simplifying the data—that is, removing a few input variables. Let's say you're predicting a boiler's consumption from a set of 20 input variables. An overfitting network strives to fit the details of that dataset, noise included. Try dropping a few variables that are less likely to impact consumption (like the day of the week) in favor of the ones that seem more relevant (like the outside temperature). The idea is that the fewer features you have, the less noise you inject into the system.

Here's another way to reduce overfitting: cut short the network's training. This idea is not as weird as it sounds. If you look at the history of the network's loss during training, you can see the system moving from underfitting to overfitting as it learns the noise in the training data. Once overfitting kicks in, the validation flattens, and then diverges from the training loss. If you stop training at that point, you'll get a network that didn't learn enough to overfit the data yet. This technique is called *early stopping*.

Finally, and perhaps surprisingly, sometimes you can reduce overfitting by increasing a neural network's learning rate. To understand why, remember that the learning rate measures the size of each GD step. With the bigger learning rate, GD takes bolder, coarser steps. As a result, the trained model is likely to be less detailed, which might help reduce overfitting.

We went through a few regularization techniques, and we'll see a couple more in the next chapter. Each of these approaches might or might not work for a specific network and dataset. Here, as in many other aspects of ML, your mileage may vary. Be ready to experiment with different approaches, either alone or in combination, and learn by experience which approaches work best in which circumstances.

### Collecting More Data

Besides the regularization techniques I describe in these pages, there is another effective approach to reduce overfitting: collect more training data. Intuitively, overfitting happens when a model fails to generalize from its training examples. It's hard to generalize from a handful of examples, and easier if you have plenty of examples. So, the bigger and more varied your training set, the less likely the system is to overfit it.

Collecting data can be expensive, both in terms of time and money. As an alternative approach, you can generate fake training data by modifying the data you already have. For example, if you're training a system to recognize images, you might double the size of your training set just by mirroring your images. Fake data don't generally work as well as real data, but they might be the next best thing in some cases.

One last thing: more data help to reduce overfitting, but it does nothing for a system that's underfitting. It's a common rookie mistake to try and fix underfitting with more training data. An underfitting system isn't sophisticated enough to make sense of the data it already has, and collecting more won't help.

## What You Just Learned

This chapter was all about *overfitting*. Overfitting happens when the system learns the *statistical noise* in the training data, and fails to generalize that knowledge to new data. The more powerful a supervised learning system is, the more likely it is to overfit. Deep neural networks are very powerful, so they're very prone to overfitting.

You can reduce overfitting by "smoothing out" the neural network's model, so that it follows the general shape of the data instead of tracking every noisy fluctuation. That idea is called *regularization*. In this chapter, we looked at a few regularization techniques:

- L1 and L2 regularization
- Simplifying the model
- Simplifying the training data
- Early stopping
- Increasing the learning rate

To understand overfitting, you should also know about the opposite problem: *underfitting*. A network underfits when its model is too simplistic for the data at hand. You recognize overfitting because the system's accuracy is better on the training set than it is on the validation set; you recognize underfitting because the system accuracy is low on both sets.

Overfitting and underfitting aren't mutually exclusive; a network can do a bit of both. However, as you keep reducing the first, you'll eventually increase the second. That catch-22 is known as the *bias-variance trade-off*. A machine learning expert will aim for the sweet spot between overfitting and underfitting.

And that's it! We confronted overfitting head-on, and came out with a nice collection of regularization methods—and a 2% improvement in accuracy. That, however, is only the beginning. Deep neural networks can take us much farther than that, as long as we get familiar with more, and more varied techniques. In the next chapter, you'll learn enough ML tricks to fill up your bag.

## Hands On: Keeping It Simple

In this chapter, we applied L1 regularization to reduce overfitting on our four-layers neural network. Now it's up to you to try a few other regularization techniques. How does early stopping work on this network? What about removing a few nodes from each layer?

Try out those techniques, keeping an eye on the accuracy on the validation set. Maybe you'll find a more accurate result than we did in this chapter. Don't worry if you don't! The point of this exercise is experimenting with regularization, not necessarily beating that 92% score.

Once you've optimized the network's accuracy on the validation set, there is one last thing that you can take care of. Do you remember what we talked about in A Testing Conundrum, on page 173? By improving the network's performance on the validation set, we run the risk of overfitting the validation set. There is only one way to find out: recover the Echidna test set, that we've been ignoring until now, and run a final test.

Edit the network's code to replace the validation set (data.X_validation and data.Y_validation) with the test set (data.X_test and data.Y_test). Check out the network's accuracy on the test set. Is it as good as the best accuracy you got on the validation set?

# CHAPTER 18

# Taming Deep Networks

In a sense, there's nothing special about deep networks. They're like shallow neural networks, only with more layers. When people started experimenting with deep networks, however, they faced an uncomfortable truth: building deep networks may be easy, but training them is not.

Backpropagation on deep networks comes with its own specific challenges that carry intimidating names such as "vanishing gradients" and "dead neurons." Those challenges rarely come up in shallow neural networks—but they're par for the course in deep neural networks.

Over the years, neural networks researchers developed a collection of strategies, or what you might call a "bag of tricks," to tackle those challenges and tame deep neural networks:

- New activation functions to replace the sigmoid
- Multiple flavors of gradient descent
- More effective weight initializations
- Better regularization techniques to counter overfitting
- Other ideas that work, though they don't quite fit any of these categories

This chapter is a whirlwind tour through these techniques. We'll spend most of our time discussing activation functions: why the sigmoid doesn't pass muster in deep neural networks, and how to replace it. Then we'll round off the chapter, and your bag of tricks, with a few choice approaches from the other categories listed here.

Let's start our tour with activation functions.

## Understanding Activation Functions

By now, you're familiar with activation functions—those cyan boxes in between a neural network's layers shown in the diagram on page 230.

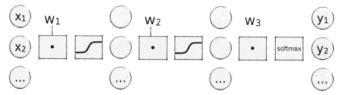

All our activation functions so far have been sigmoids, except in the output layer, where we used the softmax function.

The sigmoid has been with us for a long time. I originally introduced it to squash the output of a perceptron so that it ranged from 0 to 1. Later on, I introduced the softmax to rescale a neural network's outputs so that they added up to 1. By rescaling the outputs, we could interpret them as probabilities, as in: "we have a 30% chance that this picture contains a platypus."

Now that we're building deep neural networks, however, those original motivations feel so far away. Activation functions complicate our neural networks, and they don't seem to give us much in exchange. Can't we just get rid of them?

## What Activation Functions Are For

Let's see what happens if we remove the activation functions from a neural network. Here is the network we just saw, minus the activation functions:

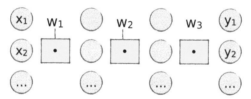

This network sure looks simpler than the earlier one. However, it comes with a crippling limitation: all its operations are *linear*, meaning that they could be plotted with straight shapes. To explore the consequences of this linearity, let's work through a tiny bit of math.

In a network without activation functions, each of the $n$ layers is the weighted sum of the nodes in the previous layer:

$$layer_2 = layer_1 \cdot weight_1$$

$$layer_3 = layer_2 \cdot weight_2$$

...

$$layer_n = layer_{n-1} \cdot weight_{n-1}$$

We can squash all those formulae together and calculate the last layer as the multiplication of the first layer with all the weight matrices in between:

$$layer_n = layer_1 \cdot weight_1 \cdot weight_2 \cdot \cdots \cdot weight_{n-1}$$

Now, here's the twist: If you take all those matrix multiplications of weights and call them w, the previous formula boils down to:

$$layer_n = layer_1 \cdot w$$

In other words, we just reduced the entire neural network to a single weighted sum:

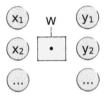

We came to a pretty stark result: No matter how many linear operations we pile up, they always add up to a single linear operation. In concrete terms, a network where everything is linear collapses to a feeble linear regression program, like the one we wrote in Chapter 4, Hyperspace!, on page 45.

Activation functions prevent that collapse because they're *nonlinear*—that is, they cannot be plotted as straight shapes. That nonlinearity is the heart and soul of a neural network.

You just learned that nonlinear activation functions are essential. However, that doesn't mean that we're stuck with the sigmoid and the softmax. We can replace them with other nonlinear functions—and in the case of the sigmoid, in particular, that might be a good idea. Let's see why.

## The Sigmoid and Its Consequences

Say hello to our old friend, the sigmoid, shown in the graph that follows:

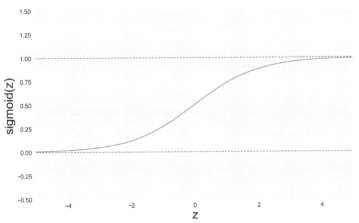

You just learned that an activation function should be nonlinear—that is, non-straight. The curvy sigmoid fits that bill.

At first sight, the sigmoid also jives well with backpropagation. Remember the chain rule? The global gradient of the neural network is the product of the local gradients of its components. The sigmoid contributes a local gradient that's nice and smooth. Slide your finger along its curve, and you'll find no hole, cusp, or sudden jump that can trip up gradient descent.

Look closer, however, and the sigmoid begins to reveal its shortcomings. Let's talk about them.

### Dead Neurons Revisited

Imagine freezing a neural network mid training and reading the values in its nodes. Earlier on, you learned an important fact: we have good reasons to want those values small. In Numerical Stability, on page 124, we saw that large numbers can overflow. Then, in Dead Neurons, on page 141, we saw that large numbers can slow down the network's training, and even halt it completely. Let's refresh our memory by recapping what dead neurons are.

If a neural network contains big numbers, those big numbers will eventually pass through a sigmoid. A sigmoid that receives a big positive or negative input can *saturate*—that is, it operates far off-center, on one of its two long tails. On those tails, the gradient is close to zero, and GD grinds to a near halt.

Here's a diagram that illustrates this situation:

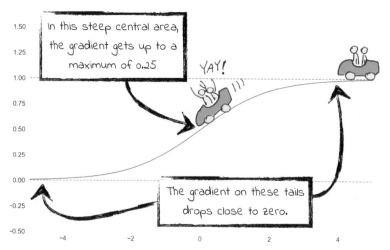

The sigmoid's gradient reaches its maximum, that happens to be 0.25, right in the center. As you move along its tails, the gradient drops quickly. If the sigmoid receives a large input, either positive or negative, it enters a vicious circle:

- The larger the sigmoid's input, the smaller the gradient.
- The smaller the gradient, the slower GD.
- The slower GD, the less the network's weights change.
- The less the weights change, the less likely it is the sigmoid's input will eventually shift back toward zero.

When the sigmoid enters this loop, the nodes uphill of the sigmoid become "dead neurons". GD is unable to update them, and they stop learning. With too many dead neurons, the whole backprop process slows to a crawl.

This problem is compound by another subtle issue: the sigmoid is "off-center." When it receives a value that's close to zero, it shifts that value close to 0.5. We said that numbers close to zero are generally better, so it would be nice if the sigmoid didn't go out of its way to push the numbers in the neural network far away from zero.

To wrap up, the sigmoid only works well when the values in the network are close to zero. That's a tough call, especially when the sigmoid itself tends to push values farther from zero. As they get farther from zero, those values slow down backpropagation and kill off the network's neurons. The deeper the network, the more sigmoids it contains—and the worse this problem becomes.

Those issues have been known since people began using sigmoids in neural networks. In a deep network, however, they contribute to a worse problem—one that stumped machine learning researchers for years.

### The Vanishing Gradient

Here's our periodic reminder of how backpropagation works: It accumulates the local gradients of all the components in the network from the output to the input layer—like this:

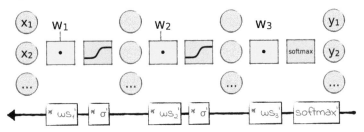

Backpropagation starts from the local gradient of the softmax in the output layer. Then it multiplies it by the gradient of the last weighted sum (that I called $ws_3'$); it multiplies the result by the gradient of the last sigmoid… and so on, all the way back to the first layer. The gradient of the first layer is the product of the accumulated local gradients.

Now, as you saw in the previous section, the local gradient of a sigmoid is a small number between 0 and 0.25. Whenever backprop traverses a sigmoid, the global gradient is multiplied by that small number, making it smaller. If the network has many layers—and many sigmoids—then the first layers in the network receive a minuscule gradient, and their weights barely change at all.

What I just described is the problem of the *vanishing gradient*. As it moves back through the network, the gradient becomes vanishingly small. This problem puts us in a catch-22: If we want a more powerful network, we should add layers to it; but the more layers we add, the smaller the gradients of the first layers become, to the point where those layers stop learning. We're damned if we add layers, and damned if we don't.

To wrap it all up, we uncovered two significant issues with the sigmoid:

- The problem of *dead neurons*: with a large input, the sigmoid's gradient tends toward zero.

- The problem of *vanishing gradients*: each sigmoid diminishes the total gradient of the network to the point where the first layers receive a gradient that's close to zero.

Both problems result in tiny gradients that slow down backpropagation, and maybe halt it for good.

### Don't Play with Explosives

The vanishing gradient has an evil twin called the *exploding gradient* problem. In that case, the gradient's absolute value grows—rather than diminishing—as it backprop-agates. Those large numbers in the network cause all sorts of trouble, including dead neurons and overflows.

Exploding gradients happen just like vanishing gradients do: when all the local gra-dients are multiplied together by the chain rule. If those local gradients are too large, then the network's gradient explodes. That can happen because the weights have been initialized to large values to begin with, or because the network contains activa-tion functions that generate large gradients. For all its shortcomings, the sigmoid is not a suspect in this case: its gradient is always small.

In Better Weight Initialization, on page 239, I'll describe a technique to minimize the risk of exploding gradients.

Thank you for staying with me! It took us some time to go through this examination of the sigmoid. On a positive note, that's nothing compared to the time it took researchers to identify some of these problems. For years they struggled to pinpoint why deep neural networks were so hard to train. Once they understood the problems, however, those researchers also came up with solutions. Let's take a look at them.

## Beyond the Sigmoid

There is no such thing as a perfect replacement for the sigmoid. Different activation functions work well in different circumstances, and researchers keep coming up with brand-new ones. That being said, one activation function has proven so broadly useful that it's become a default of sorts. Let's talk about it.

### Enter the ReLU

The go-to replacement for the sigmoid these days is the *rectified linear unit*, or *ReLU* for friends. Compared with the sigmoid, the ReLU is surprisingly simple. Here's a Python implementation of it:

```
def relu(z):
  if z <= 0:
    return 0
  else:
    return z
```

And the following diagram illustrates what it looks like:

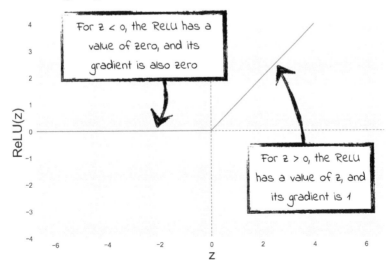

The ReLU is composed of two straight segments. However, taken together they add up to a nonlinear function, like a good activation function should be.

The ReLU may be simple, but it's all the better for it. Computing its gradient is cheap, which makes for fast training. The ReLU's killer feature, however, is that gradient of 1 for positive inputs. When backpropagation passes through a ReLU with a positive input, the global gradient is multiplied by 1, so it doesn't change at all. That detail alone solves the problem of vanishing gradients for good.

### ReLUs in Keras

In a Keras neural network, you can replace sigmoids with ReLUs by changing the activation parameters from this:

```
model.add(Dense(1200, activation='sigmoid'))
```

...to this:

```
model.add(Dense(1200, activation='relu'))
```

That's all you need. Keras will take care of calculating the ReLU's gradient, backpropagating it, and all that jazz. That's a major benefit of libraries: they make it easy to change the design of a neural network on a whim.

While the ReLU gingerly steps around vanishing gradients, it does nothing to solve dead neurons. On the contrary, it seems to have this issue even more than the sigmoid, because it flatlines with negative inputs. On a ReLU with a negative input, GD gets stuck on a gradient of zero, with no hope of ever leaving it. Isn't that a recipe for disaster?

As it turns out, that's not necessarily the case. In some cases, dead ReLUs might even be beneficial to a neural network. Researchers have stumbled on a counterintuitive result: sometimes, dead ReLUs can make training faster and more effective, because they help the network ignore irrelevant information.

That being said, there is no doubt that too many dead ReLUs can disrupt a neural network. If you suspect that's happening in your own network, you can replace the ReLU with its souped-up sibling, the *Leaky ReLU*, which is illustrated in the graph on page 237.

Did you spot the difference between the Leaky ReLU and the ReLU? Instead of going flat for negative values, the Leaky ReLU is slightly sloped. That constant slope guarantees that the gradient never becomes zero, and the neurons in the network never die. When you use a Leaky ReLU in a library such as Keras, you can change its slope, so that's one more hyperparameter that you can tune.

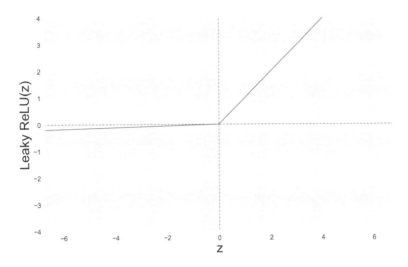

Finally, you might have noticed a blemish in the ReLU family. I said that a good activation function should be smooth—otherwise, you cannot calculate its gradient. But the ReLU and the Leaky ReLU aren't smooth: they have a cusp at the value of 0. Won't that cusp trip up GD?

That turns out not to be a problem in practice. From a mathematical standpoint, it's true that the ReLU's gradient is technically undefined at $z = 0$. However, ReLU implementations are only too happy to shrug off mathematical purity, and return a gradient of either 0 or 1 if their input happens to be exactly 0.

Bottom line: it is true that GD might experience a little bump as it transitions through that cusp in the ReLU, but it's not going to derail because of it. If you suspect that the cusp is getting in the way of your training, however, you can Google for variants of ReLU that replace the cusp with a smooth curve. There are at least two: the *softplus* and the *Swish*.

Sigmoid, ReLU, Leaky ReLU, softplus, Swish... You might feel a bit overwhelmed. Don't we have a simple way to decide which of those functions to use in a neural network? Well, not quite—but we can take a look at a few pragmatic guidelines.

## Picking the Right Function

When you design a neural network, you need to decide which activation functions to use. That decision usually boils down to a mix of experience and practical experimentation.

To begin with, however, you can follow a simple default strategy: just use ReLUs. They generally work okay, and they can help you deliver your first prototype as quickly as possible. Later on, you can experiment with other activation functions: Leaky ReLUs, maybe, or perhaps even sigmoids. Those other functions are likely to result in slower training than ReLUs, but they might improve the network's accuracy.

This "ReLU as default" approach applies to all the layers in a network, except for the output layer. In general, the output layer in a classifier should use a softmax to output a probability-like number for each class.

You can make an exception to that rule if you only have two classes. In that case, you might want to use a sigmoid instead of a softmax in the last layer. To see why, consider a network that recognizes a vocal command. When you ask the system to classify a sound snippet, a softmax would output two numbers, like this:

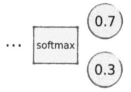

This result means "I'm 70% confident that I heard the command, and 30% confident that I didn't." In this case, however, the second output isn't very useful because it always equals 1 minus the first output. For that reason, the softmax is overkill with only two classes, and you can replace it with a sigmoid:

To recap, here's a no-nonsense default approach to picking activation functions: use ReLUs inside the network, and cap off the last layer with a softmax—or maybe a sigmoid, but only in the special case where you have two classes. This approach won't always give you the best possible network, but it generally works fine as a starting point.

We took a long tour through activation functions, and we walked out with a few useful guidelines. Now let's look at a few other techniques that can help you tame deep neural networks.

**Predicting Scalars**

The examples in this section, as in most of the book, assume we're building a classifier. However, many neural networks are not classifiers, and their output is numerical rather than categorical. For example, a network might forecast the temperature in a vat or, say, the number of pizzas sold at a restaurant.

Networks with a numerical output have a few differences from classifiers:

- They have one node in the output layer, instead of one node per class.

- Instead of the cross-entropy loss, which only works for categorical outputs, they use a loss that works for scalars, such as the mean squared error.

- Finally, and particularly relevant to this chapter, if the network's output is scalar, then you don't need an activation function in the output layer. That lonely node in the output layer—that's the output of the network.

For consistency, instead of skipping the activation function in the output layer, you can use an identity function. The identity function returns its input, so it's the same as not having an activation function at all. This is a rare case of a linear, rather than non-linear, activation function.

## Adding More Tricks to Your Bag

Picking the right activation functions is a crucial decision, but when you design a neural network, you face plenty more. You decide how to initialize the weights, which GD algorithm to use, what kind of regularization to apply, and so forth. You have a wide range of techniques to choose from, and new ones come up all the time.

It would be pointless to go into too much detail about all the popular techniques available today. You could fill entire volumes with them. Besides, some of them might be old-fashioned and quaint by the time you read this book.

For those reasons, this section doesn't aspire to be comprehensive. See it like a quick shopping spree in the mall of modern neural networks: we'll look at a handful of techniques that generally work well—a starter's kit in your journey to ML mastery. At the end of this chapter, you'll also get a chance to test these techniques first hand.

Let's start with weight initialization.

### Better Weight Initialization

You learned a few things about initializing weights in Initializing the Weights, on page 140. In case you don't remember that section, here's the one-sentence summary: to avoid squandering a neural network's power, initialize its weights with values that are random and small.

That "random and small" principle, however, doesn't give you concrete numbers. For that, you can use a formula such as *Xavier initialization*, also known as *Glorot initialization*. (Both names come from Xavier Glorot, the dude who proposed it.)

Xavier initialization comes in a few variants. They all give you an approximate range to initialize the weights, based on the number of nodes connected to them. One common variant gives you this this range:

$$|w| \leq \sqrt{\frac{2}{nodes\_in\_layer}}$$

The core concept of Xavier initialization is that the more nodes you have in a layer, the smaller the weights. Intuitively, that means that it doesn't matter how many nodes you have in a layer—the weighted sum of the nodes stays about the same size. Without Xavier initialization, a layer with many nodes would generate a large weighted sum, and that large number could cause problems like dead neurons and vanishing or exploding gradients.

Even though I didn't mention Xavier initialization so far, we already used it: it's the default initializer in Keras. If you want to replace it with another initialization method, of which Keras has a few, use the kernel_initializer argument. For example, here is a layer that uses an alternative weight initialization method called *He normal*:

```
model.add(Dense(100, kernel_initializer='he_normal'))
```

## Gradient Descent on Steroids

If something stayed unchanged through this book, it's the gradient descent algorithm. We changed the way we compute that gradient, from simple derivatives to backpropagation, but so far, the "descent" part is the same as I introduced it in the first chapters: multiply the gradient by the learning rate and take a step in the opposite direction.

Modern GD, however, can be subtler than that. In Keras, you can pass additional parameters to the SGD algorithm:

```
model.compile(loss='categorical_crossentropy',
              optimizer=SGD(lr=0.1, decay=1e-6, momentum=0.9),
              metrics=['accuracy'])
```

This code includes two new hyperparameters that tweak SGD. To understand decay, remember that the learning rate is a trade-off: the smaller it is, the smaller each steps of GD—that makes the algorithm more precise, but also slower. When you use decay, the learning rate decreases a bit at each step. A well-configured decay causes GD to take big leaps in the beginning of training, when you usually need speed, and baby steps near the end, when you'd rather have precision. This twist on GD is called *learning rate decay*, that's a refreshingly descriptive name.

The *momentum* hyperparameter is even subtler. When I introduced GD, you learned that this algorithm has trouble with certain surfaces. For example, it might get stuck into local minima—that is, "holes" in the loss. Another troublesome situation can happen around "canyons" like the one shown in the following diagram:

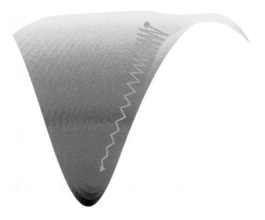

GD always moves downhill in the direction of the steeper gradient. In the upper part of this surface, the walls of the canyon are steeper than the path toward the minimum—so GD ends up bouncing back and forth between those walls, barely moving toward the minimum at all.

For this example, I drew a hypothetical path on a three-dimensional surface. However, cases such as this one are common in real life on higher-dimensional loss surfaces. When they happen, the loss might stop decreasing for many epochs in a row, leading you to believe that GD has reached a minimum, and giving up on training.

That's where the momentum algorithm enters the scene. That algorithm counters the situation I just described by adding an "acceleration" component to GD. That makes for a smoother, less jagged path, as shown in the diagram on page 242.

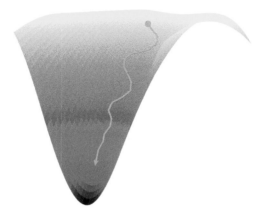

Momentum can speed up training tremendously. In some cases, it may even help GD zip over local minima, propelling it toward the lowest loss. The result is not only faster training, but also higher accuracy.

In Keras, decay and momentum are additional parameters to the standard SGD algorithm. However, Keras also comes with entirely different implementations of GD, which it calls "optimizers." One of those alternatives to SGD is the RMSprop optimizer, that implements a concept similar to momentum. I already sneakily used RMSprop when I wrote our first deep network in Chapter 16, A Deeper Kind of Network, on page 197. It made the network's training radically faster and more efficient than SGD:

```
model.compile(loss='categorical_crossentropy',
              optimizer=RMSprop(lr=0.001),
              metrics=['accuracy'])
```

That's all I wanted to tell you about optimizers. If you want to do some research on your own, another optimizer worth checking out is called Adam. It's very popular these days, and it merges momentum and RMSprop into one mean algorithm.

## Advanced Regularization

When it comes to overfitting, deep neural networks need all the help they can get. In the previous chapter you learned about the classic L1 and L2 regularization techniques. However, more modern techniques often work better. One in particular, called *dropout*, is very effective—and also somewhat weird.

Dropout is based on a striking premise: you can reduce overfitting by randomly turning off some nodes in the network. You can see dropout as a filter attached to a layer that randomly disconnects some nodes during each iteration, as illustrated by the following diagram:

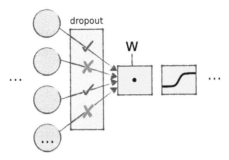

Disconnected nodes don't impact the next layers, and they're ignored by backpropagation. It's like they cease to exist until the next iteration.

To use dropout in Keras, you add Dropout layers on top of regular hidden layers. You can specify the fraction of nodes to turn off at each iteration—in this example, 25%:

```
from keras.layers import Dropout

model = Sequential()
model.add(Dense(500, activation='sigmoid'))
model.add(Dropout(0.25))
model.add(Dense(200, activation='sigmoid'))
model.add(Dropout(0.25))
model.add(Dense(10, activation='softmax'))
```

## What's a Layer?

As it turns out, the notion of a "layer" in neural networks depends on whom you ask. Look at the Keras network in Advanced Regularization, on page 242. In our convention, that network has four layers: an implicit input layer, two hidden layers that use dropout, and an output layer. Keras, on the other hand, calls "layer" everything that you add() to the model, Dropouts included. That inconsistency is unfortunate, but it's usually clear from the context whether we're talking about a layer in one or the other sense.

I've just described how dropout works—but not *why* it works. It's kinda hard to understand intuitively why dropout reduces overfitting, but here's a shot at it: dropout forces the network to learn in a slightly different way at each iteration of training. In a sense, dropout reshapes one big network into many smaller networks, each of which might learn a different facet of the data.

Where a big network is prone to memorize the training set, each small network ends up learning the data its own way, and their combined knowledge is less likely to overfit the data.

That's only one of a few possible ways to explain the effect of dropout. Whatever our intuitive understanding, however, dropout works—and that's what counts. It's one of the first regularization techniques I reach for in the presence of overfitting.

Speaking about things that work, although it's hard to see why: there is one last technique I want to tell you about in this chapter.

## One Last Trick: Batch Normalization

Think back to the idea of standardizing data, which we looked at in Preparing Data, on page 178. In a sentence, a standardized dataset is centered on zero and doesn't stray far from there. As I explained when I introduced this topic, neural networks like small, zero-centered numbers.

Standardization, however, can only go so far. As our carefully standardized data moves through the network, it changes, losing its network-friendly shape. It would be nice if each hidden layer received standardized inputs, not just the input layer. That's pretty much what *batch normalization* does: it re-standardizes each batch of data before it enters each network layer.

Batch normalization involves a few technical complexities. For one, it doesn't necessarily use an average of 0 and a standard deviation of 1, like regular input standardization. Instead, its average and standard deviation are themselves learnable parameters that are tuned by gradient descent. However, you can leave those technical details to Keras and use batch normalization as a black box:

```
from keras.layers import BatchNormalization

model = Sequential()
model.add(Dense(500, activation='sigmoid'))
model.add(BatchNormalization())
model.add(Dense(200, activation='sigmoid'))
model.add(BatchNormalization())
model.add(Dense(10, activation='softmax'))
```

When it was introduced (around 2015), batch normalization was hailed as a breakthrough. You might say that it's an advanced technique—but even beginners are keen to use it because it works so darn well. It often improves a network's accuracy, and sometimes even speeds up training and reduces overfitting. There is no such thing as an easy win in deep learning, but batch normalization comes as close as anything.

## What You Just Learned

Deep neural networks can be wild, untameable beasts. In this chapter, you learned of a few useful techniques to turn them into cute docile puppies.

We started with a lengthy discussion of *activation functions*. You learned that nonlinear functions are a necessity in neural networks, but we must choose them carefully. So far we used sigmoids inside the network, but sigmoids can cause a number of problems as the network gets deeper: saddening *dead neurons*, perplexing *vanishing gradients*, and shocking *exploding gradients*. For that reason, we looked at a few alternatives to the sigmoid—in particular, the popular *ReLU* activation function.

After that discussion of activation functions, we took a whirlwind tour through a number of other techniques that help us tame deep neural networks:

- *Xavier initialization* to initialize a neural network's weights.

- A handful of advanced GD algorithms: *learning rate decay*, *momentum*, *RMSprop*, and *Adam*.

- *Dropout*, a brilliantly counterintuitive regularization technique.

- The extremely useful technique of *batch normalization*.

You're probably itching to try out these techniques yourself. If so, then the next hands-on exercise will scratch that itch. Otherwise, prepare for the next chapter: it's going to take everything that you learned so far about neural networks and spin it on its head.

## Hands On: The 10 Epochs Challenge

Now that you have a few tricks under your belt, you can start experimenting with deep neural networks on your own. Speaking of which, I have a challenge for you.

To set up this challenge, I wrote a neural network and trained it on the MNIST dataset. You already saw plenty of MNIST classifiers, but this time, it's a deep neural network written in Keras. Go and take a look at it. It's in `network_mnist.py`, in this chapter's source code.

This network doesn't use any of the techniques from this chapter, but it still does okay. I trained it for 10 epochs and got this result:

```
loss: 0.2026 - acc: 0.9388 - val_loss: 0.2487 - val_acc: 0.9228
```

Now it's your turn. Your mission, should you choose to accept it, is to improve this network's accuracy while respecting two constraints:

- Don't change the network's layout. Keep the same number of layers and nodes per layers.

- Don't change the number of epochs or the batch size. Keep them at 10 and 32, respectively.

In all other respects, you can go wild. You can use the tricks that we described in this chapter, or even explore new ones—activation functions, optimization algorithms, or whatever else you learn by browsing Keras's documentation.[1]

Here are a few ideas to get you up and running:

- Replace the sigmoids with ReLUs or Leaky ReLUs.
- Switch from SGD to another GD algorithm.
- Add dropouts.
- Add batch normalization.

If your network does better than 97% on the validation set, then victory is yours.

Although I'm pretty sure that you can hit that 97%, I'd be surprised if you did much better than that. The techniques that we introduced in this chapter are essential, but they can only take us so far. To get radically better results, we need something more than incremental tricks—we need a fundamentally different neural network architecture. That is the subject of the next chapter.

---

1.   keras.io

# CHAPTER 19

# Beyond Vanilla Networks

At this point in the book, you're probably fairly comfortable with the structure of a neural network. Hold on tight, because we're about to shake things up a little and peek at neural networks that stray beyond that familiar structure.

All the networks that we've seen so far share the same architecture: a sequence of dense layers, where by "dense" I mean that each node in a layer is connected to all the nodes in the neighboring layers. That blueprint is also called a *fully connected* neural network—and as it turns out, it comes with a drastic limitation. Whether it's classifying images, parsing a product review, or predicting traffic congestion, a fully connected network treats all data the same, as an indistinct sequence of bytes. That generalistic approach can only go so far, and it fails when dealing with complex datasets.

Deep learning isn't just about making neural networks deeper—it's also about making them smarter, adopting different architectures to deal with different kinds of data. Deep learning researchers came up with quite a few variations to the basic fully connected network, and more are probably getting invented as you read this page. Each of those architectures would deserve its own book, and some add up to an entire field of study.

I certainly won't be able to describe or even mention all those different blueprints in this chapter. However, we can take a brief look at one of them. In keeping with the rest of this book, we'll focus on an architecture that's customized to process images: a *convolutional neural network*, or CNN for short. Where fully connected networks multiply each layer by a set of weights, CNNs are based on a more complicated operation called a *convolution*, which makes them particularly good at dealing with spatial data such as images.

Before we look at a CNN, however, we need a dataset to train it on.

### Image Classification...*Again*

You can do a lot of things with deep learning: simulate physics, generate music, caption videos, process images, summarize reviews, control robots, diagnose illnesses, kill weeds, forecast weather, translate books, drive cars...the list goes on and on. People are even experimenting with ideas straight out of science fiction, like reading a person's thoughts by interpreting her brain activity. With so many amazing examples to choose from, you might wonder why this book keeps circling back to the same classic problem: classifying images.

That was a conscious choice I made. I had the option of either giving you diverse examples of applied ML, or using the same example throughout. I decided for the second option, because it makes for a slimmer, more focused book. I picked image classification as our go-to example, because it's a cool, concrete problem—although not as cool as reading brains.

That being said, remember that deep learning goes well beyond image classification. As you become an expert, you might even come up with your own novel ways to use it.

## The CIFAR-10 Dataset

Do you remember back in Chapter 6, Getting Real, on page 77, when I introduced MNIST? Those handwritten digits looked like a formidable challenge back then. By now, our neural networks are making short work of them. Since we passed 99% accuracy on MNIST, it's getting hard to even tell apart actual improvements from random fluctuations.

What do you do when your neural networks are too cool for MNIST? You turn to a more challenging dataset: CIFAR-10.

### What CIFAR-10 Looks Like

In the field of image recognition, MNIST is considered an entry point. A tougher benchmark is the CIFAR-10 dataset.[1] CIFAR stands for Canadian Institute For Advanced Research, and 10 is the number of classes in it. A random sample of CIFAR-10 images is shown in the figure on page 249.

Like MNIST, CIFAR-10 contains 60,000 images in the training set and 10,000 in the test set, but the images in CIFAR-10 are thougher to classify. Even though they look so pixelated, they're bigger than MNIST's digits. Instead of being matrices, CIFAR-10 images are *tensors*—that is, arrays with more than

---

1.    www.cs.toronto.edu/~kriz/cifar.html

two dimensions. To be precise, they're (32, 32, 3) tensors: 32 by 32 pixels with 3 color channels for red, green, and blue. That makes for a grand total of 3,072 variables—almost four times as many as MNIST's 784.

However, the challenge of CIFAR-10 isn't in the size of its examples as much as in their complexity. Instead of relatively simple digits, the images represent real-world subjects such as horses and ships. For example, check out how different the birds (labeled 2 in our sample) look from each other. By contrast, see how similar objects can be even when they belong to different classes, like the seagull and the fighter jet, or cars and trucks. With so many confusing subjects, CIFAR-10 puts even powerful neural networks through their paces.

Let's dust off the best neural network we've built so far and see how it copes with these images.

## Falling Short of CIFAR

I retrieved our best neural network so far—the solution to Hands On: The 10 Epochs Challenge, on page 245—and modified it to train on CIFAR-10 instead of MNIST. Keras, bless its binary soul, comes with built-in support for CIFAR-10. So I only had to change a few lines, which are marked by small arrows in the left margin:

```
19_beyond/cifar10_fully_connected.py
import numpy as np
from keras.models import Sequential
from keras.layers import Dense, BatchNormalization
from keras.optimizers import Adam
from keras.initializers import glorot_normal
from keras.utils import to_categorical
➤ from keras.datasets import cifar10

➤ (X_train_raw, Y_train_raw), (X_test_raw, Y_test_raw) = cifar10.load_data()
X_train = X_train_raw.reshape(X_train_raw.shape[0], -1) / 255
X_test_all = X_test_raw.reshape(X_test_raw.shape[0], -1) / 255
X_validation, X_test = np.split(X_test_all, 2)
Y_train = to_categorical(Y_train_raw)
Y_validation, Y_test = np.split(to_categorical(Y_test_raw), 2)

model = Sequential()
model.add(Dense(1200, activation='relu'))
model.add(BatchNormalization())
model.add(Dense(500, activation='relu'))
model.add(BatchNormalization())
model.add(Dense(200, activation='relu'))
model.add(BatchNormalization())
model.add(Dense(10, activation='softmax'))

model.compile(loss='categorical_crossentropy',
              optimizer=Adam(),
              metrics=['accuracy'])

history = model.fit(X_train, Y_train,
                    validation_data=(X_validation, Y_validation),
➤                   epochs=25, batch_size=32)
```

Aside from loading CIFAR-10 instead of MNIST, the only change I made is the number of epochs. I bumped it up from 10 to 25, to give more training time to the network. When I ran this program, I had to wait for a few minutes as Keras downloaded CIFAR-10 to my computer—and then for a few hours as it churned through those 25 epochs. Here is what I got in the end:

```
Train on 50000 samples, validate on 5000 samples
Epoch 1 - loss: 1.7835 - acc: 0.3665 - val_loss: 1.9901 - val_acc: 0.3244
…
Epoch 25 - loss: 0.9512 - acc: 0.6596 - val_loss: 1.4610 - val_acc: 0.5216
```

The numbers are in: our neural network misclassifies about half the images in the validation set. Sure, it's more accurate than the 10% we'd get by random guessing, but that doesn't make it great.

It seems that CIFAR-10 is too much to handle for a fully connected neural network. Let's see what happens if we switch to a different architecture—one that's more fit to deal with images.

# The Building Blocks of CNNs

We'll spend the next few pages browsing through the core components of convolutional neural networks. To be clear, you shouldn't expect that you'll be able to build a CNN after reading through these few pages. However, you will get an idea of how they work—enough of it to run a convolutional network on CIFAR-10.

Let's start with the most important difference between a fully connected neural network and a convolutional neural network: how they look at data.

## An Image Is an Image

The first time we built a network to process images (in Chapter 6, Getting Real, on page 77), we noted a potentially surprising detail: the neural network doesn't know that the examples are images. Instead, it sees them as flat sequences of bytes. We even got into the habit of flattening the images right after loading them, and we still did that just a few pages ago:

19_beyond/cifar10_fully_connected.py
```
(X_train_raw, Y_train_raw), (X_test_raw, Y_test_raw) = cifar10.load_data()
X_train = X_train_raw.reshape(X_train_raw.shape[0], -1) / 255
```

Besides rescaling the input data, this code flattens each example to a row of bytes. CIFAR-10 contains 60,000 training images, each 32 by 32 pixels per color channel, for a total of 3,072 pixels. This code reshapes the training data into a (60000, 3072) matrix. Our network flattens the test and the validation set in the same way.

By contrast, here is the equivalent code for a CNN:

```
(X_train_raw, Y_train_raw), (X_test_raw, Y_test_raw) = cifar10.load_data()
X_train = X_train_raw / 255
```

This code still loads and rescales data, but it doesn't flatten the images. The CNN knows that it's dealing with images, and it preserves their shape in a (60000, 32, 32, 3) tensor—60,000 images, each 32 by 32 pixels, with 3 color channels. The test and validation set would also be four-dimensional tensors.

To recap, while a fully connected network ignores the geometric information in an image, a convolutional network keeps that information around. That difference doesn't stop at the input layer. The hidden *convolutional layers* in a CNN also take four-dimensional data as their input, and they output four-dimensional data for the following layer.

Speaking of convolutional layers, let's talk about the operation they're based on.

## Convolutions

In the field of image processing, a convolution is an operation that involves two matrices: an *image* and a *filter*. Here is an example:

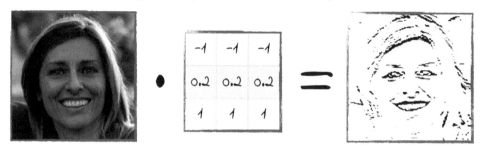

In this case, the filter is a (3, 3) matrix. When you convolve the image with the filter, you get a result like the one shown on the right. This specific filter highlights horizontal edges in the image—but a filter will give very different results depending on the numbers it contains.

In practice, convolutions work by sliding the filter over the image. For each position of the filters, it calculates the matrix multiplication of the overlapped section of the image with the filter. The outputs of those multiplications are assembled together to become the filter's output. That process is easier to grasp if you visualize it. Check out the diagram that follows:

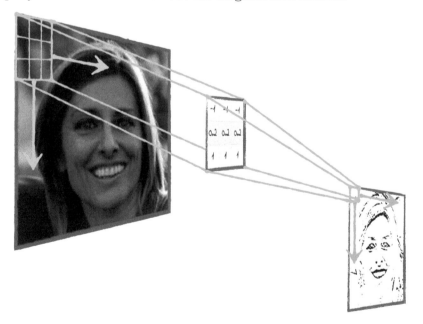

See? As the filter slides over the image, it progressively generates the output. That's the intuition behind it, and in this book I'll leave it at that. If you're curious about the technical details of convolutions, you'll find them on the ProgML[2] site. In here, it's enough that you know this core difference between fully connected networks and CNNs: in a fully connected network, the weights are multiplied by the input, and that is it. By contrast, in a CNN the weights are arranged in a filter that slides over the input, calculating the output piece by piece. That's a crucial difference, as you can read in CNNs' Secret Sauce.

Check out "Convolutional Neural Networks in Plain English" on ProgML.

### CNNs' Secret Sauce

CNNs can get complicated, but the core idea behind them is simple: instead of multiplying an input by a set of weights, like fully connected networks do, slide the weights over the input, calculating the output piecemeal. When it comes to recognizing images, that trick can make a huge difference. Here is why.

Imagine that you're building a system that recognizes human faces in pictures. To recognize a face, you must be able to recognize the peculiar shapes that a face is made of. In particular, you want to look for eyes, a nose, and other quintessentially face-y features. In practice, however, that simple notion hits a brick wall when you consider that those features might be anywhere in the image. A nose might be dead center, but it might also be tucked up in the corner of an image.

The MNIST classifiers that we built in this book work fine on images that have been carefully centered—but they'd be easily defeated if we showed them the same digits translated to different positions in a larger image. By contrast, a CNN slides its weights all over the image, like a victorian detective scanning for clues with a magnifying glass. If the digit is there, the magnifying glass will eventually pick it up, whatever its position. The same would happen with face recognition: a CNN has a chance to identify a face's defining features, no matter where they are exactly in the picture. That property is called *translation invariance*, and it's the secret sauce that allows CNNs to recognize images.

I just mentioned how a convolutional layer applies a filter to its inputs—but in reality, it doesn't need to be only one filter. In general, a convolutional layer applies multiple filters at once. The diagram on page 254 shows a stack of filters applied to an image, resulting in a stack of outputs.

As usual when you work with neural networks, it's easy to get confused by the dimensions of all the matrices and tensors involved. (In case you don't

---

2. https://www.progml.com

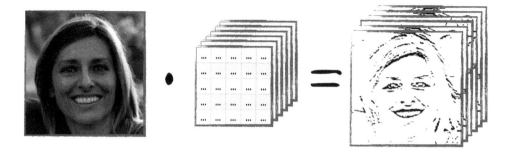

remember, a "tensor" is like a matrix, but it can have more than two dimensions.) Let's check out the dimensions of the tensors in this example. Let's say the image is 100 pixels wide and 100 pixels high with 3 color channels—a $(100, 100, 3)$ tensor. If each filter is a square of 5 by 5 numbers, and we have 6 filters, then the stack of filters is a $(5, 5, 6)$ tensor. Based on those inputs, let's calculate the dimensions of the output tensor.

There are multiple parameters to a convolution, and they can result in a tensor with different dimensions. In this book, however, we'll only use the default values of those parameters. For the default case, we can calculate the dimensions of the output like this:

- The *height* of the output is the height of the input, minus the height of the filter, plus 1. In our case, that's $100 - 5 + 1 = 96$

- The same rule applies to the *width* of the output, so that would also be 96.

- Each filter outputs one matrix, so the *depth* of the output tensor is equal to the number of filters.

Here's the convolution again, with the dimensions of all the tensors involved:

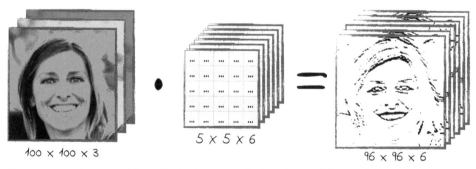

$100 \times 100 \times 3$      $5 \times 5 \times 6$      $96 \times 96 \times 6$

So now you have an idea of what a convolution looks like and how to calculate the dimensions of its result. Let's see how convolutions are used in a neural network.

## Convolutional Layers

Remember how a fully connected layer works—it's a matrix multiplication between the inputs and the weights, followed by an activation function, as shown in the diagram that follows:

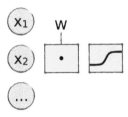

Now arrange the weights into a stack of filters, replace that matrix multiplication with a convolution (that is sometimes denoted by an asterisk), and boom! You get a convolutional layer, as shown in the next diagram:

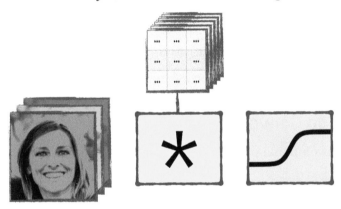

Note that both these diagrams are simplifications, because they show the input as a single image. In truth, a neural network generally processes multiple images at once, and the number of images adds another dimension to the input. So the input to a fully connected layer has not one, but two dimensions; the input to a convolutional layer has not three, but four dimensions. In both cases, we skip the first dimensions when we visualize the neural networks to avoid cluttering the diagrams.

Enough diagrams; let's see some code. Here is how you add a convolutional layer to a Keras model:

```
model.add(Conv2D(16, (3, 3), activation='relu'))
```

All the numbers in the preceding line are arbitrarily chosen hyperparameters that you can tune, and you'll get a chance to do so at the end of this chapter.

This specific convolutional layer has 16 filters, and each filter is a 3 by 3 square. Keras takes care of initializing the values in the filters, just like it does for the weights of a fully connected network. As usual, the activation is the layer's activation function—in this case, a ReLU.

Now you know what a single convolutional layer looks like. Let's put a few of those layers together and build our own CNN.

### Convolutions Can Get Complicated

As I talk about convolutions, I'm making a lot of implicit assumptions. First of all, I'm assuming that our convolutions operate on images. To process images, you need bi-dimensional convolutions called Conv2D in Keras. Different kinds of data might require higher-dimensional convolutions. For example, video has the additional dimension of time, and it could be processed with three-dimensional convolutions.

Even if you stick with bi-dimensional convolutions, there are more parameters to a convolution than just the filters. For example, a parameter named padding adds an empty frame around the input image to control the dimensions of the output.

If you decide to delve deeper into CNN, you'll take a long hard look at those variations on the main theme. In this book, we'll limit ourselves to run-of-the-mill convolutions.

## Running on Convolutions

Here is a convolutional neural network for CIFAR-10—all of it:

```
19_beyond/cifar10_cnn.py
import numpy as np
from keras.models import Sequential
from keras.layers import Conv2D, Dropout, Dense
from keras.layers import BatchNormalization, Flatten
from keras.optimizers import Adam
from keras.utils import to_categorical
from keras.datasets import cifar10

(X_train_raw, Y_train_raw), (X_test_raw, Y_test_raw) = cifar10.load_data()
X_train = X_train_raw / 255
X_test_all = X_test_raw / 255
X_validation, X_test = np.split(X_test_all, 2)
Y_train = to_categorical(Y_train_raw)
Y_validation, Y_test = np.split(to_categorical(Y_test_raw), 2)

model = Sequential()

model.add(Conv2D(16, (3, 3), activation='relu'))
model.add(BatchNormalization())
model.add(Dropout(0.5))
```

```
model.add(Conv2D(32, (3, 3), activation='relu'))
model.add(BatchNormalization())
model.add(Dropout(0.5))

model.add(Flatten())

model.add(Dense(1000, activation='relu'))
model.add(BatchNormalization())
model.add(Dropout(0.5))

model.add(Dense(512, activation='relu'))
model.add(BatchNormalization())
model.add(Dropout(0.5))

model.add(Dense(10, activation='softmax'))

model.compile(loss='categorical_crossentropy',
              optimizer=Adam(),
              metrics=['accuracy'])

history = model.fit(X_train, Y_train,
                    validation_data=(X_validation, Y_validation),
                    epochs=20, batch_size=32)
```

There were lot of decisions involved in writing this code, and to be honest, many of them were somewhat arbitrary. For example, I decided to have two convolutional layers, and to use ReLUs in every layer. I also made liberal use of the techniques from the previous chapter: batch normalization to improve accuracy, and dropout to reduce overfitting. I didn't check whether those decisions result in a better neural network than the alternatives. That exploration will be all yours, in this chapter's final exercise.

Some of the choices I made, however, are part of the default design of a CNN, and have been proven useful by many deep learning practitioners. One is the idea of building a CNN as a sequence of convolutional layers, followed by a handful of fully connected layers. Nothing prevents us from using convolutional layers throughout, but it's customary to have those fully connected layers at the end.

But wait—I'm getting ahead of myself here. Let's traverse the network from start to end, looking at each layer in detail.

First, the two convolutional layers:

```
model.add(Conv2D(16, (3, 3), activation='relu'))
model.add(BatchNormalization())
model.add(Dropout(0.5))

model.add(Conv2D(32, (3, 3), activation='relu'))
model.add(BatchNormalization())
model.add(Dropout(0.5))
```

I had to decide how many filters to use, and their size. For both layers, I used 3 by 3 filters. As for their number, I followed another common rule of thumb: the number of filters tends to grow as you traverse the network. I used 16 filters in the first layer, and 32 in the second layer. If this network had a third convolutional layer, I'd probably have used 64 filters in it.

It's always insightful, and often a bit painful, to calculate the dimensions of the tensors inside the network. If you wish, you can do that yourself, applying the rules from Convolutions, on page 252. Otherwise, let's do it together. A CIFAR-10 image is a $(32, 32, 3)$ tensor. After the first layer, its width and height become $32 - 3 + 1 = 30$, and its depth becomes equal to the number of filters. So the output of the first layer is a $(30, 30, 16)$ tensor. By the same rules, the output of the second layer is a $(28, 28, 32)$ tensor.

So far I said that convolutional layers take images as their input. To be more precise, that's only true of the input layer. From the second layer onwards, the image has become a stack of convolved data. In the next chapter, we'll consider the question of what a convolutional neural network sees in that convolved data, and how it understands images like the ones in CIFAR-10. For now, let's move forward in our examination of the neural network's code.

The next line solves the problem of passing data from the last convolutional layer to the first fully connected layer. At that point, the data must be flattened from a four-dimensional tensor of images to a bi-dimensional matrix of flat data. Keras' Flatten layer takes care of that:

```
model.add(Flatten())
```

When it reaches the Flatten layer, we calculated that each example has become a $(28, 28, 32)$ tensor. After the flattening, it becomes a row of $28 * 28 * 32 = 25088$ bytes. Those bytes pass through a couple of fully connected layers, and finally the output layer:

```
model.add(Dense(1000, activation='relu'))
model.add(BatchNormalization())
model.add(Dropout(0.5))

model.add(Dense(512, activation='relu'))
model.add(BatchNormalization())
model.add(Dropout(0.5))

model.add(Dense(10, activation='softmax'))
```

And that's it! The rest of the code comes straight from the fully connected network we had before.

Here's the result of 20 epochs of training:

```
Train on 50000 samples, validate on 5000 samples
Epoch 1 - loss: 1.7176 - acc: 0.4219 - val_loss: 1.2997 - val_acc: 0.5442
...
Epoch 20 - loss: 0.4808 - acc: 0.8305 - val_loss: 0.8315 - val_acc: 0.7334
```

It takes just one epoch for the CNN to beat the fully connected network. After 20 epochs, it blows the fully connected network out of the water.

Although it might not sound like a lot, 73% accuracy is pretty impressive considering how hard CIFAR-10 is, and the fact that I trained this network on my humble notebook. All things considered, we can grab that 73% and run with it!

## What You Just Learned

Before this chapter, we only built and trained *fully connected* neural networks, where each node is connected with all the nodes in the layers before and after it. In this chapter, we moved beyond that generic architecture to see an example of a more specialized one: a *convolutional neural network*.

Different than fully connected networks, CNNs preserve the multidimensional shape of data such as images. In a CNN, the weights are organized into structures called *filters* that detect the geometric features in the data. Each layer applies an operation called a *convolution* between its input and the filters. CNNS are better than fully connected networks at dealing with images, because they respect the spatial information in the images instead of squashing them to a mostly meaningless byte jam.

Finally, we built our own convolutional neural network. We applied a few common practices, like the idea of having a few convolutional layers followed by fully connected layers. When we trained the CNN, we were rewarded with a pretty good accuracy on the tough CIFAR-10 dataset.

Besides CNNs, deep learning spans many other architectures, each suited to different problems and different types of data. Speaking of which, we still didn't come to a conclusion on what deep learning is, how it works, and what its boundaries are. Those questions will be the subject of the closing chapter in this book.

## Hands On: Hyperparameters Galore

A CNN has more hyperparameters than you can shake a stick at. On top of the usual hyperparameters of fully connected layers, you also have to pick the number and size of filters in each layer. In case all those decisions aren't feeling overwhelming yet, also consider the additional parameters I mentioned in Convolutions Can Get Complicated, on page 256.

Your mission is to experiment with the hyperparameters of the CNN we built in this chapter. Tune those that you already know about, and maybe search online for the meaning of those we skipped. You probably won't be able to do very fine hyperparameters tuning, because that would require training the CNN for a long time—but you'll get to understand those options a little bit better, and maybe get a sense of how they impact the network's loss, accuracy, and training speed. Also take a chance to investigate how those hyperparameters impact the shape of a convolution's output.

This is the last Hands On in this book. It doesn't set a specific goal, and you won't find a solution for it in the book's source code, like you did for the others. Deep learning is still a brave new world, fit for people who like experimenting. This Hands On asks you to start experimenting yourself.

This experiment is also a chance to explore the material that's available on the Internet so that you'll be prepared when you finish this book and embark on a path to deep learning mastery. There's a lot of information out there—so take it easy, and have fun exploring!

# CHAPTER 20

# Into the Deep

Part III of this book has been a build-up to a revolution. In this last chapter, we'll finally examine the breakthrough known as *deep learning.*

With an additional car chase or two, the story of deep learning would make a great Hollywood movie. You know its beginning from Chapter 8, The Perceptron, on page 99: the clash between connectionists and symbolists, and how the connectionists were discredited and pushed into the basements of research.

You might remember the follow-up to that story from Part II of this book. In the 1970s, ML researchers discovered how to train neural networks with backpropagation. After years of struggle, they could finally overcome the limitations of perceptrons and tackle nonlinear data! For a while, it looked like connectionism was back—but as it happened, that new spark was also bound to fizzle out.

This chapter continues the story, up to the birth of deep learning. It also explains, to the best of what we know today, what makes deep learning so effective and such an improvement upon earlier methods. Finally, the last pages will point at a few trails you can walk after closing this book to delve deeper into this brave new world.

## The Rise of Deep Learning

In the 1990s, neural network research was in a rut again. After the discovery of backpropagation, connectionists had reaped a few high-profile successes, including a system to read handwritten numbers for the U.S. Postal Service.[1] And yet, the AI community at large still scoffed at neural networks.

---

1. yann.lecun.com/exdb/publis/pdf/lecun-89e.pdf

The general consensus was that yeah, regular neural networks could solve simple problems—but that was about as far as they could go. To tackle more interesting problems, you needed *deep* neural networks, and those were a pain in the neck. They were slow to train, prone to overfitting, and riddled by frustrating problems such as the vanishing gradient. Connectionists had cracked backpropagation, but they still couldn't win over their peers.

Then a few things happened that changed everything.

## Building Up to a Perfect Storm

The progress of machine learning from the 1990s to the early 2010s is the stuff of lore. In spite of the general skepticism around neural networks, a covenant of researchers kept advancing the field. Today, some of their names are famous: Geoffrey Hinton, Yahn LeCun, Yoshua Bengio, and many others.

One problem after the other, those stubborn pioneers tackled the most pressing issues of deep networks. They discovered novel weight initialization methods and activation functions like ReLUs to counter vanishing and exploding gradients. They sped up networks with better optimization algorithms and—again—better activation functions. They invented new regularization techniques such as dropout to keep overfitting in check.

At the same time, those trailblazers invented or perfected radically different ways to build neural networks. Fully connected networks struggled with complex data like images, text, and speech. Early deep network practitioners developed architectures that were custom-fit to those data, such as convolutional neural networks (which we looked at in the previous chapter), and recurrent neural networks (which I'll mention a few pages from now). Those new architectures made quick progress in corners of AI that had barely seen any improvement in dozens of years.

Besides their formidable skills and resolve, the pioneers of deep networks also had a fair share of luck. During those years, the world of computing underwent two sea changes that buoyed up their efforts: the diffusion of graphics processing units (GPUs), and the explosive rise of the Internet.

GPUs are the massively parallel graphics processors popularized by 3D computer games. In the 2000s, as progress on CPUs slowed down, GPUs were getting faster and faster—and they happened to fit neural networks like a glove. Like neural networks, 3D graphics rendering is mostly about churning through matrix operations, and doing it fast. Deep networks took forever to train on a CPU, but they could be trained dozens of times faster on a GPU.

The second boost to the connectionists' efforts came from the Internet, which helped solve a critical problem with early deep networks: even with all those clever regularization techniques, they kept overfitting their small datasets. In Collecting More Data, on page 225, you learned that the first defense against overfitting is collecting more data. When Internet companies burst onto the scene, they flooded researchers with previously unthinkable amounts of data—and the economic resources to process them.

In 2012, all those factors came together to form a perfect storm.

## The Tipping Point

In 2012, three deep networks researchers (Geoffrey Hinton, Alex Krizhevsky, and Ilya Sutskever) entered the high-profile ImageNet computer vision competition.[2] Up to then, ImageNet had been dominated by traditional techniques that boasted accuracies well below 75% on the benchmark dataset. The new challenger, a convolutional deep network called AlexNet, wiped the floor with the competition, with an astounding 84.7%. Nobody had ever seen anything like that.

It was a watershed moment. The name "deep learning," which replaced the disreputed name "neural networks," suddenly became a buzzword. As the research funds exploded, companies like Google and Facebook swept up the pioneers of the field, putting them at the helm of their nascent AI departments. Deep networks got deeper, reaching hundreds of layers—numbers that would have seemed ludicrous a few years before. Their evolution became hard to keep up with as they pulverized long-standing records across all fields of AI.

Soon enough, neural networks had become the most popular idea in machine learning. In the first chapter of this book, Chapter 1, How Machine Learning Works, on page 3, you learned that ML has three main branches: supervised learning, which is the subject of this book; reinforcement learning, which is all about learning by trial and error; and unsupervised learning, which is a collection of algorithms to make sense on unlabeled data. Deep neural networks seeped into all three, often displacing long-time established techniques.

Since the 1960s, connectionist ideas had been mostly cast out of the field of AI. In hindsight, AI had been impoverished by that exile. Over dozens of years, the brightest minds of artificial intelligence had gained a reputation for over-promising and underdelivering. Now, for the first time since Minsky's book on perceptrons, connectionists ideas were popular again—and AI was leaping

---

2. en.wikipedia.org/wiki/ImageNet

forward. Neural networks quickly displaced ineffective symbolist AI in crucial fields like natural language processing, image recognition, and medical diagnosis. Voice-controlled digital assistants, automatic photo captioning, and sophisticated recommendation systems became the new normal. Previously unthinkable technologies, such as self-driving cars, became a matter of public discussion. After all those years, connectionism was back with a vengeance.

## To Be Continued…

The rest of the story is still left to be written. In 2020, as I finish this book, the progress of deep learning shows no sign of slowing down. It's been hailed as a revolution in AI—a strangely enthusiastic definition from the traditionally staid academic community. For better or worse, deep learning is changing the world.

I mentioned a few factors behind this upheaval:

- Backpropagation, which allowed people to train neural networks in the first place.

- Dozens of novel techniques such as ReLUs, dropout, and Xavier initialization, which paved the way to deeper neural networks.

- New powerful architectures such as convolutional and recurrent neural networks, which boosted accuracy on complex datasets.

- More processing power, especially thanks to GPUs, which made deep networks not just possible, but practically feasible.

- Large datasets, which allowed deep networks to spend their power generalizing the training data, instead of overfitting it.

All those elements were important. However, they would have amounted to little if not for another, less concrete factor: the tenacity of the trailblazers who advanced machine learning through a decades-long pushback. They swam against the tide for all those years, cracking the problems that most of their colleagues deemed unsolvable. If we have deep learning today, it's thanks to them.

And that's how deep neural networks took over AI. But we still didn't investigate the secret sauce that makes them so good at what they do.

## Unreasonable Effectiveness

As you read through this book, you might have been surprised by the capabilities of simple programs like our first MNIST classifier. And yet, little prepares you for the uncanny capabilities of modern deep networks. In the words of one famous researcher, those networks are "unreasonably effective."[3] In a sense, they do nothing more than recognize patterns—and yet, they increasingly beat us at quintessentially human tasks, like facial recognition or medical diagnosis. How is that even possible?

Here's the short answer: we don't really know. As I write, nobody understands why deep neural networks work so well on so many tasks. Indeed, there's a lot of ongoing research bent to explain that fact.

At first sight, it's not even obvious why deeper networks work better than more shallow ones. A famous theorem from 1989 (called the "universal approximation theorem") proves that, with enough hidden nodes, even a humble three-layered network can approximate any function—that is, any possible dataset.[4] If shallow networks are good enough for any dataset, at least in theory, then why are deeper networks so much more accurate?

That question has been traditionally hard to answer because neural networks are mostly *opaque*—that is, it's hard to understand why a network takes a certain decision. You might be able to explain a small network by peeking at its internals, but as the numbers of nodes and layers grow, it quickly becomes impossible to wrap your mind around all those numbers. Indeed, researchers spend a lot of time inventing techniques to explain the decision making of neural networks in human terms.

A scientific paper from 2016 made a leap forward in explaining how deep networks see the world ("Towards Better Analysis of Deep Convolutional Neural Networks," by Mengchen Liu, Jiaxin Shi, Zhen Li, Chongxuan Li, Jun Zhu, and hixia Liu).[5] Using novel techniques, the authors visualized the "thinking" of a deep CNN, and showed that its layers work like levels of abstractions. As an image moves through the network, the first layers identify basic geometric features, like vertical or horizontal lines. Deeper layers identify more complex geometries, like circles. And even deeper layers catch higher-level details, like a human face, the fins of a Cadillac, or the beak of a platypus. In other words, each layer in a network outputs higher-level features for the next layer to work on, as illustrated in the diagram on page 266.

That's a striking discovery for a few reasons. First, that process resembles the workings of our visual cortex. As far as we know, neurons in the visual cortex are organized hierarchically, with lower-level neurons catching simple

3.    karpathy.github.io/2015/05/21/rnn-effectiveness

4.    www.academia.edu/9573599/On_the_approximate_realization_of_continuous_mappings_by_neural_networks

5.    arxiv.org/abs/1604.07043

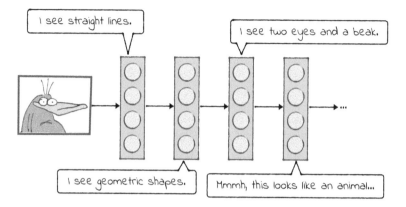

details, and higher-level neurons arranging those details into the face of our loved one, or the dismal sight of a fine on our windshield.

So, are neural networks similar to the wetware in our craniums? That's still hard to tell. On the one hand, it seems unlikely that our brains involve a mechanism similar to backpropagation. On the other hand, there are a few parallels between brains and neural networks, and this hierarchy of abstractions seems to be one of them.

There is a more practical reason why this progressive abstraction is crucial to AI. For many years, artificial intelligence has required a preliminary step of human analysis. For example, speech recognition usually required painstaking preparation: a human had to divide speech samples into sentences, words, and phonemes so that the computer could work on the basic building blocks of speech. This process is called *feature engineering*, or *feature extraction*. As you can imagine, it's error-prone and time-consuming.

Deep learning, however, made feature engineering mostly obsolete. Why bother breaking down a sentence into phonemes, or an image into geometric shapes, when the layers in a deep network do that on their own, unassisted? By now, we know that's one of the reasons that makes deep networks so good on unstructured data: they identify relevant features on their own, often better than a human could.

This book opened with a story. In Chapter 1, How Machine Learning Works, on page 3, I told you about my friend's impossible mission, when she was asked to code a pneumonia detector for X-ray scans. That task seemed impossible because we can't really spell out an algorithm to recognize pneumonia—so we can't code a computer to do it. Deep learning solved this problem by turning it on its head: you don't have to tell the computer which features are important. It will find out on its own.

And that, as far as we understand today, is what makes deep learning tick.

## Where Now?

You're reaching the end of this book, but I bet you're up for more. You have no shortage of things to learn. In fact, even if you track the field closely, it's hard to keep up with the barrage of exciting new ideas and techniques across the many areas of deep learning.

With so many possible paths to mastery, you might wonder which one to take. The next sections describe a few of those paths, including some topics I didn't even mention so far. See if any of these pique your interest.

### Learning a Machine Learning Library

For most of this book, we didn't use machine learning libraries at all. And when we finally got around to using Keras, we only learned the bare minimum we needed. As you continue exploring ML on your own, however, learning a library should be one of your priorities.

To begin with, I suggest you pick a popular, mainstream library. When I first delved into ML, I strived to find libraries and tutorials that supported my favorite languages. In hindsight, that was a waste of time, as I struggled to find well-maintained code and documented examples. In the end, I learned to go with the flow, and turned to the most widely used languages and libraries.

As I write, the two commonly used ML libraries are TensorFlow[a] and PyTorch.[b] Both are primarily Python libraries, even though TensorFlow expanded to become a platform that supports multiple languages. Unless you read this book while it's fresh off the presses, the situation might have changed already—so you'll have to do a bit of investigation to find what the state of the art is.

---

a.    www.tensorflow.org
b.    pytorch.org

### The Path of Vision

Your first option is to stay on the trail that we walked in the previous 270 or so pages: computer vision and CNNs. I picked image recognition as the storyline for this book because it makes for nice concrete examples—but even then, we only scratched the surface.

There is a lot more to do and learn in computer vision beyond recognizing images. One prominent subfield of computer vision these days is *object detection*. While image recognition answers questions like: "Does this picture represent a platypus?", object detection answers questions like: "Where are the platypuses in this picture?" As you can imagine, that's a crucial technology for self-driving cars, especially Australian ones. (As this book comes to a close, I admit the quality of my jokes is degrading.)

Computer vision isn't just about static images—it's also about video. There are many fascinating use cases for computer vision applied to video, including *pose estimation*, which detects the position of a human figure, and *motion estimation*, which tracks the movement of objects.

If you want to delve deeper into computer vision, you should learn more about CNNs. You should also look up a technique called *transfer learning*, which allows you to reuse a pretrained model on a different dataset. Transfer learning allows you to download a model that might have been trained on a large cluster of GPUs, and complete the training on your home machine. That technique can be useful in all areas of supervised learning, but it's most commonly used with CNNs.

## The Path of Language

Another area of ML that's in full bloom these days is the processing of natural language, such as speech or text. Just like computer vision has been upheaved by CNNs, natural language processing is the domain of *recurrent neural networks*—or RNNs for short.

Language works like a sequence of information, where the meaning of a word depends on the words before and after it. Fully connected networks don't jive well with this kind of data because they don't have memory. A training network takes a batch of independent examples, tweaks its weights to approximate them, and then all but forgets about them. With no memory of what's come before, a fully connected network gets stumped in the middle of a sentence, staring at a word out of context, without hope of grokking its meaning.

By contrast, recurrent neural networks have a form of memory. While the information in a regular network only moves forward, the information in RNNs can loop back into the same layer or an earlier one, as shown in the diagram on page 269.

Because of those loops, an RNN can process sequence-like data. It understands a piece of information based on the information that came before it—like your brain is doing right now as you read these sentences.

Loops make a neural network more complicated. In a sense, they also make it deeper. Think about it: if a layer feeds back into itself from one iteration to

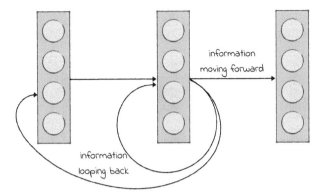

the other, then you can imagine unrolling it into a sequence of regular layers, each of which represents one iteration of the original layer:

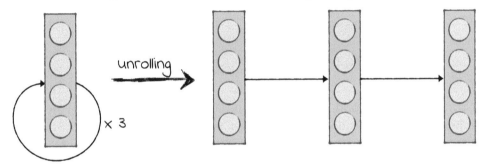

For that reason, even pretty shallow RNNs suffer from the same problems as deeper networks, like the vanishing gradient. Only in the late 1990s did researchers find a reliable a way to ameliorate those problems when they invented the weirdly named *long short-term memory* architecture. That architecture is the basis of today's surprisingly accurate text processing systems, such as Google Translate.

So, in general, you should focus more on CNNs if you're attracted by computer vision, and RNNs if you're fascinated by natural language processing. Now let's look at another option that's a bit more far out.

## The Path of Image Generation

Image generation is all about synthesizing images, either by modifying existing ones, or by creating new ones from scratch. To me, the most amazing invention in this field are *generative adversarial networks*, or GANs, invented by a young researcher called Ian Goodfellow in 2014. GANs are the technology behind those uncanny fake pictures and videos that you might have seen on the Internet.

Here is a concrete example to help you understand GANs. To experiment with this concept, I started by selecting a bunch of horse pictures from the CIFAR-10 dataset. Here are a few of those:

Imagine building a CNN to tell these horse pictures from other pictures that don't contain a horse. Let's call this network the *discriminator*, as shown in this diagram:

Now imagine a second, somewhat unusual, neural network. This network takes a random sequence of bytes as input, and passes it through its parameterized model to turn it into an image. It might use an architecture similar to a regular CNN, only tweaked to generate images as output instead of taking them as input, as shown in the next diagram:

This second network is called the *generator*, even though all it generates before it's trained is random pixel jam.

Now comes the brilliant idea behind GANs. Connect the output of the generator to the input of the discriminator, and train the two networks in tandem as shown in the diagram on page 271.

The trick of this architecture is that the loss functions of the two networks are carefully chosen to pit them against one another:

- The discriminator is receiving a random mix of horse pictures and pictures from the generator. It gets a lower loss when it correctly tells apart the horses from the generated images.

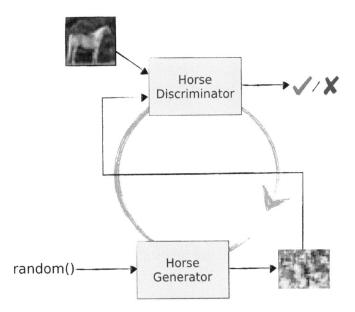

- On its part, the generator gets rewarded when the discriminator gets it wrong. Its loss is higher if the discriminator identifies its output as generated, and lower if the discriminator confuses it for a horse.

Do you see where this is going? The whole systems works like a competition between an expert that identifies fake images, and a forger that attempts to counterfeit them. As a result, the discriminator and the generator improve together as you train them.

I assembled such a contraption myself. Following are a few randomly chosen images from the generator, taken every 50 iterations of training:

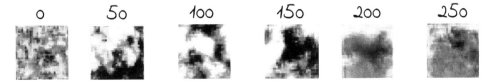

In the beginning, the generator outputs meaningless noise. After 200 iterations, it already seems to output images that are mostly green at the bottom, mostly blue at the top, and contain vague brownish shape. Those are common traits of horse pictures, which usually involve blue skies and grassy fields. At the same time, the discriminator is improving at weeding out synthetic pictures.

After a few hours and about one million iterations of training, the generator
has become pretty darn good:

Just to be clear, none of these pictures are a straight copy of a CIFAR horse.
Indeed, the generator has never ever seen a horse picture—it just learned
what a horse looks like by learning how to cheat the discriminator. As a result,
it forged these weirdly crooked, but undisputedly horse-like creatures.

These images come from my humble laptop and a pair of sloppily hacked
neural networks. If you want to see the state of the art, the Internet has more
generated images than you can shake a stick at. The site known as "This
person does not exist," for one, generates jaw-droppingly realistic human
faces.[6] GANs also power Google's famous Deep Dream image generator.[7]

That's it about GANs. Before leaving the topic of image generation, I have to
at least mention *style transfer*—another brilliant idea that became popular
in the last few years. You've seen it before: it's the technique that redraws
photos in the style of pencil drawings, watercolor, or famous painters. Style
transfer uses an algorithm similar to neural networks, but instead of optimizing the network's weights, it works directly on an image's pixels. Here's my
portrait as painted by Edvard Munch:

I don't really have that red face and thick mustache, but this picture is still
an artistic improvement over my original muzzle. Once again, the Internet

6.  thispersondoesnotexist.com
7.  deepdreamgenerator.com

has more examples, tutorials, and style transfer web apps than you probably need. If you're willing to take the path of image generation, then you're well covered.

### The Broad Path

I strove to make this book feel like a straight, narrow road through the vast landscape of ML. We focused on supervised learning, and specifically on supervised learning with neural networks. If you're a "big picture" kind of person, however, you might aim for broader knowledge, as opposed to deeper knowledge. In that case, you might want to look at other machine learning flavors and techniques off the path of this book.

For one, the field of reinforcement learning deserves more attention than I could grant it in these pages. Its recent successes compete with those of supervised learning. To mention one story that hit the front pages: AlphaGo, the program that made a sensation by beating a human at the ancient game of Go, uses reinforcement learning.[8]

Unsupervised learning is ML applied to unlabeled data, and it's also a hot topic these days. Among other things, people are coming up with clever ways to use neural networks to compress or cluster data.

Another exciting branch of ML is called *semi-supervised learning*, and it uses a mixture of labeled and unlabeled data to train a machine learning system. It's often easier to collect large amounts of unlabeled data than labeled data, and semi-supervised learning can be a brilliant way to use all those extra data.

Even if you stick to supervised learning, however, you have plenty to look at, especially if you like computer science or statistics. While this book focused on neural networks, there are other algorithms worth learning, and some of them still work better than neural networks in specific circumstances. For a couple of examples, take a look at *support vector machines* and *random forests*.

### The Hands-On Path

Last but not least, here is one final path into the world of machine learning, and the one that I find most exciting as a developer. Instead of cherry-picking a subfield of ML up front, keep your options open, and join a competition on Kaggle—a popular platform that organizes ML challenges.[9]

---

8. en.wikipedia.org/wiki/AlphaGo
9. www.kaggle.com/competitions

Kaggle competitions are a great way to dip your toes into concrete problems. Some of those competitions are high-level business, targeted to academic teams armed with state of the art techniques. Others, clearly marked for beginners, are ideal introductions to pragmatic ML.

As you expect, the realities of a project tend to be twistier and messier than the streamlined story in this book. As you go through your first competition, you might feel like an absolute beginner again. You might need to prepare your data in ways that you didn't expect. Instead of being either numerical or categorical, your input variables might be a mix of both. You'll have to decide how to attack each problem on your own. You might need to study new techniques, and even when you don't, those first lines of code may give you the dreaded blank page effect.

Don't let those early difficulties frustrate you. Deep learning is huge—as vast a topic as programming—but by going through this book, you laid a foundation that you can now build upon. It might take you time to find your bearings on a real project, but keep going. You'll soon feel comfortable dealing with a variety of data, architectures, and libraries.

## Your Journey Begins

This book began with a wide-eyed look at the earlier machine learning ideas of the 1950s. It ends on the shores of deep learning and today's cutting-edge techniques. That was quite the journey!

Now another journey begins, and it's entirely your own. I've pointed at a few possible trails worth following, but the choice is yours. It's time for us to part ways. (Well, not quite. You can always reach me on Twitter, if you wish. My handle is *@nusco*.)

Congratulations for coming this far, and accept my humble thanks for reading this book. It's been a pleasure introducing you to these world-changing techniques. May they change your own world for the better.

Godspeed!

# Just Enough Python

Welcome to Python! These days, Python is *the* language for machine learning. From the research labs to the biggest AI companies, Python snaked its way everywhere. (See what I did here?)

Python is a great language all around, but it fits ML particularly well—for two reasons. First, it comes with powerful numerical and scientific libraries. Second, Python is powerful, but also easy to approach. Many people in the ML community lack a background in programming, and would be intimidated by a less friendly language.

Don't get me wrong: Python isn't a toy language that you can learn in a day. It comes with sophisticated features that take time to learn and master. The examples in this book, however, avoid those features in favor of a small subset of Python. This appendix is a day trip through that mini-Python. Read it, and you'll know just enough of the language to read and modify the code in this book.

Here is what we'll talk about:

- We'll see what Python code looks like, and describe the fundamental features of the language.

- We'll get a whirlwind tour of Python's basic building blocks: types such as strings and collections, and control structures such as loops.

- We'll learn to define and call Python functions.

- We'll learn how to work with multiple files and how to install libraries.

- Finally, we'll take a quick look at Python's object oriented features.

At the end, I'll tell you where to look for more in-depth information.

This appendix moves at a much faster pace than the rest of the book. We won't linger on basic programming concepts that you already know. In most

> ## Jupyter Notebooks
>
> Being a developer, you're accustomed to coding with IDEs, or maybe a combo of a text editor and the command line. By contrast, most people in the ML community write their code in a tool called Jupyter Notebook.[a] Jupyter allows you to type and run Python code in a web page, mixed with descriptive text. Imagine a simple in-browser text editor that also executes code snippets, and you pretty much get the idea.
>
> Jupyter has two advantages over the classic developer's toolset:
>
> 1. It allows you to mix Python code with formatted text, images, and data visualizations like charts and tables. That's a big deal for data scientists, who often need to explain the context, input, and output of their system.
>
> 2. With their gigantic toolbars and hundreds of keyboard shortcuts, IDEs are intimidating. As for text editors like vim… if you're into those, then you know that they can positively scare off a beginner. By contrast, Jupyter is friendly and welcoming, especially to people who lack a programming background. Jupyter allows them to type and run code in the familiar context of a web page.
>
> You don't have to use Jupyter to read this book. All the examples in these pages come as *.py files, and you should feel free to edit them in your favorite IDE or text editor. If you prefer to use Jupyter, however, you have that option: you'll find notebook versions of all the examples in the notebooks directory.
>
> ----
>
> a.    jupyter.org

cases, we'll glance at a few lines of code, see what Python's syntax looks like, and move forward. Maybe have a browser handy as you read through, in case you want to dig a bit deeper into a specific Python feature.

While you're at your computer, you might want to type Python statements as you read through. Open a terminal and check that you have Python 3 installed.

```
python3 --version
```

If the python3 command fails, then try the python command, without a version number—but make sure that your version of Python is 3.7 or later. If you don't have Python, or you have an earlier version, then look for an installation method that works for you and your system. You'll find a few on the official "Installing Python" page.[1] If you want to go with the flow, you can also do like most people in the machine learning community, and install Python via the Conda package manager.[2]

----

1.    realpython.com/installing-python
2.    conda.io

There are two main ways to run Python code. One is to write a Python program in a file with a *.py* extension, and execute it:

```
python3 my_code.py
```

You can also execute Python code in an interactive Python interpreter. Start it with the `python3` command, without a file name. Once the interpreter is running, you can execute Python statements on the fly—like this one:

```
print("Hello, Python!")
```

Oh, by the way: it's always embarrassing when you don't know how to close an interactive interpreter. In Python, you do that with the exit() command, or by pressing Ctrl-D.

## What Python Looks Like

Python code is famously easy to read. It has even been described half-jokingly as "executable pseudocode." For example, you can probably understand a lot of the following program, even if you have no Python experience at all:

```
just_enough_python/find_prime_numbers.py
# Import the square root function
from math import sqrt

# Return True if the argument is a prime number, False otherwise
def is_prime(n):
    # n is prime if it cannot be divided evenly by any number in
    # the range from 2 to the square root of n.
    max_check_value = sqrt(n)
    # range(a, b) goes from a included to b excluded. Both a and b
    # must be integers, so we convert max_check_value to an integer
    # with the in-built int() function.
    for x in range(2, int(max_check_value) + 1):
        # Check the remainder of the integer division of n by x
        if n % x == 0:
            return False  # n can be divided by x, so it's not prime
    return True  # n is prime


MAX_RANGE = 100
primes = []
print("Computing the prime numbers from 2 to %d:" % MAX_RANGE)
for n in range(2, MAX_RANGE):
    if is_prime(n):
        primes.append(n)
print(primes)
```

This program finds the prime numbers in the range from 2 to 100. It's short, but it uses most of the features of Python that you need for this book. If you can understand all of it, then you shouldn't have trouble understanding the examples in this book. If you can't... well, that's what this appendix is all about.

A lot of Python's readability is a consequence of two features of the language: dynamic typing, and significant whitespace. Let's discuss them.

## Python Is Dynamically Typed

In Python, you don't declare the types of variables. You just assign a value to them, and they spring into existence:

```
x = "Hello!"
x = 42
```

In the preceding code, the variable x doesn't have a type constraint, so it can hold values of any type—in these two lines, a string and an integer.

As a programmer, you probably have a strong opinion about type systems. If you're used to languages such as JavaScript or Ruby, then you might appreciate the terseness and versatility of dynamic typing. On the other hand, if your daily languages is Java, C#, or C, then you might favor the safety and consistency of explicit type declarations, such as int x = 42.

If you're not used to dynamic typing, I suggest you give it a fair chance. It's always worth having a dynamically typed language like Python in your toolbox.

## In Python, Indentation Matters

Python has a unique way to delimit a block of code, like the body of a function, or the body of a loop. For that purpose, most languages use special characters such as curly braces, or keywords like begin and end. By contrast, you delimit Python blocks by indenting them. Look at this contrived snippet of code:

```
x = 7
if x > 5:
    print("x is greater than 5")
    print("And while we're here...")
    if x < 10:
        print("...it's also smaller than 10")
else:
    print("x is less or equal than 5")
```

The code between the if x > 5 statement and the else statement is a single block, because it's all indented the same. The line after the if x < 10 statement is a nested one-line block, because it's indented further. The line after the else is also a one-line block. This program prints:

```
x is greater than 5
And while we're here...
...it's also smaller than 10
```

You can indent the lines in a block with either spaces or tabs, as long as you do so consistently. Whitespace actually has a meaning in Python!

Significant whitespace is by far the most controversial feature of the language. Some programmers love it. For others... well, it can be an acquired taste. If you're in the second camp, consider the advantages of significant whitespace: it keeps the indentation style consistent across different programmers, and it removes the need for noisy braces and semicolons.

Now that you know what Python code looks like, let's get into a bit more detail.

### Readable by Convention

Look at Python code from multiple programmers, and you'll see that it tends to have a common, uniform style. We discuss one reason for that consistency in the section In Python, Indentation Matters, on page 278. Another reason is that the Python community is serious about coding conventions. They even have an official stylesheet that is revered by coders and automatically checked by IDEs.[a]

Here are a couple of examples of consistent style in Python. Almost all programmers use "snake case" for the names of Python's variables and functions, as in this_is_a_variable, or is_prime(). As a second example, Python has no language-level support for constants, but if you want to let the reader know that a variable is meant to be a constant, then you name it with uppercase letters separated by underscores, as in MAX_RANGE.

Fair warning: ignoring these naming conventions will expose you to frowning by vocal Pythonistas.

---

a.     www.python.org/dev/peps/pep-0008/

## Python's Building Blocks

I don't know about you—for me, the boring part of learning a new language is the mandatory listing of basic types, operators, and control structures. Whenever I try to memorize the finer points of loop syntax and operator precedence, that information slips right off my brain. It only sticks once I start writing code.

For that reason, I won't bog you down in details that you can look up yourself later, when you're confronted with real code. I'll keep this section on types, operators, and control structures as brief as possible, providing a broad overview and only zooming in on those few details that are important for this book.

## Data Types and Operators

Python comes with the data types you expect: integers, floating-point numbers, booleans, strings—the works:

```
an_integer = 42
a_float = 0.5
a_boolean = True
a_string = "abc"
```

As for Python's operators, you'll probably find them familiar across the board:

```
an_integer + a_float    # => 42.5
an_integer >= a_float   # => True
a_float * 2             # => 1.0
an_integer / 10         # => 4.2
an_integer % 10         # => 2
not a_boolean           # => False
a_boolean or False      # => True
a_string + 'def'        # => 'abcdef'
```

Compared to some other dynamic languages like JavaScript or Perl, Python is strict about mixing types. While the language does cast types automatically in some cases, potentially ambigous operations usually result in an error:

```
# Implicit cast from an integer to a boolean:
not 10     # => False

# Failing implicit cast from an integer to a string:
"20" + 20  # => TypeError: must be str, not int
```

If you need to convert Python values from one type to the other, you generally do so explicitly, with functions such as str(), int(), and bool():

```
"20" + str(20)  # => '2020'
```

We'll get a closer look at Python's strings in a minute—but first, let's look at variables that contain multiple values.

## Collections

Every modern language supports variables with multiple ordered values, usually called "arrays," "lists," or "vectors." Python has two such multi-valued collection types: *lists* and *tuples*.

Here is what tuples look like:

```
just_enough_python/collections.py
a_tuple = (3, 9, 12, 7, 1, -4)
len(a_tuple)  # => 6
a_tuple[2]    # => 12
a_tuple[2:5]  # => (12, 7, 1)
```

You create a tuple by wrapping a sequence of comma-separated values in round brackets. The preceding code demonstrates a couple of things you can do with tuples: getting their length, and getting one or more of their elements (using zero-based indexes).

Tuples are immutable: once you create one, it cannot change. If you want a mutable collection of values... that's what lists are for. They look similar to tuples—only they use square brackets, and they are mutable:

```
a_list = [10, 20, 30]
a_list[1] = a_list[1] + 2
a_list.append(100)
a_list  # => [10, 22, 30, 100]
```

Python being dynamic, tuples and lists can contain values of any type, or even a mix of types. As an example, each element in the following list has a different type, including a tuple and another list:

```
a_mixed_list = ['a', 42, False, (10, 20), 99.9, a_list]
```

Lists and tuples will both appear in this book's source code—but they won't get the spotlight. The most common collection we'll use, by far, is the powerful array type from the NumPy library. There's no need to linger on arrays here, because you're going to get familiar with them as you read the book. Just know that they look a bit like Python's lists, but they have multiple dimensions—so they're perfect to represent matrices, which are a common data structure in ML.

In this appendix, we're going to skip over the *dictionary*—Python's take on key–value collections. The reason we're passing over dictionaries is that we don't happen to use them in the book. However, if you want to do some Python coding of your own, then dictionaries are one of the first features you should look up.

We're almost done with Python's basic types. We only need to give a closer look at strings.

## Strings

You can define a string with either double or single quotes:

```
just_enough_python/strings.py
s1 = "This is a string"
s2 = 'this is also a string'
s1 + " and " + s2  # => 'This is a string and this is also a string'
```

Python programmers tend to use double quotes, and switch to single quotes when the string itself contains double quotes:

```
print('Yup, this is yet another "Hello, World!" example')
```

A string behaves pretty much like a tuple of characters, which is why we looked at collections first. In particular, you can index a string's individual characters:

```
s3 = s2[8:12]
s3  # => 'also'
```

There is another way in which Python's strings look like tuples, and it will please the functional programmers among you (you know who you are): strings are immutable. You cannot modify a string in place—you have to create a new string, as I did in the preceding code.

One feature that we use a lot in this book is string interpolation—a way to embed variables in a string. Python offers a few ways to do string interpolation, but we're going to stick with the "classic" style, because it's compatible with all modern versions of Python. It looks like this:

```
a = 1
b = 99.12345
c = 'X'
"The values of these variables are %d, %.2f, and %s" % (a, b, c)
# => The values of these variables are 1, 99.12, and X
```

The % sign separates the string from a tuple of values that must be embedded in it. The embedding positions are marked by special codes, that are also prefixed by a %. In particular, %d means "embed as a decimal number," %s means "embed as a string," and %.2f means "embed as a floating-point number rounded to two decimal places."

Finally, if you want to print a percent sign inside an interpolated string, you need to escape it by typing double percent signs:

```
"Less than %.d%% of ML books have a hammer on the cover" % a
# => Less than 1% of ML books have a hammer on the cover
```

## Loops

Python comes with the usual C-style control structures: if, while, for, and their ilk. We already saw how to use if in our first Python example, in What Python Looks Like, on page 277. As for while, we won't use it in this book.

On the other hand, we'll use for loops all the time. Here is what they look like:

just_enough_python/loop.py
```
for i in range(4):
    if i % 2 == 0:
        print("%d is an even number" % i)
    else:
        print("%d is an odd number" % i)
```

The for loop iterates over the values in the range:

```
0 is an even number
1 is an odd number
2 is an even number
3 is an odd number
```

Note that the range includes 0, but excludes 4.

Experienced Python coders tend to shun for loops, in favor of more elegant constructs inspired by functional programming. We won't use those constructs in this book. If you're curious, check out Python's list comprehension.[3]

With that, we've completed our tour of Python's basic types, operators, and control structures. Let's move on to another fundamental feature of the language: functions.

## Defining and Calling Functions

In most programming languages, you cannot go far without defining and calling your own functions. In Python, you define a function with the def keyword:

just_enough_python/functions.py
```
def welcome(user):
    PASSWORD = "1234"
    message = "Hi, %s! Your new password is %s" % (user, PASSWORD)
    return message
```

This function generates a password for a new user. (Admittedly, the default password isn't the most secure—but hey, at least it's popular.) Then it composes a welcome message, and returns the message to the caller.

3. docs.python.org/3/tutorial/datastructures.html

Pythonically, you don't need to delimit the function's body with brackets—you just indent it. Also, being Python dynamically typed, you don't need to specify the type of the user parameter, or the type of the function's return value. Taken together, these features make for a very concise function declaration.

Once you have a function defined, you can call it:

```
welcome("Roberto")  # => 'Hi, Roberto! Your new password is 1234'
```

Python has a few different flavors of function arguments. Let's look at them.

> ## Changing Your Arguments
>
> In case you're wondering, Python's function parameters are passed by reference, not by copy. That means that if you pass a mutable argument to a function, the function might modify it. Here is a function that adds an element to a list:
>
> ```
> def modify_list(l):
>     l.append(42)
>
> a_list = [1, 2, 3]
> modify_list(a_list)
> a_list  # => [1, 2, 3, 42]
> ```
>
> In most cases, you don't want to have your arguments modified behind your back. Polite functions generally don't modify their arguments, and treat them as if they were read-only—unless modifying the argument is the entire point of the function, as in the case here.

## Named Arguments

You can use *named arguments*, also called *keyword arguments*, to make a function call easier to read. Let's look at an example.

Assume that your boss just saw the welcome() function from the previous section, and he really liked it—but he's concerned that the password isn't very secure. He proposes a solution: add a secure argument to the function. If secure is True, then the function should generate a more secure password.

Here is the updated welcome() function:

```
def welcome(user, secure):
    if secure:
        PASSWORD = "123456"
    else:
        PASSWORD = "1234"
    return "Hi, %s! Your new password is %s" % (user, PASSWORD)
```

We don't mess around with security here, buddy. Now we can call the function with the secure flag on:

```
welcome("Roberto", True)  # => Hi, Roberto! Your new password is 123456
```

Note, however, that the function call here has a readability issue: if you don't know what that True argument means, then you have no way of finding out, short of looking at the function definition. It would be nice to show clearly that True is the value of the secure argument. You can do that by using named arguments:

```
welcome("Roberto", secure=True)  # => Hi, Roberto! Your new password is 123456
```

Now the call is more readable. As an added bonus, named arguments allow us to change the order of the arguments in the call—although I'll leave it to you to decide whether that's a good idea in general:

```
welcome(secure=False, user="Mike")  # => Hi, Mike! Your new password is 1234
```

We're not quite done with function arguments yet. There is one last useful feature related to them, and we use it a lot in this book.

## Default Arguments

The boss just asked for a few more changes to the security system. He wants the function to work even if we don't provide the user's name. Besides, he wants the password to be secure by default, unless the caller specificies otherwise.

We can implement both features by specifying the arguments' default values in the function definition:

```
def welcome(user="dear user", secure=True):
    if secure:
        PASSWORD = "123456"
    else:
        PASSWORD = "1234"
    return "Hi, %s! Your new password is %s" % (user, PASSWORD)
```

Now we can skip one or both arguments, and they'll take their default values:

```
welcome()  # => Hi, dear user! Your new password is 123456
```

You can even mix and match named arguments and default arguments:

```
welcome(secure=False)  # => Hi, dear user! Your new password is 1234
```

With that, you know everything you need about Python functions and their arguments. And just to be clear: I do not recommend this code to generate passwords in production. You never know... it might contain non-obvious security bugs.

# Working with Modules and Packages

A short Python program can happily live in a single file—but as soon as you write a larger program, you need a way to organize its code. Above functions, Python has two more levels of code organization: functions and other code live in *modules*, and modules live in *packages*. Let's start by looking at modules.

## Defining and Importing Modules

A module defines entities such as constants and functions that you can import and use in a program. Aside from some of the in-built modules of the Python interpreter, a module is a Python file.

For example, here is a module named my_module.py:

just_enough_python/my_module.py
```
THE_ANSWER = 42

def ask():
    return THE_ANSWER
```

This file defines a function and a constant. Now imagine that we have a Python program in the same directory. This program can import either (or both) definitions with the import keyword:

just_enough_python/my_program.py
```
from my_module import ask, THE_ANSWER
```

When you import a module, two things happen:

- First, the code in the module is executed.
- Second, the names you imported become available in your program.

For example, now my_program can call the ask() function:

```
ask()        # => 42
```

Note that the code in the module is executed only the first time you import it. If you import a module more than once, Python marks it as "already imported" the first time around, and ignores subsequent imports.

Instead of cherry-picking the names you want to import, as we did before, you could instead import the entire module:

just_enough_python/import_everything.py
```
import my_module
```

This line will import all the names defined in my_module.py. When you import an entire module like that, however, those names might clash with other names in the main program, or in another module. To avoid those clashes, Python forces you to prefix the names with the name of the module, like this:

```
my_module.ask()        # => 42
my_module.THE_ANSWER   # => 42
```

To avoid prefixing the same long module name dozens of time, you can give a shorter name to the module when you import it, like this:

just_enough_python/module_renaming.py
```
import my_module as mm
mm.ask()   # => 42
```

For example, the numpy library is almost always shortened to np, like this:

```
import numpy as np
```

After the renaming, you can make a reference to the NumPy functions with the np prefix, as in np.multiply(x, y).

## The Standard Library

Python prides itself on being "batteries included," meaning that it comes with a bunch of useful modules right out of the box. For example, the math module gives you the basic mathematical functions and constants:

```
import math
math.sqrt(16)   # => 4.0
math.pi         # => 3.141592653589793
```

Note that math.pi doesn't follow Python's conventions for the names of constants—if it did, then it would be called math.PI. The standard library is showing its years here, as that name dates back earlier than the current naming conventions.

## The main Idiom

When it comes to modules, we have one last topic to mention. It concerns a very common Python idiom.

We said that a file of Python code can be either a program, or a module, depending on how you use it. You execute a program directly, with a command like python3 my_code.py. By contrast, you use a module by importing it in another file.

However, it's common for the same Python file to play both roles. A file with this binary nature can either be run as a stand-alone program, or imported as a module. Here is one such file:

```
just_enough_python/greetings.py
print("Executing the code in greetings.py")

def greet(name):
    print("Hello,", name)

if __name__ == "__main__":
    greet("human")
```

Ignore the last two lines in the file for a minute. If we import greetings.py from another file, the usual things happen: first, the code in greetings.py is executed; and second, we can access the greet() function:

```
just_enough_python/greetings_demo.py
import greetings
greetings.greet("Bill")
```

If you run python3 greetings_demo.py, you get:

```
Executing the code in greetings.py
Hello, Bill
```

However, you can also run greetings.py as a stand-alone program, by typing python3 greetings.py. In that case, you get:

```
Executing the code in greetings.py
Hello, human
```

The secret to running the file as a program is in the idiom if __name__ == "__main__". (That's a double underscore both before and after name and main.) This idiom stands for: "only execute the following code if this file is run directly." By contrast, if the file gets imported, then the Python interpreter skips the if block.

To see how this idiom is useful, imagine writing a program that defines a bunch of functions, and then uses those functions to interact with the user. When you load the file from another program, you want to skip the user interaction—but you still want to access the functions, to reuse or test them. You can fence the user interaction behind the if... "__main__" idiom, and it will be executed only when the file runs as the main program.

You'll see the if... "__main__" idiom throughout this book, and in the source code of most Python libraries.

## Managing Packages

Above modules, packages are the next level of code organization. A package is essentially a bundle of modules, organized in a directory structure.

In this book, we don't define our own packages—but we use them all the time, for one reason: when you install a Python library, that library comes in the form of a package.

There are multiple ways to install Python libraries. Most Python developers use the *pip* package manager. Others prefer an alternative tool named Conda, which I already mentioned as one way to install the Python language itself. Let's look at both tools.

### Installing Packages with *pip*

*pip*[4] is Python's official package manager. Its name is a recursive acronym that stands for "pip Installs Packages." (Yup, the Python community has a warped sense of humor. After all, the name of the language is a homage to the Monty Pythons.)

If you have Python installed, chances are you also have pip. You can use it to install one of the many packages from PyPI,[5] that stands for "Python Package Index"—Python's official package repository. For example, this command installs version 2.3.1 of the Keras machine learning library:

```
pip3 install keras==2.3.1
```

Once you have Keras installed, you can use its modules from a Python program. This line imports the serialize() function from the keras.metrics module:

```
from keras.metrics import serialize
```

To be precise, keras is a module in the Keras library, and metrics is a submodule of keras.

pip has all the features you expect in a package manager: you can install a specific version of a package, list the packages installed, and so on. If you're looking for a simple out-of-the-box system to install libraries, pip has you covered. If you want something more sophisticated... then keep reading.

### Installing Packages with Conda

Conda[6] is the package manager of choice in the ML community. It's part of a hefty Python distribution called Anaconda[7] that's especially tailored to data science.

---

4.   pip.pypa.io
5.   pypi.org
6.   conda.io
7.   www.anaconda.com

Anaconda comes with a lot of bells and whistles, including an IDE and its own repository of packages, separated from the official Python repository. If you don't need the extras, then you can install Miniconda,[8] which is a much slimmer install that only includes Conda and Python.

When it comes to installing a package, Conda works pretty much the same as pip:

```
conda install keras=2.3.1
```

However, Conda has a couple of selling points over pip. For one, where pip focuses on Python libraries, Conda can handle data science packages written in different languages. Also, Conda allows you to create "environments" that you can activate and deactivate on the fly. Each environment can have a different set of libraries. By contrast, packages installed with pip are global: all the Python code on your machine sees the same version of the package.

Conda also integrates well with pip: if you want a package that's only available in the PyPI repository, but not in Conda's repository, you can run pip install in a Conda environment, and the package will only be visible in that environment.

To sum it up, the choice between pip and Conda usually boils down to this: if you're okay with globally installed packages, then use pip; if you prefer to maintain separate environments that contain different packages (for example, a different set of packages for each project), then use Conda.

You'll need to install a few packages to run the code in this book. Setting Up Your System, on page 11 contains instructions to install them with pip. If you opt for Conda, then take a look at the readme.txt in the book's source code.

## Creating and Using Objects

Python is an *object-oriented* language. The code in this book, however, is targeted at programmers from all walks of life, including those who aren't used to objects—so I avoided object-oriented programming in most of this book. There are only a few examples where I used object-oriented programming, because some library required it. This short section tells you everything you need to understand those examples.

You can see a Python *object* as a special kind of variable. Regular variables belong to the language's built-in types, such as float or bool. By contrast, objects belong to types that are defined by yourself, or by a library. These higher-level types are called *classes*.

---

8. docs.conda.io/en/latest/miniconda.html

For example, Python has no built-in type for dates—but the standard library datetime defines a class named date. Import that library, and you can create date objects:

```
just_enough_python/objects.py
from datetime import date
moon_landing = date(1969, 7, 20)
```

Running these two lines creates a variable called moon_landing that contains a date. To create that date, we passed it a year, a month, and a day.

In some other languages, you use the keyword new to create an object. In Python, you just use the name of the class, followed by parentheses. You pass the object creation parameters inside the parentheses, just like you would for a regular function call.

Once you have an object, you can call its *methods*. Methods are like functions that are specific to the object's class. For example, dates have a weekday() method that returns the day of the week, from 0 to 6:

```
moon_landing.weekday()   # => 6
```

Now we know that the moon landing happened on a Sunday.

Just like functions, some methods take arguments. For example, the date class has a replace() method that returns a copy of the date with a different year, month, or day. It also has a method called strftime() that formats the data according to a format string. Here's a snippet of code that uses those two methods:

```
viking_1_mars_landing = moon_landing.replace(year=1976)
viking_1_mars_landing.strftime("%d/%m/%y")   # => 20/07/76
```

Also like functions, methods can have default arguments, and can be called with named arguments.

For historical reasons, the name of the date class is all lowercase—but today it's customary to use camel case for class names, as in ThisIsAClass. For example, the Keras library that we use in Part III of this book defines classes with names like Sequential, BatchNormalization, and MaxPooling2D.

In some languages, such Java and C#, you cannot even write a basic program without classes and objects. By contrast, Python's object-oriented features are almost optional. You can easily write a procedural Python program without any objects or classes… Or at least, that's until you take a deeper look, and you find out that objects and classes are woven right into Python's fabric. For example, strings are actually objects with their own methods:

```
'strings are objects'.upper()  # => 'STRINGS ARE OBJECTS'
```

Even if objects and classes are core to Python, however, you can go pretty far without paying them much attention. In particular, we use objects in a very limited fashion in this book. We don't define our own classes—we just import classes from libraries such as Keras. We use those classes to create objects, and we call those objects' methods. That's pretty much all the object-oriented programming you need here.

## That's It, Folks!

Congratulations for reading this far! Now you know enough Python to hack the code in this book.

Admittedly, we've only scratched the surface of this beautiful programming language. We didn't look at the more advanced and elegant Python constructs. We didn't even mention some of the features that you need to write professional software, such as error management. However, those features aren't necessary to understand the examples in this book. You can study them later, once you decide to get deeper into Python.

Enjoy the book, and enjoy Python!

---

### Becoming a Python Expert

Your first experiences with Python might whet your appetite. If you decide to learn more about the language, then you have only one problem: too many choices. Python is one of the most popular learning topics around. You can find Python courses, primers, and tutorials all around the Internet, and in your local bookshop. The popular online training hubs, such as Coursera, Udacity, and Pluralsight, all have their own Python online courses—sometimes many of them, often available for free.

With so many options, your best bet is to Google for something that fits your needs. If you prefer to browse through a list of resources, however, you can find one on the official Python site.[a] The same site carries a list of introductory books,[b] and even an official tutorial.[c]

---

a. wiki.python.org/moin/BeginnersGuide/Programmers
b. wiki.python.org/moin/IntroductoryBooks
c. docs.python.org/3/tutorial

# The Words of Machine Learning

One of the first hurdles for machine learning rookies is learning the vocabulary. So many words in ML sound familiar, and yet subtly foreign. You'll probably ask yourself questions like: "Am I supposed to already know what a *feature* is?", or "What does *numerically stable* mean, exactly?"

This appendix gives you quick definitions of common terms and expressions of ML. Most entries also refer you to the section in the book where a term is first introduced, in case you need something more than a quick reminder. These definitions have no pretense to be Wikipedia-worthy. They're here just to trigger your memory and point you at additional information.

You won't find *all* the terms from the book in here—only those that I thought you might want to review. If you can't find the word you're looking for, then look it up in the book's index.

In the definitions, terms written in *italic* have their own entry in this appendix.

*Activation function*
> The function that follows the *weighted sum* in each *layer* of a *neural network*—in this book, typically a *sigmoid*, a *softmax*, or a *ReLU*. I introduce the name "activation function" in Chapter 8, The Perceptron, on page 99—but a detailed discussion of activation functions comes much later, in Understanding Activation Functions, on page 229.

*Accuracy*
> One of the performance metrics that you can use to evaluate a *classifier*. For example, if a program correctly classifies one fourth of the test examples, you can say that it has 25% accuracy.

*Adam*
> A variant of *gradient descent*. See Gradient Descent on Steroids, on page 240.

*Artificial neural network*

A more technically precise name for a *neural network*. There was a time where people felt the need to specify that they're talking about an "artificial" neural network, as opposed to a biological one.

*Asymptotic*

A curve is asymptotic when it approaches a value without ever quite reaching it. If I say, for example, "this *loss* asymptotically approaches a value of 10," that means that the loss gets closer and closer to 10, but it never quite reaches it.

*Backpropagation*

The fundamental algorithm for training *neural networks*. Backpropagation—or "backprop," for friends,—calculates the gradients of the *loss* with respect to the *weights*. Chapter 11, Training the Network, on page 129 is dedicated to backpropagation.

*Batch gradient descent*

The "plain vanilla" version of *gradient descent*, where the gradient is calculated based on all the training examples, taken together as a single batch. By contrast, see *mini-batch gradient descent* and *stochastic gradient descent*.

*Batch normalization*

One of the most effective techniques for improving neural networks. We briefly talk about it in One Last Trick: Batch Normalization, on page 244.

*Bias*

In many ML systems, including the ones in this book, the bias is one of the learnable *parameters* of the *model*. To see its mathematical meaning, check out Adding a Bias, on page 26 and Adding More Dimensions, on page 46. However, the term "bias" also has a second meaning in machine learning: you can say that a system has "high bias" when it *underfits* the training data, as I explain in Bias and Variance, on page 217.

*Bias-variance trade-off*

*Bias* and *variance* are alternative terms for *underfitting* and *overfitting*. The "trade-off" between them is a pragmatic concern: in many *supervised learning* systems, reducing overfitting can cause the system to underfit the training data, and vice versa. This balancing act is explored in Chapter 17, Defeating Overfitting, on page 211.

*Bias column*

In some machine learning models, the *bias* is a special case among *parameters*: other parameters are used in the *weighted sum*, but the bias stands on its own. In Bye Bye, Bias, on page 59, I introduce a trick to get rid of this special case: by adding a column full of 1s to the inputs, we turn the bias into a *weight* like any other. This ad hoc column is called the "bias column."

*Binary classifier*

A *classifier* with an boolean output—for example, one that classifies the state of a hardware component as either "working" or "broken." If the classifier has more than two classes, then it's a *multiclass classifier*.

*Broadcasting*

A feature of some numerical libraries such as NumPy. Broadcasting allows you to treat arrays like you would treat individual values. For example, you can subtract two NumPy arrays: each element in the result is the subtraction of the matching elements in the two original arrays. You can see examples of broadcasting throughout this book, starting with Implementing Prediction, on page 21 and Upgrading the Loss, on page 56.

*Categorical label*

See *label*.

*Chain rule*

The chain rule is the foundation of the *backpropagation* algorithm. It says that the *derivative* of a composite function is the product of the derivatives of the component functions. See From the Chain Rule to Backpropagation, on page 131.

*Classes*

The word "class" has different meanings in machine learning and programming. In ML, the classes are the categories that you use to organize data. For example, a *classifier* that recognizes digits has 10 classes, one for each digit; a classifier that recognizes dog breeds has one class per breed; and so on. By contrast, a class in programming is something else entirely—see Creating and Using Objects, on page 290.

*Classifier*

A system that assigns data to one of a limited set of *classes*. For example, you might label a movie review as "positive," "negative," or "neutral." The machine that reads the review and applies that label is a classifier. I introduce the concept in Chapter 5, A Discerning Machine, on page 63.

*CNN*

See *convolutional neural network*.

*Computational graph*

A notation to visualize the flow of data and operations in a system. Computational graphs are used often to represent neural networks, especially in the context of frameworks such as TensorFlow. I use computational graphs for the diagrams in Chapter 11, Training the Network, on page 129.

*Computer vision*

The scientific field that studies how computers can recognize images and videos. Today, most computer vision problems are solved with machine learning.

*Convergence*

In general, an algorithm converges when it finds a result, as opposed to running forever. In machine learning, this word is usually associated with algorithms like *gradient descent*. If GD converges, this means that it manages to minimize the *loss*; if it doesn't, that means that it oscillates indefinitely around the minimum loss, or even that it steps further and further from the minimum.

*Convex*

A mathematical function is convex when you can pick any two points on it, join them with a line, and the line won't cross any other point in the function. Intuitively, that means that the function has a single "cavity" (like, say, the exponential function) as opposed to multiple ones (like the sine function).

*Convolution*

A mathematical operation that serves as the basis for *convolutional neural networks*. We broadly show what convolutions look like in Convolutions, on page 252.

*Convolutional Neural Network*

A *neural network* architecture that is often used to learn data with a bi-dimensional or three-dimensional shape—in particular, images. Check out Chapter 19, Beyond Vanilla Networks, on page 247 for the details.

*Cross-entropy loss*

One of the formulae that we use to calculate the *loss*. It's a generalization of the *log loss*, and it's used for *multiclass classification* problems. See Writing the Classification Functions, on page 124.

*Dead neuron*

The phenomenon of dead neurons happens when an *activation function* in a neural network gets *saturated*, and its *gradient* gets close to 0. When that happens, the *gradient descent* algorithm gets stuck, and the *nodes* that are downhill of the activation function stop learning. We describe this phenomenon in Dead Neurons, on page 141 and The Sigmoid and Its Consequences, on page 231.

*Decision boundary*

A *classifier* does its job by partitioning the space of the *examples* into areas. The decision boundary is the border between those areas. It's called "decision boundary" because data points on different sides of the boundaries are assigned to different *classes*. I know, that's a pretty abstract definition—but you can find concrete examples in Tracing a Boundary, on page 149.

*Deep learning*

To put it simply, "deep learning" is a short name for "machine learning done with *neural networks* that have many *layers*." More broadly, the term indicates a large set of techniques that are used today in ML, such as *convolutional neural networks*, *recurrent neural networks*, and many more. For a better definition, read Chapter 20, Into the Deep, on page 261.

*Dense layer*

The same as a *fully connected layer*.

*Dev set*

Another name for the *validation set*.

*Derivative*

See the definition for *gradient*, and also the one for *partial derivative*.

*Differentiable*

A function is differentiable when you can calculate its *derivative* at any point. Intuitively, that happens when the function is smooth, and it doesn't have sudden jumps or holes. I use this term in When Gradient Descent Fails, on page 42.

*Dropout*

A bizarre (but powerful) *regularization* technique that randomly turns off *nodes* in a training *neural network*. See Advanced Regularization, on page 242.

*Early stopping*

A technique to counter *overfitting*, described in A Regularization Toolbox, on page 224. Early stopping is about finding the best moment to stop the *training phase*—after the system has learned enough to be useful, but before it starts overfitting the *training set*.

*Epoch*

In *mini-batch gradient descent* (or *stochastic gradient descent*), a training iteration processes only a fraction of the entire training set. By contrast, an "epoch" is a pass through the entire training set. For example, if you have 10,000 training examples, and you process them in batches of 10, it will take 1,000 iterations to complete an epoch.

*Examples*

See *supervised learning*.

*Exploding gradient*

A counterpart to the *vanishing gradient* problem. In the case of the exploding gradient, the *gradient* grows quickly as it *backpropagates* through a *neural network*. See Don't Play with Explosives, on page 234.

*Feature*

A common name to indicate the *input variables* in a machine learning system. For example, the pizza forecasting problem from Adding More Dimensions, on page 46 has three features: "Reservations," "Temperature," and "Tourists." In an image recognition problem, such as the one in Chapter 7, The Final Challenge, on page 87, you can treat each pixel as a separate feature.

*Feature engineering*

Also known as "feature extractions." The process by which a human extracts basic *features* from data, that are then processed by a computer. One of the selling points of *deep learning* is that it often makes feature engineering unnecessary, as I explain in Unreasonable Effectiveness, on page 264.

*Feature scaling*

ML systems tend to work better if their input *features* span a similar range—for example, from 0 to 1. On the other hand, if some features can take much larger values than others, then you might want to rescale them to the same range. That's what "feature scaling" means. Read Preparing Data, on page 178 for more details, or check out the entry on *standardization* for an broader data preparation technique.

*Forward propagation*

The process by which data move from the input to the output of a supervised learning system. I use this term for the first time in Confidence and Doubt, on page 67—but it really starts making sense when I introduce *neural networks*, because it parallels the process of *backpropagation*.

*Fully connected layer*

A *layer* in a neural network where each *node* is connected to all the nodes in a neighboring layer. Also called a *dense layer*.

*Fully connected network*

A traditional *neural network*, made up entirely of *fully connected layers*. You usually say that a neural network is "fully connected" to tell it apart from other architectures, like *convolutional neural networks*.

*Generative Adversarial Networks*

One of the most striking ideas in deep learning, GANs are systems that generate realistic artificial data, usually images. See The Path of Image Generation, on page 269.

*Global minimum*

The minimum value over an entire function. For example, imagine a function that takes a date and returns the temperature in Chicago on that day. The global minimum of that function is on January 20, 1985, when the thermometers dropped to −27 °F—the lowest temperature ever recorded in Chicago. By contrast, a *local minimum* is a value that's lower than the ones around it. If the temperature drops a bit one one day, and then raises again on the following day, that's a local minimum.

*Glorot initialization*

Another name for *Xavier initialization*.

*Gradient*

Intuitively, imagine the gradient as an arrow pointing "uphill" on a curve. The idea of a gradient is tightly connected to the concept of the *derivative*, that measures how a function changes as its input changes. If the derivative of the curve is zero at a specific point, that means the curve is flat at that point. If the derivative is positive, the curve is sloped upwards. If the derivative is negative, the curve is sloped downwards. The larger the derivative, the steeper the slope.

*Gradient descent*

One of the fundamental algorithms of machine learning. Gradient descent iteratively calculates the *gradient* of a system's *loss*, and changes the weights to step in the direction where the loss diminishes. GD is the subject of Chapter 3, Walking the Gradient, on page 31, and some of its variations are described in Chapter 13, Batchin' Up, on page 159 and Gradient Descent on Steroids, on page 240.

*Ground truth*

Observations collected from real-world data, as opposed to predictions. You often hear the term "ground truth" to refer to the *labels* in a *supervised learning* dataset, as in: "The system would have predicted 300 millimeters of rain for last year, but the ground truth was actually 400."

*Hidden layer*

Any layer in a *neural network* that is "inside" the network—that is, neither the *input layer* nor the *output layer*. See Chaining Perceptrons, on page 113.

*Hyperparameters*

In machine learning, there are two important types of parameters. On one side, there are the parameters of the *model function*, that the system learns during the *training phase*. On the other, there are parameters that you configure yourself before training—such as the *learning rate*, the number of training iterations, and the number of nodes in the *hidden layers* of a *neural network*. To avoid confusion between the two kinds of parameters, people use different names: the learnable parameters are often called *weights*, and the parameters that you configure yourself are called "hyperparameters."

*Identity function*

The function that outputs the same value as its input. It can be used as an *activation function* in some corner cases, as we mention in Picking the Right Function, on page 237.

*Input layer*

The first *layer* in a *neural network*. It takes the values of the *input variables*. See Chaining Perceptrons, on page 113.

*Input variable*

See *supervised learning*.

*L1/L2*

Two common *regularization* techniques, explained in L1 and L2 Regularization, on page 220. They can be wrapped up like this: keep the *weights* in a *neural network* small, so that the network generates a smoother function.

*Label*

In *supervised learning*, each example is composed of an input and an expected output. The label is the expected output. A label can be either numerical or categorical. For example, in a dataset that tracks the effect of temperatures on precipitation, the temperature would be the input variable, and the precipitation wold be a numerical label. On the other hand, a database of dog pictures might have dog images as the inputs, and the dog's breeds as their categorical labels.

*Layers*

The main units of organization of the *nodes* in a *neural network*. See the diagram in Here's the Plan, on page 118 for an example of a three-layered network. Other entities such as *dropouts* are sometimes called "layers" in the context of some machine learning libraries.

*Leaky ReLU*

See *ReLU*.

*Learning rate*

One of the most important *hyperparameters* of the *gradient descent* algorithm. At each step of GD, the gradient of the weights is multiplied by the learning rate—hence, the bigger the learning rate, the bigger the step. You meet this hyperparameter very early in the book, in Closer and Closer, on page 24. Later on, in Hands On: Tweaking the Learning Rate, on page 30 and Tuning the Learning Rate, on page 185, I discuss the trade-offs involved in making the learning rate smaller or larger.

*Learning rate decay*

A variant of plain vanilla *gradient descent* where the *learning rate* progressively decreases during training. See Gradient Descent on Steroids, on page 240.

*Linear*

Intuitively, a function is linear when it can be plotted as a straight shape. Also check out *nonlinear*.

*Linear regression*

A technique that predicts an input from an output by approximating the relation between input and output with a line—or with a higher-dimensional *linear* shape. In this book, linear regression is the first concrete example of *supervised learning*, in Chapter 2, Your First Learning Program, on page 15. Later on, in Chapter 4, Hyperspace!, on page 45, I introduce higher-dimensional *multiple linear regression*.

*Linearly separable*

A dataset is linearly separable if it can be partitioned with a "straight" shape. For example, imagine a plane populated with two different kinds of data: circles and triangles. If the data are linearly separable, then you can trace a straight line that has all the circles on one side, and all the triangles on the other. Check out Tracing a Boundary, on page 149 for visual examples.

*Local gradient*

In the context of the *chain rule*, the local gradient is the gradient of an operation's output with respect to its input. I use this concept to explain *backpropagation* in From the Chain Rule to Backpropagation, on page 131.

*Local minimum*

See *global minimum*. I talk about both kinds of minima there.

*Log loss*

One of the formulae that we use to calculate the *loss*. It works well for *binary classification* problems. See Smoothing It Out, on page 69.

*Logistic function*

A more technically accurate name for the *sigmoid*.

*Logistic regression*

Logistic regression is a statistics technique to model a binary variable. I don't really use the name "logistic regression" in the main text of this book, except in passing—but this technique is the theoretical underpinning for the binary classifier in Chapter 5, A Discerning Machine, on page 63.

*Logits*

The inputs of a *softmax*.

*Loss*

A function that measures the error in a machine learning system—in other words, a number that measures how bad the system's forecast is. The *training phase* of a machine learning system is all about minimizing the loss, by tweaking the *weights* with techniques such as *gradient descent*. In this book, we use different formulae to calculate the loss, including the *mean squared error* and the *log loss*.

*Matrix*

A bi-dimensional array, like a grid.

*Matrix multiplication*

A frequent operation in ML. It operates on two *matrices* of shapes (a, b) and (b, c), and results in a third matrix of shape (a, c). Check out the details in Multiplying Matrices, on page 49.

*Matrix transpose*

An operation that flips a *matrix* over its diagonal. For an example, see Transposing Matrices, on page 51.

*Mean squared error*

One of the common formulae used to calculate the *loss*. I introduce it in How Wrong Are We?, on page 22.

*Mini-batch gradient descent*

A variation of *gradient descent* where each step calculates the gradient on a subset of the training examples, rather than all of them. For example, you might have 10,000 training examples, but only feed them to GD in batches of 50. The exact number of examples for each mini-batch is a *hyperparameter* of the system. I introduce batch GD in Batch by Batch, on page 162.

*Model function*

*Supervised learning* works by approximating data with a function. That function is also called the "model." For example, in Chapter 2, Your First Learning Program, on page 15, we use a line as our model.

*Model selection*

The process of choosing an algorithm, and hence a *model function*, for a ML system. For example, you might compare the results of *linear regression*, a *neural network*, and some other algorithm, and pick the algorithm that gives the most accurate predictions.

*Momentum*

In the context of machine learning, momentum (or "gradient descent with momentum") is a variant of plain vanilla *gradient descent*. See Gradient Descent on Steroids, on page 240.

*Multilayer perceptron*

An alternative (and somewhat old-fashioned) name for a *neural network*.

*Multiclass classifier*

Also called *multinomial classifiers*, multiclass classifiers assign data to many classes, as opposed to *binary classifiers*. For example, if you're deciding which brand a car belongs to, then you're doing multiclass classification—unless you only have one or two brands, that is. Chapter 7, The Final Challenge, on page 87 is all about multiclass classification.

*Multinomial classifier*

Another name for a *multiclass classifier*.

*Multiple linear regression*

*Linear regression* on a function that takes more than one input variable. Chapter 4, Hyperspace!, on page 45 is dedicated to multiple linear regression.

*Neural network*

Neural networks are a popular architecture for *supervised learning*, and the main characters in this book. We introduce them in Chaining Perceptrons, on page 113, and use them throughout the rest of the book. Neural networks are usually defined as "shallow" when they consist of three *layers*, and "deep" when they have more.

*Neuron*

Sometimes, people use the word "neuron" to indicate a *node* in a neural network. More precisely, the neuron is the component that includes a *node*, its preceding nodes, and the operations in between—a *weighted sum* and an *activation function*. Check out Chaining Perceptrons, on page 113 for a picture.

*Node*

The values inside a neural network, that are arranged in *layers*. See Chaining Perceptrons, on page 113 for a picture.

*Nonlinear*

A function is nonlinear when it cannot be plotted as a straight shape. When we talk about nonlinearity in *neural networks*, that's usually in the context of *activation functions*.

*Normalization*

In general, you normalize something when you scale its value to be between 0 and 1. For example, the *softmax* function normalizes a bunch of variables so that each variable is in that range, and their sum equals 1. However, sometimes the term "normalization" is used in place of the term "standardization," that is more specific. For example, the technique known as *batch normalization* should arguably be called batch *standardization*.

*Numerical stability*

Technically, a computation is "numerically unstable" when it tends to amplify small fluctuations in its inputs. In concrete, that means that the computation tends to generate values that are very large or very small, and those values can cause an overflow or an underflow. For example, the *softmax* that we code in this book is numerically unstable because it can easily generate huge values that are too large for Python to handle. For more, see Numerical Stability, on page 124.

*One-hot encoding*

An encoding technique that converts a set of *categorical* values to a set of arrays, each containg a single 1 and a bunch of 0s. For example, the array [1, 2, 3] could be one-hot encoded as [[1, 0, 0], [0, 1, 0], [0, 0, 1]]. One-hot encoding is useful to encode the labels in certain machine learning problems, for reasons I discuss in One-Hot Encoding, on page 89.

*Outlier*

In a dataset, an outlier is a data point that's significantly different from its siblings. For example, imagine a dataset that shows a programmer's income and the number of hours she worked. On most months, there is a strict correlation between the two—except on one lucky month, when the programmer happened to win a few thousands bucks at the lottery while she was on vacation. That month would be an outlier.

*Output layer*

The last *layer* in a *neural network*. See Chaining Perceptrons, on page 113.

*Overfitting*

A machine learning system is "overfitting" when it's more accurate on the training data than it is on new, unknown data. For example, a face-recognition system might become good at recognizing faces in the pictures that it's been trained on, and then fail when confronted with new pictures of the same people. Overfitting happens because the system "knows" the training data, so it ends up memorizing the accidental details of that data instead of generalizing out of it. To use a metaphor, the system is acting like a student who memorizes a concept by rote learning, without really understanding it. Chapter 17, Defeating Overfitting, on page 211 is entirely dedicated to overfitting.

*Partial derivative*

Take a function with more than one variable, such as a * b. The partial derivative is the derivative of that function with respect to only one variable—either a or b. For more details, and an intuitive description of this concept, see Partial Derivatives, on page 38.

*Perceptron*

Historically, the perceptron was one of the first working ML systems. It's also the base for *multilayer perceptrons*—that is, *neural networks*. Chapter 8, The Perceptron, on page 99 is dedicated to the perceptron.

*Prediction phase*

The prediction phase (as opposed to the *training phase*) is the phase of *supervised learning* where you get your money back—the time when you ask the system to make an inference from *unlabeled data*. For example, during a speech recognizer's prediction phase, the system could take a sound and "predict" the vocal command in it. I talk about the two phases of supervised learning in Supervised Learning, on page 6.

*Recurrent Neural Networks*

RNNs are one of the most important types of *neural network* architectures today, especially in the field of natural language processing. I don't talk about RNNs in this book, but I mention their basic principles at the end of the book, in The Path of Language, on page 268.

*Recursion*

See *recursion*.

*Reinforcement learning*

A style of machine learning where the algorithm learns by trial and error. I talk briefly about reinforcement learning in Programming vs. Machine Learning, on page 4.

*Regularization*

A family of approaches to reduce *overfitting*. More precisely, "regularization" is any change that you make to a system like a *neural network* to reduce the distance between its performance on the *training set* and its performance on the *validation set*. For the details, read Regularizing the Model, on page 217 and A Regularization Toolbox, on page 224.

*ReLU*

One of the most popular *activation functions*, described in Enter the ReLU, on page 235. Also comes in a few variants, like the *Leaky ReLU* and the *softplus*.

*RMSprop*

A variant of *gradient descent*. See Gradient Descent on Steroids, on page 240.

*Saturation*

An *activation function* saturates when it receives an input that's outside its "ideal" range, which pushes its *gradient* close to zero. The best way to understand this concept is to see a concrete example of it. Read Dead Neurons, on page 141 for an example of a saturating *sigmoid*.

*Scalar*

A single number you might represent in your code with an integer or floating point value. By contrast, a value that's composed of multiple scalars is called a "vector"—but in programming, it's more likely to be called an "array."

*Sigmoid*

The sigmoid is a function that takes any number and converts it to the range from 0 to 1, excluded. It's often used as an *activation function*. I introduce it in Invasion of the Sigmoids, on page 66.

*Softmax*

The softmax is a function that takes an array of numerical inputs (called *logits*) and returns an array of the same size, where the inputs have been rescaled to the range from 0 to 1, excluded. It's often used as the last *activation function* in a *neural network*. I introduce it in Enter the Softmax, on page 116.

*Softplus*

See *ReLU*.

*Standard deviation*

A measure of how "spread out" a variable is. A variable with a low standard deviation rarely strays too far from its average value. One example from Chapter 15, Let's Do Development, on page 177 is the height of humans compared to the height of plants. The second has higher standard deviation than the first, because plants have wildly different heights, while humans don't: nobody is hundreds of times taller than anyone else.

*Standard normal distribution*

A distribution of data with a mean of 0 and a standard deviation of 1. I briefly mention it in Weight Initialization Done Right, on page 143.

*Standardization*

A technique to rescale data before feeding it to a machine learning system. In the strictest sense, you standardize a bunch of input *features* when you rescale them so that their mean is zero, and their *standard deviation* is 1. However, the term is used often to mean slightly different techniques. For an example, read Preparing Data, on page 178.

*Statistical noise*

Here is an example to explain what statistical noise is: every time you weigh yourself, you're likely to get a different weight. Some of these differences might be meaningful, and they depend on the fact that you're gaining or losing weight. Other differences might be due to irrelevant factors: you weighed yourself at different times during the day, your scale doesn't have perfect accuracy, and so on. These irrelevant fluctuations in real-world data are called "statistical noise." We talk about this concept in our discussion of *overfitting*, in The Causes of Overfitting, on page 212.

*Stochastic gradient descent*

For most people, "stochastic gradient descent" means "*mini-batch gradient descent* with a batch size of 1." In chapters such as Chapter 13, Batchin' Up, on page 159, I refer to that meaning. However, some ML practitioners (and some libraries, including Keras) use "stochastic gradient descent" as a synonym to "mini-batch gradient descent," regardless of the batch size. We'll have to live with the confusion, and hope that one of those conflicting meanings fades with time.

*Strictly increasing/decreasing*

Intuitively, a function is strictly increasing if it always points "upward," and strictly decreasing if it always points "downward." More formally, as the input grows, the value of a strictly increasing function always grows, and the value of a strictly decreasing function always drops. For example, if I say "the amount of food we consume increases with the number of dogs we own," that means that once we get a new dog, we'll need the same or more food—never less food. If we say that "the amount of food *strictly* increases with the number of dogs," that means we'll need more food—never the same or less food.

*Supervised learning*

A style of machine learning where a system takes a set of *examples* in the form of *input variables* and *labels* and learns the relation between the input variable and the label. For example, the input variable could be the number of reservations at a restaurant, and the label could be the number of pizzas sold; or, the input variable could be an X-ray scan, and the label could be a boolean value that tells whether the scan shows pneumonia. This style of ML is called "supervised" because somebody, supposedly a human, took care of preparing and labeling the examples.

*Swish*

See *ReLU*.

*Tensor*

A multidimensional array. A tensor with one dimension is usually called a "vector," and a tensor with two dimensions is usually called a *matrix*—so people tend to reserve the name "tensor" for arrays with three or more dimensions.

*Test set*

The subset of *examples* you use to test the system. In general, you shouldn't use the same examples to test and train the system, for reasons I explain in Training vs. Testing, on page 79.

*Training set*

The subset of examples you use to train the system. In general, you shouldn't reuse them to test the system as well, for reasons I explain in Training vs. Testing, on page 79.

*Training phase*

The training phase (as opposed to the *prediction phase*) is the phase of *supervised learning* where the system goes through the *examples* and learns the relation between the *input variables* and the *label*. For example, during a speech recognizer's training phase, the system could sort through a large number of sound clips, each labeled with the vocal command in the clip. I talk about the two phases of machine learning in Supervised Learning, on page 6.

*Translation invariance*

A property of *convolutional neural networks* that allows them to identify shapes wherever they are inside an image. See CNNs' Secret Sauce, on page 253.

*Tuple*

A Python type that is similar to a list, but immutable. See Collections, on page 280.

*Underfitting*

Simply put, a machine learning system is "underfitting" when it's not powerful enough to make accurate predictions—either because of its architecture, or because its hyperparameters haven't been tuned correctly. For example, imagine trying to predict fluctuations in ice cream sales with linear regression. Ice cream sales are mostly periodical—higher in summer and lower in winter—so it's hard to approximate them with a straight line. If you try, then your predictions aren't likely to be very good in most cases. That's a case of underfitting. Contrast that concept with the concept of *overfitting*.

*Unsupervised learning*

A style of machine learning where the machine finds patterns in unlabeled data. I talk about it in What About Unsupervised Learning?, on page 11.

*Validation set*

The set of examples that is used to choose a system's model and hyperparameters during the development process. (Also see *model selection*.) The validation set should be different from the *test set*, that is only used at the very end of the process. The reason for that difference is that you don't want your system to *overfit* the test data. For a more detailed explanation, see A Testing Conundrum, on page 173.

*Vanishing gradient*

A problem that plagued deep *neural networks* for years. The vanishing gradient slows down training to a crawl as you increase the number of *layers* in a network. It was partially solved by switching from *sigmoid*-like *activation functions* to other functions such as the *ReLU*. For the nitty gritties, see The Vanishing Gradient, on page 233.

*Variance*

In machine learning, you can say that a system has "high variance" when it *overfits* the training data, as I mention in Bias and Variance, on page 217.

*Weight*

One of the learnable *parameters* in a *perceptron*, or a *neural network*.

*Weighted sum*

An operation that consists in adding together a number of elements, each multiplied by a *weight*: element1 * weight1 + element2 * weight2 + ...

*Xavier initialization*

Xavier (or "Glorot") initialization is a method to initialize the *weights* in a *neural network*. It helps reduce problems such as *dead neurons* and *vanishing* or *exploding gradients*. For the details, see Better Weight Initialization, on page 239.

# Index

# Thank you!

How did you enjoy this book? Please let us know. Take a moment and email us at support@pragprog.com with your feedback. Tell us your story and you could win free ebooks. Please use the subject line "Book Feedback."

Ready for your next great Pragmatic Bookshelf book? Come on over to https://pragprog.com and use the coupon code BUYANOTHER2020 to save 30% on your next ebook.

Void where prohibited, restricted, or otherwise unwelcome. Do not use ebooks near water. If rash persists, see a doctor. Doesn't apply to *The Pragmatic Programmer* ebook because it's older than the Pragmatic Bookshelf itself. Side effects may include increased knowledge and skill, increased marketability, and deep satisfaction. Increase dosage regularly.

And thank you for your continued support,

Andy Hunt, Publisher

# Genetic Algorithms and Machine Learning for Programmers

Self-driving cars, natural language recognition, and online recommendation engines are all possible thanks to Machine Learning. Now you can create your own genetic algorithms, nature-inspired swarms, Monte Carlo simulations, cellular automata, and clusters. Learn how to test your ML code and dive into even more advanced topics. If you are a beginner-to-intermediate programmer keen to understand machine learning, this book is for you.

Frances Buontempo
(234 pages) ISBN: 9781680506204. $45.95
*https://pragprog.com/book/fbmach*

# Python Testing with pytest

Do less work when testing your Python code, but be just as expressive, just as elegant, and just as readable. The pytest testing framework helps you write tests quickly and keep them readable and maintainable—with no boilerplate code. Using a robust yet simple fixture model, it's just as easy to write small tests with pytest as it is to scale up to complex functional testing for applications, packages, and libraries. This book shows you how.

Brian Okken
(214 pages) ISBN: 9781680502404. $43.95
*https://pragprog.com/book/bopytest*

# Complex Network Analysis in Python

Construct, analyze, and visualize networks with networkx, a Python language module. Network analysis is a powerful tool you can apply to a multitude of datasets and situations. Discover how to work with all kinds of networks, including social, product, temporal, spatial, and semantic networks. Convert almost any real-world data into a complex network—such as recommendations on co-using cosmetic products, muddy hedge fund connections, and online friendships. Analyze and visualize the network, and make business decisions based on your analysis. If you're a curious Python programmer, a data scientist, or a CNA specialist interested in mechanizing mundane tasks, you'll increase your productivity exponentially.

Dmitry Zinoviev
(260 pages) ISBN: 9781680502695. $35.95
*https://pragprog.com/book/dzcnapy*

# Software Estimation Without Guessing

Developers hate estimation, and most managers fear disappointment with the results, but there is hope for both. You'll have to give up some widely held misconceptions: let go of the notion that "an estimate is an estimate," and estimate for your particular need. Realize that estimates have a limited shelf-life, and re-estimate frequently as needed. When reality differs from your estimate, don't lament; mine that disappointment for the gold that can be the longer-term jackpot. We'll show you how.

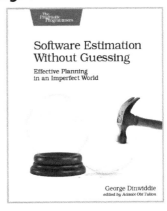

George Dinwiddie
(246 pages) ISBN: 9781680506983. $29.95
*https://pragprog.com/book/gdestimate*

# Agile Web Development with Rails 6

Learn Rails the way the Rails core team recommends it, along with the tens of thousands of developers who have used this broad, far-reaching tutorial and reference. If you're new to Rails, you'll get step-by-step guidance. If you're an experienced developer, get the comprehensive, insider information you need for the latest version of Ruby on Rails. The new edition of this award-winning classic is completely updated for Rails 6 and Ruby 2.6, with information on processing email with Action Mailbox and managing rich text with Action Text.

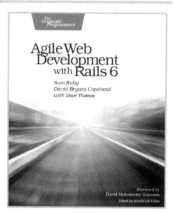

Sam Ruby and David Bryant Copeland
(494 pages) ISBN: 9781680506709. $57.95
*https://pragprog.com/book/rails6*

# Programming Flutter

Develop your next app with Flutter and deliver native look, feel, and performance on both iOS and Android from a single code base. Bring along your favorite libraries and existing code from Java, Kotlin, Objective-C, and Swift, so you don't have to start over from scratch. Write your next app in one language, and build it for both Android and iOS. Deliver the native look, feel, and performance you and your users expect from an app written with each platform's own tools and languages. Deliver apps fast, doing half the work you were doing before and exploiting powerful new features to speed up development. Write once, run anywhere.

Carmine Zaccagnino
(368 pages) ISBN: 9781680506952. $47.95
*https://pragprog.com/book/czflutr*

# Modern Systems Programming with Scala Native

Access the power of bare-metal systems programming with Scala Native, an ahead-of-time Scala compiler. Without the baggage of legacy frameworks and virtual machines, Scala Native lets you re-imagine how your programs interact with your operating system. Compile Scala code down to native machine instructions; seamlessly invoke operating system APIs for low-level networking and IO; control pointers, arrays, and other memory management techniques for extreme performance; and enjoy instant start-up times. Skip the JVM and improve your code performance by getting close to the metal.

Richard Whaling
(260 pages) ISBN: 9781680506228. $45.95
*https://pragprog.com/book/rwscala*

# Fixing Your Scrum

Broken Scrum practices limit your organization's ability to take full advantage of the agility Scrum should bring: The development team isn't cross-functional or self-organizing, the product owner doesn't get value for their investment, and stakeholders and customers are left wondering when something—anything—will get delivered. Learn how experienced Scrum masters balance the demands of these three levels of servant leadership, while removing organizational impediments and helping Scrum teams deliver real-world value. Discover how to visualize your work, resolve impediments, and empower your teams to self-organize and deliver using advanced coaching and facilitation techniques that honor and support the Scrum values and agile principles.

Ryan Ripley and Todd Miller
(240 pages) ISBN: 9781680506976. $45.95
*https://pragprog.com/book/rrscrum*

# The Pragmatic Bookshelf

The Pragmatic Bookshelf features books written by professional developers for professional developers. The titles continue the well-known Pragmatic Programmer style and continue to garner awards and rave reviews. As development gets more and more difficult, the Pragmatic Programmers will be there with more titles and products to help you stay on top of your game.

# Visit Us Online

### This Book's Home Page
*https://pragprog.com/book/pplearn*
Source code from this book, errata, and other resources. Come give us feedback, too!

### Keep Up to Date
*https://pragprog.com*
Join our announcement mailing list (low volume) or follow us on twitter @pragprog for new titles, sales, coupons, hot tips, and more.

### New and Noteworthy
*https://pragprog.com/news*
Check out the latest pragmatic developments, new titles and other offerings.

# Save on the ebook

Save on the ebook versions of this title. Owning the paper version of this book entitles you to purchase the electronic versions at a terrific discount.

PDFs are great for carrying around on your laptop—they are hyperlinked, have color, and are fully searchable. Most titles are also available for the iPhone and iPod touch, Amazon Kindle, and other popular e-book readers.

Send a copy of your receipt to support@pragprog.com and we'll provide you with a discount coupon.

# Contact Us

Online Orders: *https://pragprog.com/catalog*
Customer Service: *support@pragprog.com*
International Rights: *translations@pragprog.com*
Academic Use: *academic@pragprog.com*
Write for Us: *http://write-for-us.pragprog.com*
Or Call: +1 800-699-7764

Milton Keynes UK
Ingram Content Group UK Ltd.
UKHW052057230924
448749UK00001B/1